The Company of Strangers

The Company of Strangers

A NATURAL HISTORY OF ECONOMIC LIFE

Paul Seabright

PRINCETON UNIVERSITY PRESS

PRINCETON AND OXFORD

Copyright © 2004 by Princeton University Press
Published by Princeton University Press, 41 William Street, Princeton, New Jersey 08540
In the United Kingdom: Princeton University Press, 3 Market Place,
Woodstock, Oxfordshire OX20 1SY
All Rights Reserved

Third printing, and first paperback printing, 2005
Paperback ISBN 0-691-12452-3

The Library of Congress has cataloged the cloth edition of this book as follows

Seabright, Paul.
The company of strangers : a natural history of economic life / Paul Seabright.
p. cm.
Includes bibliographical references and index.
ISBN 0-691-11821-3 (alk. paper)
1. Social capital (Sociology).   2. Economics — Sociological aspects.
3. Sociobiology.   4. Strangers.   5. Trust.   I. Title.
HM708.S43 2004
302 — dc22   2003055550

British Library Cataloging-in-Publication Data is available

This book has been composed in Sabon

Printed on acid-free paper. ∞

pup.princeton.edu

Printed in the United States of America

10 9 8 7 6

ISBN-13: 978-0-691-12452-0 (pbk.)

ISBN-10: 0-691-12452-3 (pbk.)

To Alice, Edmond, and Luke

Contents

Acknowledgments

I have been exceptionally fortunate to have so many colleagues and friends who gave their time, energy, and ideas to encourage and improve this book. Diane Coyle, Isabelle Daudy, Barbarina Digby-Jones, Jeremy Edwards, Stanley Engerman, Mark Greenberg, Denis Hilton, David Howarth, Sheilagh Ogilvie, Anne Péchou, Diana Seabright, Jack Seabright, Keith Stenning, and several anonymous readers all made detailed comments on the whole manuscript. In addition, the following read some or all of the manuscript at various stages in its preparation and gave me very useful information or reactions to some of its arguments: Giuseppe Bertola, Susan Blackmore, Wendy Carlin, John Covell, Nicholas Crafts, Sophie Dawkins, Jeff Dayton-Johnson, Denis Eckert, Guido Friebel, Murray Fulton, Azar Gat, Karen Gold, Andrew Goreing, Geoffrey Hawthorn, Paul Hirsh, Marc Ivaldi, Kostas Karantininis, Hélène Lavoix, Jean Leduc, Tanya Luhrmann, James McWhirter, Patricia Morison, Elizabeth Murry, Francesca Nicolas, Andrew Schuller, Alice Seabright, Edmond Seabright, Victor Sarafian, and Kay Sexton. The following responded kindly and promptly to requests for information and advice: Kaushik Basu, Ravi Kanbur, Paul Klemperer, and Leigh Shaw-Taylor. Jennifer Gann provided a massive input to the notes, bibliography, and index as well as many wise comments on the text.

It has been a pleasure to work with Richard Baggaley, my editor at Princeton. He followed the project from an embryonic stage and has been an untiring source of advice; the book's title was his coinage. His colleague Peter Dougherty has also taken a keen interest in the project, and I have benefited greatly from his experience as a publisher and writer. The book was steered through production by Linny Schenck and Kathleen Cioffi with the immensely professional copy-editing skills of Vicky Wilson-Schwartz and the design talents of Leslie Flis. Carolyn Hollis provided valuable administrative support.

Thanks to the intermediation of Patricia Morison and Felicity Bryan, Catherine Clarke began acting as my agent before we had ever had more than email and telephone contact. My daughter Alice found this strange: "How can you trust to represent you someone you've never even met?" She then thought a moment and added, "I suppose that's what your book's all about, really." She was right only up to a point: I've been lucky to find an agent whose personal and professional qualities exceed anything for which social institutions can possibly take the credit.

I began writing this book in Cambridge, England, and completed it in Toulouse, at the outstanding research environment of the Institut d'Economie Industrielle. Its founder Jean-Jacques Laffont and current director Jacques Crémer, its scientific director Jean Tirole, the President of the University of Toulouse-1 Bernard Belloc, and their colleagues Marc Ivaldi and Michel Moreaux were all instrumental in enabling me to move to Toulouse. I am grateful to them all, and to the many other researchers in Toulouse who have made it such a personally as well as an intellectually stimulating place.

Besides those named above, I am grateful to the following who, in many diverse ways that only they can know, have given me information, ideas, practical support or inspiration, sometimes all four: David Begg, Robert Boyd, Sam Bowles, Florence Chauvet, Sabrina Choudar, Partha Dasgupta, Jayasri Dutta, Jon Elster, Rosalind English, Ernst Fehr, Christiane Fioupou, David Hart, Lucy Heller, Angela Hobbs, Peregrine Horden, Susan Hurley, John Kay, Joanna Lewis, Sylvie Mercusot, Alice Mesnard, Jim Mirrlees, Damien Neven, Nicholas Rawlins, Gilles St. Paul, Larry Siedentop, John Sutton, Susie Symes, and John Vickers.

Isabelle Daudy has been a constant support and sounding board for ideas. She urged me for many years to write a book for the general reader and has often helped me resist the pressure for the urgent to drive out the important. Our children, Alice, Edmond, and Luke Seabright, have constantly reminded me that the world around us is strange and needs explaining; this book is dedicated to them.

And finally, thanks to all the agricultural laborers, banana-growers, carpenters, dentists, engineers, flower-sellers, grocers, handbag-makers, inspectors, jewelers, knife-grinders, lathe-operators, midwives, night-watchmen, organists, potters, quantity surveyors, reed-makers, seamstresses, tattooists, undertakers, vets, window-cleaners, xylophonists, yogurt-makers and zoologists (to name but a few) that I have met and talked with in the course of thinking about the issues discussed in this book.

The Company of Strangers

Introduction

THE GREAT EXPERIMENT

Our everyday life is much stranger than we imagine, and rests on fragile foundations. This is the startling message of the evolutionary history of humankind. Our teeming, industrialized, networked existence is not some gradual and inevitable outcome of human development over millions of years. Instead we owe it to an extraordinary experiment launched a mere ten thousand years ago.* No one could have predicted this experiment from observing the course of our previous evolution, but it would forever change the character of life on our planet. For around that time, after the end of the last ice age, one of the most aggressive and elusive bandit species in the entire animal kingdom began to settle down. It was one of the great apes — a close cousin of chimpanzees and bonobos, and a lucky survivor of the extinctions that had wiped out several other promising branches of the chimpanzee family.[1] Like the chimpanzee it was violent, mobile, intensely suspicious of strangers, and used to hunting and fighting in bands of close relatives. Yet now, instead of ranging in search of food, it began to keep herds and grow crops, storing them in settlements that limited the ape's mobility and exposed it to the attentions of the very strangers it had hitherto fought or fled. Within a few hundred generations — barely a pause for breath in evolutionary time — it had formed social organizations of startling complexity. Not just village settlements but cities, armies, empires, corporations, nation states, political movements, humanitarian organizations, even internet communities. The same shy, murderous ape that had avoided strangers throughout its evolutionary history was now living, working, and moving among complete strangers in their millions.

Homo sapiens sapiens is the only animal that engages in elaborate task-sharing — the division of labor as it is sometimes known — between genetically unrelated members of the same species.[2] It is a phenomenon as remarkable and uniquely human as language itself. Most human beings now obtain a large share of the provision for their daily lives from others to whom they are not related by blood or marriage. Even in poor

---

* This is equivalent to about two and a half minutes ago on a twenty-four-hour clock that began ticking when our evolution diverged from the rest of the animal kingdom.

rural societies people depend significantly on nonrelatives for food, clothing, medicine, protection, and shelter. In cities, most of these non relatives crucial to our survival are complete strangers. Nature knows no other examples of such complex mutual dependence among strangers. A division of labor occurs, it is true, in some other species, such as the social insects, but only among close relatives (the workers in a beehive or an ant colony are sisters).[3] Modern biology has provided a convincing account of the evolutionary mechanisms by which such cooperation between close relatives must have evolved: it is known as the theory of kin selection.[4] This theory has shown that cooperation through a division of labor between close genetic relatives is likely to be favored by natural selection, since close relatives share a high proportion of genes, including mutant genes, both good and bad.[5] But for a cooperative division of labor to evolve among genetically unrelated individuals would be very surprising indeed, since individuals with mutant genes favoring dispositions to cooperate would help others who had no such dispositions and offered nothing in return. And sure enough, cooperation through a division of labor has never evolved in any species other than man.

Some species, it is true, practice a small degree of cooperation between unrelated individuals on very precise tasks. It has been seen among sticklebacks, vampire bats, and lions, for example — albeit only in very small groups.[6] But these rudiments bear as much relation to the elaborate human division of labor between relatives, nonrelatives, and complete strangers as do the hunting calls of chimpanzees to the highly structured human languages spoken all over the globe. Nature is also full of examples of mutual dependence between *different* species — such as that between sharks and cleaner fish (this is known as symbiosis).[7] But members of the same species occupy the same environment, eat the same food, and — especially — pursue the same sexual opportunities; they are rivals for all of these things in a much more intense way than are members of different species. Nowhere else in nature do unrelated members of the same species — genetic rivals incited by instinct and history to fight one another — cooperate on projects of such complexity and requiring such a high degree of mutual trust as human beings do.

No solution to this puzzle can be found in evolutionary biology alone. Ten thousand years is too short a time for the genetic makeup of *Homo sapiens sapiens* to have adapted to his new social surroundings. If it were somehow possible to assemble together all your direct same-sex ancestors — your father and your father's father and so on if you're male, your mother and your mother's mother and so on if you're female; one for each generation right back to the dawn of agriculture — you and all of these individuals could fit comfortably in a medium-sized lecture hall.[8] Only half of you would have known the wheel, and only 1 percent of you the motor car. But you would be far more similar to each other—genetically, physically, and instinctually—than any group of modern men or women who might have assembled there by chance. Apart from a small number of genes that have been subject to unusually strong selective pressures over the last ten millennia (such as the gene for lactose tolerance—the ability to digest milk—in adults)[9] and the effects of improved nutrition and other environmental developments over the centuries, the biological differences between you and your furthest ancestor would be very hard to distinguish from random variation within the group. If you are reading this book in a train or an airplane, this means your most distant ancestor from Neolithic times was almost certainly more like you, biologically, than the stranger sitting in the seat next to you now.

Yet evolutionary biology has something important to tell us all the same. For the division of labor among human beings has had to piggyback on a physiology and a psychology that evolved to meet a far different set of ecological problems. These were problems faced by hunter-gatherers, mainly on the African woodland savannah, over the six or seven million years that separate us from our last common ancestor with chimpanzees and bonobos. Some time in the last two hundred thousand years or so—less than one-thirtieth of that total span—a series of changes, minuscule to geneticists, vast in the space of cultural potential, occurred to make human beings capable of abstract, symbolic thought and communication.[10] The changes themselves must have occurred before the last common ancestor of the human beings alive today. This implies that they occurred at least 140,000 years ago.[11] But the first evidence of the new cultural capabilities to which they gave rise is found in the cave paintings, grave goods, and other symbolic artifacts left by hunter-gatherer communities of anatomically modern man (Cro-Magnon man, as he is sometimes known), which are no older than sixty or seventy thousand years—and most are much younger.[12] These capabilities seem to have made a move toward agriculture and settlement possible once the environmental conditions became favorable, after the end of the last ice age. Indeed, the fact that agriculture was independently invented at least seven times, at close intervals, in different parts of the world suggests it was more than possible; it may even have been in some way inevitable.[13] These capabilities also enabled human beings to construct the social rules and habits that would constrain their own violent and unreliable instincts enough to make society possible on a larger, more formal scale. And they laid the foundation for the accumulation of knowledge that would provide humanity as a whole with a reservoir of shared skills vastly greater than the skills available to any single person. But these cultural capabilities did not evolve *because* of their value in making the modern division of labor possible. Quite the contrary: modern society is an opportunistic experiment, founded on a human psychology that had already evolved before human beings ever had to deal with strangers in any systematic way. It is like a journey to the open sea by people who have never yet had to adapt to any environment but the land.

THE ARGUMENT OF THIS BOOK

The chapters that follow explore what made this remarkable experiment possible and why, against all the odds, it did not collapse. They also explore why it could collapse in the future, and what might be done to prevent that from happening. Part 1 shows why the division of labor is such a challenge for us to explain. It looks at the way in which even some of the simplest activities of modern society depend upon intricate webs of international cooperation that function without anyone's being in overall charge. On the contrary, they work through eliciting a single-mindedness from their participants—a tunnel vision—that is hardly compatible with a clear and nonpartisan vision of the priorities of society as a whole. It seems hard to believe that something as complex as a modern industrial society could possibly work at all without an overall guiding intelligence, but since the work of the economist Adam Smith in the eighteenth century, we have come to realize that this is exactly how things are. Like medical students studying the human body, therefore, we have to understand and marvel at the degree of spontaneous coordination displayed in human societies before we can even begin to investigate its pathologies. This coordination comes about simply because of a willingness of individuals to cooperate with strangers in a multitude of small but collectively very significant ways.

Part 2 looks at what makes such cooperation possible, given the psychology we have inherited from our hunter-gatherer ancestors. The answer consists of institutions—sets of rules for social behavior, some formal, many informal—that build on the instincts of the shy, murderous ape in ways that make life among strangers not only survivable but attractive, potentially even luxurious. These rules of behavior have made it possible for us to deal with strangers by persuading us, in effect, to treat them as honorary friends. Some of the institutions that make this possible have been consciously and coherently designed, but many have grown by experiment or as the by-product of attempts to achieve something quite different. Nobody can claim they are the "best" institutions that human beings could ever devise. They are simply the ones that happen to have been tried, and that, given the psychology and physiology of the creatures that tried them, happen to have survived and spread.[14]

The explanation begins by showing how the division of labor can create great benefits for those societies that can make it work. These benefits come mainly from specialization, the sharing of risk, and the accumulation of knowledge. But advantages to society as a whole cannot explain why a division of labor evolved. We also need to understand why individuals have an interest in participating. A division of labor needs to be robust against opportunism — the behavior of those who seek to benefit from the efforts of others without contributing anything themselves. In other words, participants need to be able to trust each other — especially those they do not know. Social cooperation depends on institutions that have exactly such a property of robustness. Given the facts of human psychology, they ensure that cooperation not only happens but is reliable enough for others to be willing to take its presence for granted, at least most of the time. One such robust human institution will be described in detail: it is the institution of money. Another is the banking system. We shall look at the foundations of trust in financial institutions, and examine the delicate balance between the natural incentives of individuals to signal their trustworthiness to others and the need for outside supervision to enforce trust. Effective institutions rely on a minimum of outside supervision, knowing that a little outside supervision can make natural incentives go a long way.

The rest of part 2 completes the task of explaining how human cooperation is possible by addressing the paradox of tunnel vision. Not only does widespread social trust arise in spite of the limitations of people's individual perspectives, but it even *requires* tunnel vision in order to persist. This is because the most effective mechanisms for ensuring trust rely not just on incentives but on people's internalization of values through education and training. This process entrenches commitment to professional values and at the same makes them resistant to change. Codes of professional ethics can therefore make individual acts of local cooperation more reliable, while generating a degree of systematic blindness to the more distant consequences of our actions. Such blindness — tunnel vision — has dangers that are a natural by-product of its inherent virtues.

Part 2 has therefore argued that we can understand why human beings have proved capable of cooperating with strangers, thanks to institutions that build on their already evolved hunter-gatherer psychology. Part 3 goes on to look at global consequences — at what happens when human beings equipped with this psychology, and responding to the presence of these institutions, come together in the mass. Our mutual interdependence has produced effects that utterly surpass what any of the participants can have intended or sometimes even imagined. The growth of cities, the despoliation of the environment, the sophisticated functioning of markets, the growth of large corporations, and the development of stocks of collective knowledge in the form of science and technology: all are part of the landscape of human interaction even though nobody has planned them to look the way they do, and all have contributed to the dramatic historical improvement in the prosperity of mankind. But since nobody has planned them, we should not be surprised that while some of them look encouraging, others look very troubling indeed. For instance, the growth of cities — the result of countless uncoordinated individual decisions about where to live and work — has led to some of history's most creative and innovative environments. It has also produced pollution and disease on an unprecedentedly concentrated scale. Cities themselves have often been able to organize collective action to overcome these by-products of their affluence, but only by living off a hinterland whose resources they exploit and to which they export their waste. But the world as a whole cannot do as cities have done, for it has no hinterland. The example of water, which we shall look at in detail, shows us that problems of global pollution and resource depletion will prove extremely dangerous unless we can find ways of calculating and accounting for the cost of the resources we use and the pollution we cause. For this we need to draw on one of the other great unintended characteristics of modern society: the capacity of markets to calculate prices that summarize the information necessary for allocating resources in a world of scarcity. Markets, when they work well, have a remarkable ability to allow their participants — who may never even physically meet — to pool information about the scarcity of the goods and services they are exchanging. It is precisely this kind of information that we need in order to treat our limited environmental resources wisely.

Nevertheless, there are other aspects of the division of labor that markets on their own cannot effectively coordinate. Many kinds of productive activity take place inside firms, which represent islands of planning and coordination — often also between strangers — in the sea of unplanned market transactions around them. What makes some activities suitable for large firms, whose members are more anonymous to each other, while others are suitable for small firms? The answer is that successful firms adapt to their economic environment by channeling information between people in a way that market transactions cannot do. Information, and the spectacular accumulation of knowledge across the centuries, is another of the remarkable by-products of modern society: how has it happened, what are its benefits, and what are its dangers?

Finally, the last chapter in part 3 explores the paradox that a society whose members are interconnected as never before can nevertheless exclude some of its most vulnerable members — the unemployed, the poor, the sick.

So, although part 3 will give us many reasons to be impressed by the achievements of modern society, it will also show us urgent reasons for concern. The persistence of desperate poverty in a world of plenty, the destruction of the world's environmental assets, and the spread of weapons of large- and small-scale destruction (resulting from the diffusion of information into the hands of those who would use it for aggressive ends) all call for conscious reflection on solutions, using that same capacity for abstract reasoning that has created so many of the problems in the first place. So part 4 looks at the institutions of collective action — states, communities, and other political entities — and considers their virtues and their weaknesses in the face of the need to design collective solutions to the common problems of our species. At first, it may look as though we have abundant reasons to be optimistic. For while part 3 indicated the daunting scale of these common problems, part 2 has already shown us that the emotional and cognitive capacities for cooperation, and for rational reflection on the proper uses to make of that cooperation, have a solid foundation in human evolution.

Unfortunately, however, the human capacity for cooperation is double-edged. It is not only the foundation of social trust and peaceful living but also what makes for the most successful acts of aggression between one group and another. Like chimpanzees, though with more deadly refinement, human beings are distinguished by their ability to harness the virtues of altruism and solidarity, and the skills of rational reflection, to the end of making brutal and efficient warfare against rival groups. What modern society needs, therefore, is not more cooperation but better-directed forms of cooperation. The book concludes by asking just how optimistic we can reasonably be, knowing that some of the very qualities that have made the great experiment of modern life possible are also those that now threaten its very existence. Just how fragile is the great experiment on which our species set out ten thousand years ago? And what can we do to make it less fragile now?

Understanding the delicacy of our social institutions and their roots in our evolutionary past helps us to think constructively about the pressing problems of the world today. Take globalization — one of those rare abstract nouns that can bring people out marching in the streets in their hundreds of thousands. The anxieties provoked by globalization are not new but have been with us for ten thousand years — anxieties about powerful individuals and groups of whom we know little but who may intend to do us harm or who may undermine our security and our prosperity even if they have no intentions toward us of any kind. Terrorism, too, is a modern name for a phenomenon that provokes in us an age-old fear: that among our enemies are numbered not only those who bear us personal grudges but also those who do not know us or even care about us as individuals at all. Living with these fears requires us to deploy abstract reasoning in the service of institution-building, today as throughout the last ten thousand years. As our world has grown more complex, we now have to do more than create the simple local marketplaces where the first strangers could meet in enough security to justify the risk of dealing with each other. We have to create a marketplace where tribes, corporations, and whole nations can meet in relative security and do the deals that underpin their collective prosperity. But though the scale of the challenges has grown, they retain much of their old character. And the last ten millennia have shown repeatedly how those who have not learned from their history may never notice their deficiency until, fatally, they are pitted against adversaries who have.

The argument of this book rests, therefore, on four pillars:

First, the unplanned but sophisticated coordination of modern industrial societies is a remarkable fact that needs an explanation. Nothing in our species' biological evolution has shown us to have any talent or taste for dealing with strangers.

Second, this explanation is to be found in the presence of institutions that make human beings willing to treat strangers as honorary friends.

Third, when human beings come together in the mass, the unintended consequences are sometimes startlingly impressive, sometimes very troubling.

Fourth, the very talents for cooperation and rational reflection that could provide solutions to our most urgent problems are also the source of our species' terrifying capacity for organized violence between groups. Trust between groups needs as much human ingenuity as trust between individuals.

This book draws together a large range of findings by scholars working in history, biology, anthropology, and, especially, economics and economic history. The outline of the story told here is not new and in many respects has been part of the shared understanding of economists since the work of Adam Smith in the eighteenth century. But the growing specialization of disciplines has meant that many people outside the mysterious world of professional economics have not realized how directly our subject speaks to the past and the future of our human species. We are believed to deal only in the rational skeleton of human life and to avoid addressing the flesh and blood it bears. At the same time, some scholars working within economics are surprised to discover how starkly and expressively the writings of other disciplines illustrate the dilemmas that we have been in the habit of studying in our often somewhat bloodless way.

To help bridge this gap I have chosen to discuss economic arguments using as little economic terminology as possible and citing evidence drawn mainly from outside economics — from history, biology, and other sources, including literary ones. The endnotes are designed not just to support the claims made in the text but also to give sources and suggestions for further reading. While the book's individual chapters are designed to be read as self-contained essays, the prologues to parts 2, 3, and 4 situate the chapters to come within a structured argument. Epilogues at the end of these parts link the themes that have been discussed to the more formal literature of economics. They offer suggestions for further reading to those who would like to see the economic arguments made more explicit, to see the logical skeleton under the flesh.

PART I

Tunnel Vision

CHAPTER 1

Who's In Charge?

THE WORLD'S NEED FOR SHIRTS

This morning I went out and bought a shirt. There is nothing very un-usual in that: across the world, perhaps 20 million people did the same. What is more remarkable is that I, like most of these 20 million, had not informed anybody in advance of what I was intending to do. Yet the shirt I bought, although a simple item by the standards of modern tech-nology, represents a triumph of international cooperation. The cotton was grown in India, from seeds developed in the United States; the arti-ficial fiber in the thread comes from Portugal and the material in the dyes from at least six other countries; the collar linings come from Bra-zil, and the machinery for the weaving, cutting, and sewing from Ger-many; the shirt itself was made up in Malaysia. The project of making a shirt and delivering it to me in Toulouse has been a long time in the planning, since well before the morning two winters ago when an In-dian farmer first led a pair of ploughing bullocks across his land on the red plains outside Coimbatore. Engineers in Cologne and chemists in Birmingham were involved in the preparation many years ago. Most remarkably of all, given the obstacles it has had to surmount to be made at all and the large number of people who have been involved along the way, it is a very stylish and attractive shirt (for what little my judgment in these matters may be worth). I am extremely pleased at how the project has turned out. And yet I am quite sure nobody knew that I was going to be buying a shirt of this kind today; I hardly knew it myself even the day before. Every single one of these people who has been laboring to bring my shirt to me has done so without knowing or indeed caring anything about me. To make their task even more chal-lenging, they, or people very much like them, have been working at the same time to make shirts for all of the other 20 million people of widely different sizes, tastes, and incomes, scattered over six continents, who decided independently of each other to buy shirts at the same time as I did. And those were just today's clients. Tomorrow there will be an-other 20 million — perhaps more.

If there were any single person in overall charge of the task of supply-ing shirts to the world's population, the complexity of the challenge facing them would call to mind the predicament of a general fighting a war. One can imagine an incoming president of the United States being presented with a report entitled *The World's Need for Shirts*, trembling at its contents, and immediately setting up a Presidential Task Force. The United Nations would hold conferences on ways to enhance international cooperation in shirt-making, and there would be arguments over whether the UN or the U.S. should take the lead. The pope and the archbishop of Canterbury would issue calls for everyone to pull together to ensure that the world's needs were met, and committees of bishops and pop stars would periodically remind us that a shirt on one's back is a human right. The humanitarian organization "Couturiers sans Frontières" would airlift supplies to sartorially challenged regions of the world. Experts would be commissioned to examine the wisdom of making collars in Brazil for shirts made in Malaysia for re-export to Brazil. More experts would suggest that by cutting back on the wasteful variety of frivolous styles it would be possible to make dramatic improvements in the total number of shirts produced. Factories which had achieved the most spectacular increases in their output would be given awards, and their directors would be interviewed respectfully on television. Activist groups would protest that "shirts" is a sexist and racist category and propose gender- and culture-neutral terms covering blouses, tunics, cholis, kurtas, barongs, and the myriad other items that the world's citizens wear above the waist. The columns of newspapers would resound with arguments over priorities and needs. In the cacophony I wonder whether I would still have been able to buy my shirt.

In fact there is nobody in charge. The entire vast enterprise of supplying shirts in thousands and thousands of styles to millions and millions of people takes place without any overall coordination at all. The Indian farmer who planted the cotton was concerned only with the price this would subsequently fetch from a trader, the cost to him of all the materials, and the effort he would have to put in to realize an adequate harvest. The managers of the German machinery firm worry about export orders and their relations with their suppliers and their workforce. The manufacturers of chemical dyes could not care less about the aesthetics of my shirt. True, there are certain parts of the operation where there is substantial explicit coordination: a large company like ICI or Coats Viyella has many thousands of employees working directly or indirectly under a chief executive. But even the largest such company accounts for only a tiny fraction of the whole activity involved in the supply of shirts. Overall there is nobody in charge. We grumble sometimes about whether the system works as well as it could (I have to replace broken buttons on my shirts more often than seems reasonable). What is truly astonishing is that it works at all.[1]

Citizens of the industrialized market economies have lost their sense of wonder at the fact that they can decide spontaneously to go out in search of food, clothing, furniture, and thousands of other useful, attractive, frivolous, or life-saving items, and that when they do so, somebody will have anticipated their actions and thoughtfully made such items available for them to buy. For our ancestors who wandered the plains in search of game, or scratched the earth to grow grain under a capricious sky, such a future would have seemed truly miraculous, and the possibility that it might come about without the intervention of any overall controlling intelligence would have seemed incredible. Even when adventurous travelers opened up the first trade routes and the citizens of Europe and Asia first had the chance to sample each other's luxuries, their safe arrival was still so much subject to chance and nature as to make it a source of drama and excitement as late as Shakespeare's day. (Imagine setting *The Merchant of Venice* in a supermarket.)

In Eastern Europe and the countries that used to belong to the Soviet Union, even after the collapse of their planning systems, there has been persistent and widespread puzzlement that any society could aspire to prosperity without an overall plan. About two years after the break-up of the Soviet Union I was in discussion with a senior Russian official whose job it was to direct the production of bread in St. Petersburg. "Please understand that we are keen to move towards a market system," he told me. "But we need to understand the fundamental details of how such a system works. Tell me, for example: who is in charge of the supply of bread to the population of London?" There was nothing naive about his question, because the answer ("nobody is in charge"), when one thinks carefully about it, is astonishingly hard to believe. Only in the industrialized West have we forgotten just how strange it is.

COOPERATION WITH NOBODY IN CHARGE

This book is about the human capacities that have made such cooperation possible, about their advantages and their dangers. One way to capture their paradoxical quality is to think of them as embodying a kind of tunnel vision. By "tunnel vision" I mean the capacity to play one's part in the great complex enterprise of creating the prosperity of a modern society without knowing or necessarily caring very much about the overall outcome. We may be — and often are — interested in broader questions about the point and purpose of it all, but the answers to such questions have comparatively little effect on our ability to do our jobs well. Our activities are part of a network; we can play our part just by knowing how to behave toward our neighbors in the network. Sometimes we rationalize this to ourselves by thinking that someone else is taking care of the network as a whole; if so, we are usually mistaken.

Tunnel vision is not the same thing as the profit motive, though a concern for profit to the exclusion of all else is one rather unattractive form that tunnel vision can take. Nor is it the same as self-interest. Economists have often found it convenient to assume that individuals are purely self-interested, if only to contrast the egoism of their motivation with the unwitting benefits created for others by the pursuit of that motivation. In truth human motivation is much richer than this simplification allows — but it cannot escape tunnel vision even so. We all have a strong component of self-interest, and we also care about other things: the welfare of our families and friends, the physical and moral health of our communities, the future of our world. Sometimes this concern expresses itself in strong views about the way in which the production or distribution of economic resources should be organized, as when we protest against the closure of a local hospital. But the altruism of our gesture is no guarantee that we have thought through its wider implications: single-minded obsessiveness can be just as prevalent among those whose goals are not narrowly selfish ones, such as crusaders for a charitable cause, as among profit-oriented businessmen. More often, we neither know nor care very much about the details. If I work in a furniture factory, it is more important to me to have a good working environment, pleasant colleagues, and reasonable pay than to know how the furniture I produce will be used to decorate the homes of those who buy it. I may, of course, derive job satisfaction from understanding how my work contributes to the activities and aspirations of others. People can often strengthen their sense of their own worth by understanding how their work fits into some larger frame of things; this was an important message of the book *Working*, in which the American writer Studs Terkel interviewed people from all corners of life to find out how their jobs affected them.[2] But Terkel's book also showed how solitary this satisfaction can be for many people in modern occupations; it may affect their happiness without making much difference to the quality of their work. It is both an admirable and a melancholy fact that training and the standardization of working methods are designed to reduce the impact of personal idiosyncrasy on the job.[3]

Tunnel vision, then, covers a range of states of mind, from a mere capacity for detachment at one end to an obsessive single-mindedness at the other. As we shall see in later chapters, our understanding of the way modern economies work shows us two things. First, that modern society needs tunnel vision: the prosperity that the world's citizens rightly demand rests upon institutions that are not only compatible with tunnel vision but even encourage it. Secondly, that tunnel vision is also dangerous: it is the source of many of the gravest threats to our security and happiness. How can this be? To begin uncovering the answer we must go back to shirts.

How should we react when we ask about some activity, "Who's in charge?" and receive the answer "No-one"? It clearly depends on what kind of activity is in question. If I were an airline passenger, I would be concerned to discover that no one was in charge of the airplane. But it is good to know there is nobody in charge of creating modern English poetry. What is surprising is that supplying shirts to the world is — in this respect — closer to poetry than to piloting an aircraft. Why? What explains why these different activities provoke these particular responses?

The details of the answer will occupy most of this book. But here's a start. First of all, the passengers in an aircraft share more or less the same clear goal: they want to get to their destination quickly and, above all, safely. Some of them may be more willing than others to travel slowly to avoid turbulence, but compared with the overriding shared goal of safe arrival, all differences of emphasis between them are minor. Secondly, in the event of danger all the passengers and crew are in the same — as it were — boat. If I don't like the way the lefthand side of the aircraft is tilting, I can't just go and sit on the right. The right hand side of the aircraft will be traveling in the same direction as the left. In other words, the activities and fates of the passengers are interconnected in an inextricable way: such interconnections may make tunnel vision quite dangerous. However, some of this interconnection of our destinies may actually be welcome: if I don't have a parachute, I shall be somewhat reassured to know that the pilot doesn't have one either.

Thirdly, there is enough uncertainty in the aircraft's environment to make us unwilling to trust any purely mechanical set of rules for coordinating its flight — such as those embodied in the autopilot. Even sophisticated fly-by-wire technologies can cope only with conditions precise enough for the programmers to foresee in detail, but there are others (such as the failure of the autopilot itself) where only the presence of someone in charge will do. The relative importance of the unforeseeable explains why there are driverless trains but not yet pilotless passenger airplanes,* and this difference is significant for many aspects of social life.

Fourthly, although being in charge of an aircraft is a complex responsibility that requires considerable training and experience, it is still sim-

---

* However, pilotless passenger aircraft are likely to enter production soon (see *The Economist*, 21 December 2002, pp. 81–83), even if their entry into general service may take many years. Adam Brown of Airbus in Toulouse tells me that in the near future the only inhabitants of the cockpit will be a man and a dog. The man's job will be to feed the dog, while the dog's job will be to bite the man if he dares to touch the controls.

ple enough for one person to be capable of discharging it in most circumstances. This is because of the relative simplicity of the overall goal, the limited number of controls to be operated, the limited number of ways of operating them, and the relatively limited number of signals to which the operator needs to respond. The job of being in charge is within a single individual's capacity.

These four features together imply that the task of flying the aircraft is simple enough for one person but too complex and unforeseeable for a machine. (There are many such tasks — cleaning a hotel room and weeding a flowerbed, to name but two.) But why does this mean one person has to be in charge? Why can't everyone be in charge together? The moment one asks this question it becomes obvious what the answer is: if backseat driving is a nuisance, backseat flying is potentially disastrous. Trying to reach agreement on how to fly the aircraft would involve arguments and delays that the passengers, in their desire to reach their destination safely, simply cannot afford.

Creating poetry is very different in a number of obvious ways, of which only some matter for the question we are concerned with here. First of all, there is no clear goal that poetry is trying to achieve, for all that literary critics may try to impose an order upon it. That's not just an accident or an unfortunate omission: poetry would not be valuable if it lost the subversive, unsettling quality of an activity whose goals are always open to question and renewal. Individual poets who are not free to reinvent and rediscover their own activity cease to be poets and become speechwriters. If the poetry of any era or culture has a pattern, it is not one that can be planned and imposed but one that emerges from the interplay of many individual voices.

Secondly, because the voices are many and individual, the connections between them are subtle and detachable. Poets influence each other, certainly; but if the poet laureate writes a bad poem, it's a bad poem, not a collective disaster.

Thirdly, even if there were reasons to wish to do so, being in charge of a nation's or a culture's poetry is a task of such complexity that no individual could discharge it except by simplifying it to a point of crudity. That is why cultural commissars set up by dictatorships always begin by giving themselves some clear task: poetry should aim to restore national pride or uplift the toiling and exploited masses. Then they realize that monitoring the pursuit of this task is going to be very difficult if there is no limit to the number of people who can write poetry, so the next thing they do is to stipulate that all poets must be members of a Writers' Union. Even without invoking any rights of free expression, it takes very little imagination to see that commissars are bad for poetry.

There may also be a more subtle reason why a single individual could not be in charge of a culture's poetry. One reason why so few critics of art or literature have also been great artists or writers is that the breadth and flexibility of vision that make a critic—the ability to see virtues in opposing styles and movements and to understand something of the roots of their opposition—tends to be incompatible with the single-minded energy that creates great works. Creativity seems to require more tunnel vision than criticism can usually afford.

What about the production of the world's shirts? The goal of this activity cannot be summed up simply in the phrase "producing shirts." The quality, the design, the variety of styles, the durability of the cloth, and the location of the different people with their different tastes represent a whole array of dimensions along which decisions must be taken on behalf of all the twenty million people a day who buy shirts—dimensions that are at least as important as the sheer quantity of shirts produced. There is no agreed-upon goal. This, incidentally, is a first step toward understanding why the Soviet Union was able to achieve much more impressive economic growth, relative to Western countries, in its early days, when the priority was to produce items like coal, steel, and electricity and the goals could be summed up relatively uncontroversially in quantitative terms, than in its last decades, when the emphasis had switched toward consumer goods. Chinese planners were more farsighted: the Mao jacket simply imposed on consumer fashions the logic of coal and steel.

By comparison with the passengers in the aircraft, there is also very little direct interconnection between the activities of all the world's wearers of shirts, other than that they are all participants in the market for shirts. Shirts are quite different in this respect from some other products: if your power station pollutes the atmosphere in the course of producing electricity, this has a direct effect on everyone else and not just yourself, but the chances are that you will ignore most of these effects on others when managing your power station. Modern life is full of instances where the direct interactions between individuals mean that in pursuit of their own goals all end up worse off. Consider:

- Everyone else drives to work, so the bus and rail services are infrequent, so I drive to work as well, and the roads are packed.
- Each side in the civil war fears the other side cannot be trusted to keep the truce, so each side prepares to break the truce rather than risk allowing the other side to fire first.
- Any secondhand car for sale must be of dubious quality, so worth only a low price, but if used cars can only fetch a low price, only cars of dubious quality will be offered for sale.
- He drinks in an attempt to forget her infidelity, and she is unfaithful because he drinks.

- The owner of each trawler would prefer the fish stocks to be allowed to regenerate, but each knows that one person's restraint will make no difference, so all of them fish heavily, and the stocks decline.
- Each company hopes that a recession can be avoided, but just in case it can't, all of them cut back on their orders, so a recession occurs.

Shirts are comparatively free of such interactions (though not entirely free of them, as we shall see in chapter 2). You may be somewhat scornful of my taste, but by and large this does not affect your own ability to buy and wear the shirts you prefer, and almost all the rest of the world's shirt-wearers could not care less what shirt I buy. It is true that it may take only one photograph of Cindy Crawford or Claudia Schiffer wearing a particular style of shirt for there to be a surge in demand for it, but that surge will still amount to no more than a ripple on the surface of the vast industry that turns out shirts for the world as a whole, and we can be sure that Cindy and Claudia will be photographed wearing a different shirt tomorrow.

The sheer number and variety of shirts produced in the world is an essential part of the reason why no single individual could be in charge. There are over six billion people in the world, and anyone who thinks it is possible to imagine that number of people might reflect that six billion is roughly the same as the number of postage stamps that could be laid end to end around the equator, or the number of days it would take your hair to grow from London to Casablanca. This vast number means that the variety of needs and styles and tastes that the shirt-making industry has to cater to lies far beyond the capacity of any individual to comprehend, let alone to organize. As anyone who has worked in a large organization knows, people who are put in charge of a complex activity that would be better left alone never do nothing; they seek to justify their existence by simplifying and restricting that activity so that it can be controlled. That is what Soviet planners did: they created large firms, much larger than any equivalent firms in the West, simply in order not to have to deal with too many of them.

By contrast with the overwhelming nature of the problems that would face an individual put in charge of global shirt production, each of us can carry out our task of choosing a shirt fairly effectively without outside guidance. A shirt is an item whose quality is more or less visible to inspection before it is bought (whatever reservations one may have about the quality of the buttons). This is more than can be said for medicines, for instance, and indeed the inability of ordinary buyers to discern the properties of a medicine just by looking at it is central to explaining why we usually choose to delegate at least part of the responsibility for our health to those more expert than ourselves.

Large numbers also help us to understand one of the most mysterious features of a system with no one in charge: its apparent ability to anticipate my desire when I have done nothing to communicate that desire to anyone. We may like to think of ourselves as individuals quite unlike others, but in many respects our behavior is highly predictable. Partly this is because of our biology: we have physical needs that are by and large common to other members of our species. Social conventions also play a part: nothing in our biology obliges us to have our meals when other people are having theirs, but it makes life more pleasant if we do. But finally it is the sheer number of us that makes our behavior predictable, for large numbers of people tend under many conditions to behave in much more regular ways than do any of the particular individuals of which such crowds are composed. Statisticians of the early nineteenth century were fascinated by the fact that even such profoundly personal actions as suicide occurred in a sufficiently regular way in large populations as to be predictable within certain limits.[4] And our more banal activities of working, dressing, shopping, cooking, and traveling turn out, in the mass, to display a regularity sufficiently striking for whole centers of productive activity to be based upon it. If I had not bought my shirt this morning, somebody rather like me would very probably have bought it within a few days. It is on that conjecture that my shirt-maker has built a business.

These four factors—large numbers, great complexity, few direct interconnections between the actions of the different buyers of shirts, and a reasonable ability on the part of ordinary buyers to assess the quality of what they are buying—provide the beginning of an answer to our earlier question: why is it a relief to know that no one is in charge of making the world's shirts? One of the great intellectual achievements of modern economics has been to work out very precisely the circumstances under which decentralized systems of market exchange can produce results that are efficient, in the sense of improving the condition of every individual as far as possible whenever this can be done without harming someone else. This definition of efficiency was originally proposed by the Italian economist and sociologist Vilfredo Pareto and is now known as Pareto-efficiency. The intellectual achievement of economics in showing how and when market exchange can achieve Pareto-efficiency is not the same thing as a practical achievement, for as we shall see, all real-life systems of market exchange fail to live up to these demanding conditions, sometimes to a disturbing degree. But shirts are a pretty good advertisement for decentralized market exchange. They are also a remarkable reminder of how much of the pattern of modern life has emerged without ever having been consciously willed by anyone.

Two Reasons for Doubt

Arguments such as these may still not be enough to remove a nagging doubt. Can we be sure that shirt-making shows us the virtues of tunnel vision rather than the vices of central control? Does the shirt-making system really work so well? There are two serious grounds for wondering whether it works as well as it could. The first is that, while the system produces shirts well given the circumstances at any particular time, it may be unstable across time. Swings of fashion and small divergences between producers in their costs of production can result in large shifts of demand away from some producers and in favor of others. In particular, the very internationalization of shirt production described at the beginning of this chapter has led to the loss of many jobs in rich countries whose textile industries have been in steep decline for several decades.[5] Some years ago *The Economist* expressed vividly the anxiety underlying this criticism on its front cover, which portrayed an emaciated, poorly dressed, and dark-skinned man under the caption: "He wants your job." There is often much inconsistency (not to mention xenophobia) in such sentiments, especially when they assert that other countries should buy our products without presuming to make any of their own — as if they could afford to do the one without also doing the other. But there is also a potentially more serious and well-founded point. Even though, on average, shirts made through international cooperation are shirts that correspond better to what their wearers want, if the system that creates them increases instability, that may be bad for everyone. In former ages people faced major hazards affecting their productive abilities (mainly disease and the failure of the harvest). As these hazards have declined, people face threats not so much to their ability to produce as to their ability to sell what they have produced. In an internationally integrated set of markets, people may develop their skills at producing good-quality shirts but find that these skills have become worthless because of unexpected shifts in the decisions of buyers on the other side of the world.

So the growing international division of labor has certainly not removed the threat of instability for those who make shirts, or grow food, or build cars. But that does not mean it has *increased* instability relative to some realistic alternative. The risks of disease and harvest failure are *much* lower today in almost all parts of the world than they were a century or two ago (the exceptions being parts of Africa). And we should not underestimate how often farmers, traders, and artisans in preindustrial societies suffered from the collapse of the market for what they produced.[6] When markets were typically more local, fragmented and cut off from the outside world than they are today, their failures did not show up as world or even as national events. But they could be just as catastrophic for the individuals caught in their wake. True, the instability of some modern markets is indeed a serious problem for the world economic system. But one reason it seems so serious is that a number of problems that once seemed even larger now trouble us much less.

The second ground for dissent about the effects of tunnel vision would challenge my description of the system as delivering the shirts that wearers want. A much more sinister interpretation is possible: the system teaches wearers to want what the system can deliver. If I believe that I can buy almost everything I want without traveling more than a short distance from my home, that may only show how effectively I have been brainwashed, since it apparently never occurs to me to want something I would have to travel further to get. In the 1950s Vance Packard's popular and riveting book *The Hidden Persuaders* persuaded people that they were in the grip of advertisers who were not only unscrupulous but extraordinarily powerful. Advertisers were achieving in the West what commissars were trying less successfully to do in the East.[7]

These two arguments, though sometimes made by the same people, cannot be simultaneously right, at least not to any important degree. If producers are capable of persuading the public to want whatever they produce, they cannot at the same time be vulnerable to being deserted by the public at any moment for the wares of a rival producer. This same inconsistency pervades Naomi Klein's influential book *No Logo*, which claims that through the process of creating worldwide brands, corporations have become all-powerful, but that they are at the same time engaged in a desperate struggle to survive in the face of competition from each other.[8] Indeed, some of the examples she used to illustrate the unassailable power of brands (such as Levi's jeans) were already looking weak even by the time her book was published.

In fact both arguments express a deep-rooted anxiety at the powerlessness of individuals in the face of a large and anonymous world economic system, and it is the fact that such powerlessness strikes a chord among today's citizens that has made Naomi Klein a millionaire. But the two arguments give different and incompatible accounts of that powerlessness. *The Hidden Persuaders* told us we were powerless because someone else had the power. The instability thesis tells us we are powerless because no one has power. In fact the instability thesis is a more persuasive account of the dangers in tunnel vision, though we shall see in later chapters that *The Hidden Persuaders* may also have an important lesson for us. But for the time being let me return to shirts and reiterate the simple message they bring us. Even if tunnel vision has dangers, an understanding of those dangers has to start with an explanation of the remarkable fact that many thousands of productive and useful activities work *at all* with no one in overall charge.

Is that really because of tunnel vision or in spite of it? Could it be that they work because people are public-spirited, because they understand what the system needs and do their best to contribute? The difficulty with this suggestion is not the assumption that people may be public-spirited. There is plenty of evidence that, in the right circumstances, people can be persuaded to behave in very selfless ways. The real problem lies not with the idea that there is public spirit so much as with the assumption that people have no difficulty knowing what public spirit requires. If the shirt-making system as a whole is too hard for a single individual to understand, it is no easier for each of a large number of people to do so. The only reason why the system works better with no one in charge is that each of the many individuals who contribute need worry about only a small part of the task, and it is much easier to worry about a part than to worry about the whole. The sense of being responsible for the whole world could easily become a disabling burden.

THE ROLE OF GOVERNMENT

It may seem strange to suggest that no one is in charge, since we may well wonder what politicians are for. Every country has a finance minister, or a treasury secretary, or chancellor, whose job it is to look after the nation's economy. There may be no one in charge of the world economy, but that is because there is no world government. At the level of the nation state, one might think, it is surely clear who is in charge.

Yet is it really so clear? There is a lost look sometimes that flits across the brow of those senior politicians who have not managed to attain perfect facial self-control. It is the look of a small boy who has dreamed all his life of being allowed to take the controls of an airplane, but who discovers when at last he does that none of the controls he operates seems to be connected to anything, or that they work in such an unpredictable way that it is safer to leave them alone altogether. Politicians have very little power, if by power we mean the capacity to achieve the goals they had hoped and promised to achieve. Another such admission came from the dismissed British chancellor Norman Lamont, who accused the government he had left (after the U.K.'s forced exit from the European Exchange Rate Mechanism in 1992) of being "in office but not in power." He meant it as an accusation against a particular government, but to a greater or lesser degree it characterizes the predicament of any government of a complex modern society. It is a predicament that begins at the most simple level of all, that of knowing what is happening around us — for as the economist Sir Josiah Stamp once observed, "the Government are very keen on amassing statistics. They collect them, add them, raise them to the nth power, take the cube root and prepare wonderful diagrams. But you must never forget that every one of these figures comes in the first instance from the village watchman, who just puts down what he damn well pleases."[9] Without eyes and ears of their own, politicians are touchingly dependent on the cooperation of those they supposedly govern. It is cooperation that precedes government and not the other way round.

Politicians are in charge of a modern economy in much the same way as a sailor is in charge of a small boat in a storm. The consequences of their losing control completely may be catastrophic (as civil war and hyperinflation in parts of the former Soviet empire have recently reminded us), but even while they keep afloat, their influence over the course of events is tiny in comparison with that of the storm around them. We who are their passengers may focus our hopes and fears upon them, and express profound gratitude toward them if we reach harbor safely, but that is chiefly because it seems pointless to thank the storm.

Politicians' inability to control events is not an accidental and regrettable feature of modern society. It is a consequence of the very complexity and the consequent tunnel vision, that have given us both the rewards and the dangers of prosperity in its modern form, in the same way as storms are an inevitable danger once a boat leaves port and heads for the open sea. Many of the most anguished debates over the way society should be organized have turned upon the choice between the often irreconcilable attractions of the port and the open sea. The eternal verities of the countryside versus the adventure and decadence of the city; the virtues of national self-sufficiency versus the rewards of integration into the world economy; the security of traditional forms of order and community versus the flexibility and lack of constraint implicit in modernity: these tensions are too deeply rooted in humanity to be resolved simply by a bold declaration in favor of one or the other pole. Politicians who declare in favor of one or the other may ride a temporary wave but risk an eventual turn of the tide: in the case of Marxism, the wave lasted half a century, with help from the secret police, while its successor liberal democracy is little over a decade old in the former Soviet empire and the nationalist tide is gathering force. Nationalism is, after all, just tunnel vision with costumes and flags, but it is driven principally by a fear of the anonymous open sea.

It should by now be clear that this book is not a hymn to tunnel vision. Tunnel vision is what makes it possible for all the participants in the task of supplying the world's need for shirts to respond to that need in the many ways it expresses itself, without having continually to check back to base; there is no base. But tunnel vision is also what makes it possible for us to pollute the earth without thinking of the costs. Tunnel vision is what enables a worker in a factory making land mines, and a civil servant authorizing their export, not to think of themselves as accessories to the murder of the small child who will step on the land mine in five years' time. Tunnel vision is what makes us all vulnerable to the sudden disappearance of a market for those skills we have, with much effort, managed to build.

Tunnel vision in this sense is a skill (and a predicament) that was unknown to our hunter-gatherer ancestors. It is a social rather than a biological talent, though it channels powerful biological capacities, and it has developed during the ten thousand or so years that separate us from the first farmers of the Neolithic era. Before we look at its consequences for life in the modern world, it is important to consider why it evolved at all.

Prologue to Part II

What makes trusting strangers a reasonable, instead of a suicidal, thing to do? It's not enough to show that societies in which people can trust one another reap the benefits of peace and prosperity on a scale unimaginable to our distant ancestors. They do, but trust would soon unravel if individuals could enjoy the benefits of other people's cooperative behavior while making no contribution of their own. Making mistakes about the trustworthiness of others is not just costly but extremely dangerous, and more so for human beings than for almost any other species. The evidence that will be reviewed in part 2 suggests that, in the absence of incentives to the contrary, human beings can behave so violently toward one another that no sane person would trust others based on their natural dispositions alone. If we do so, it is because we have created structures of social life in which such judgments of trust make sense. Still, the structures work — most of the time — because they do not run against the grain of our natural dispositions but build on them in a constructive way.

Two kinds of disposition have proved important to our evolution: a capacity for rational calculation of the costs and benefits of cooperation, and a tendency for what has been called *reciprocity* — the willingness to repay kindness with kindness and betrayal with revenge, even when this is not what rational calculation would recommend. Neither disposition could support cooperation without the other. People given to calculation without reciprocity would be too opportunistic, so nobody would trust them. People given to reciprocity without calculation would be too easily exploited by others. It seems likely that natural selection favored the evolution of a balance between these two dispositions in our ancestors. It did so because such a balance was important to the development of social life even before these ancestors ever began to deal with strangers in any systematic way. But once the dispositions were there, they could be put to work to make exchange between strangers possible.

In the chapters that follow we look at how the balance between reciprocity and calculation underpins our social life. No social institution can function on calculation alone, but well-designed social institutions can make a little reciprocity go a long way. They do so, in effect, by making it reasonable for us to treat strangers as though they were honorary relatives or friends. We frame rules for behavior toward strangers that mimic the way we treat our family and our friends, and we reinforce these rules by explicit systems of incentives, as well as by education and training—an apprenticeship for social life that is designed to make opportunistic behavior more uncomfortable for us. By training us to follow the rules of social cooperation, this apprenticeship makes our behavior reliable enough for others to count upon. At the same time, and disturbingly, it reinforces our tunnel vision, giving us a power to influence our world at a distance that exceeds our capacity to care much of the time about the damage we can do, a power whose consequences we shall explore more fully in part 3.

The knowledge that most people can be trusted much of the time to play their part in the complex web of social cooperation has had dramatic effects on the psychology of our everyday life. Our ancestors of twelve thousand years ago have left no novels, diaries, or travelogues, but it is a reasonable bet that when they moved across the plains of Africa and Eurasia they did so cautiously, in small bands, taking care not to expose themselves to those strangers they might occasionally hear or see in the distance. Their brains had evolved under selective pressures favoring caution and mistrust, since opportunistic murder and organized warfare were almost certainly at least as common among early humans as they are among chimpanzees.[1] Those brains were physically almost indistinguishable from the brains of their descendants who are alive today.[2] Yet any one of these descendants may step nonchalantly out of the front door of a suburban house and disappear into a city of ten million strangers, every one of whom is as much his biological rival as the strangers of whom his ancestors were so justly wary two hundred centuries ago.

PART II

From Murderous Apes to Honorary Friends: How Is Human Cooperation Possible?

CHAPTER 2

Man and the Risks of Nature

JUDGING CHANCES

It is notoriously hard to make scientifically robust statements about something as complex and multifaceted as human intelligence, and even more so to compare the intelligence of different groups. But here are two statements we can be reasonably confident are true. First, over the course of human evolution in the 6 or 7 million years since our last common ancestor with chimpanzees and bonobos, children have been, on average, very slightly less intelligent than their parents. Secondly, over that same period, grandchildren have been, again on average, very slightly *more* intelligent than their grandparents.

How can these statements both be true? Grandchildren are just the children of children, after all. Here's the explanation. Children bear the genes of their parents in a random combination. This combination might make them either more or less intelligent than their parents, but there's no reason to expect one outcome more than the other. When averaged over the many billions of children who have ever been born, combinations of parental genes can be expected to have the same intelligence as the parental genes themselves. In addition, a very few children will be the bearers of genetic mutations. A tiny fraction of these genetic mutations will be favorable ones, enhancing the intelligence of their bearers. But the overwhelming majority will be damaging, for the same reason that a random blow delivered to a television set is much more likely to damage it than to improve its reception. The combined effect of combination and mutation, again over billions of children, is to bring the average intelligence of children to a level very slightly below that of their parents.

What about the children's children? Their intelligence will be slightly below that of *their* parents, certainly, and for the same reasons. But those parents were not just the randomly selected children of the grandparents' generation; they were the children who survived and succeeded in reproducing. *Given that they had survived to reproduce*, those children were likely to be slightly more intelligent than their own parents, and they would have transmitted this slight advantage to their children in turn. This advantage, though slight, would nevertheless have been large enough across the population to outweigh the negative effect of mutations. Again, this is a statement about averages, one we know to be true since modern man has a higher intelligence than the chimpanzee, even if it may not have been true for any particular generation of the three hundred thousand that separate us from our last common ancestor. There's nothing particularly mysterious about this fact, nor does it indicate any kind of historical inevitability. It's just that what we *call* intelligence is a mixed group of mental capacities for anticipating and manipulating our environment — precisely the capacities that, in the long run, tend to promote survival and reproduction. Indeed, we can be more confident about the comparison of intelligence between humans and chimpanzees than we could ever be about the comparison of intelligence between human beings, which underlines the fact that our statement is about averages and not about any given pair of generations.

This explanation not only encapsulates the essentials of the theory of natural selection; it also makes use of the two most fundamental ideas in statistics. The first idea is embodied in the law of large numbers, which states, roughly, that the average behavior of a large group of similar individuals will be more predictable than the behavior of a small group, or of any one individual in that group. (It is sometimes known informally as the law of averages.) Consider a seaside town whose citizens can choose at the weekend between going to the beach, going to the park, and staying at home. On any particular weekend it may be very hard to predict what one individual will do, but it is comparatively easy to predict, within a reasonable margin, what proportion of citizens will choose each of the three options. Any one individual may decide to go to the park, but for the whole town to go to the park would require a massive and implausible correlation between their individual decisions (implausible, that is, unless they were all there for the Fourth of July parade). Similarly, over the course of a whole year, if we try to predict what proportion of weekends any one individual might choose to go to the park, we would expect a lot of variation between individuals, and our margin of error would be large. If we try to predict the total proportion of the citizens who go to the park over the whole year, the margin of error would be much smaller. This is another way of saying that, if we decide how close to the true proportion our prediction has to be to count as successful, we will be successful more often when predicting the behavior of all citizens than when predicting the behavior of any one of them. Ice cream sellers and deck chair attendants have a much more predictable future in a large town than a small one.

The second statistical idea is known as conditional probability. If we try to predict what proportion of a group will behave in a certain way, our prediction will (and should) be sensitive to what other information we have. We may know that, on average over the year, 5 percent of the town's citizens go to the beach at the weekend. However, if we consider just weekends in summer, that proportion rises to 10 percent. If we consider weekends on which the temperature rises above thirty degrees, the proportion rises to 20 percent. So, conditional on information about the season or the temperature, the proportion of citizens going to the beach is different from the proportion we would calculate if we had no such information. Likewise, if we know it is the Fourth of July, we will realize that the town's citizens are not behaving independently; that their behavior is correlated — meaning that to find them all at the park would not require an extraordinary coincidence, just a peculiarity of the calendar.

We can also calculate probabilities conditional not on information about external events but about a particular subgroup of people. For example, the proportion of beachgoers among those citizens who cannot swim is lower than among all citizens as a whole. Similarly, the average intelligence of children among those who survive to reproduce is different from the average among all children who are born.

The effect of conditional probability depends on what unconditional probabilities we start with. Knowing that it is a hot weekend in summer makes us guess that 20 percent of the population will go to the beach — given that we started from a baseline of 5 percent in the first place. If we had taken a different town, miles from the sea, in which over the year as a whole only 1 percent go anywhere near a beach, our assessment for a hot weekend in summer would have been much lower. This kind of sensitivity to initial conditions notoriously bedevils medical diagnosis. If you test positive for a fairly common disease on a test with 99 percent reliability, the chances are that you have the disease. If you test positive on a test with the same reliability, but for an extremely rare condition, the chances are overwhelmingly *against* your having the disease, even though the probability is greater than it was before you took the test. This is because the 99 percent of people with the disease who are found by the test may still be few in number compared to the 1 percent of "false positives" generated by the rest of the population. So if the disease is rare, you're much more likely to be a false positive than a true one.[1] This idea is embodied in the statistical theorem known as Bayes Law.

Using the laws of statistics does not require a sophisticated mathematical education: people and animals use the law of large numbers and the idea of conditional probability all the time. They may not know they are doing so, any more than a pool player necessarily knows he is using mechanics and trigonometry. Fish swimming in schools for safety are instinctively using the law of large numbers, while working with conditional probability is central to animal survival. My predators are distributed across the savannah in such a way that if I wander around at random, I shall come across a predator perhaps once a day. But if I make an unnecessary sound or stand upwind of the waterhole, that frequency will rise to a dangerous level. Not only does it help me to know this, but I may even be able to manipulate the conditional probabilities in my favor—by using camouflage, say, or mimicking the appearance of a poisonous or aggressive animal.

Human society has also evolved in ways that reflect these powerful statistical ideas. In particular we have developed to take advantage of the benefits of large numbers, through a vastly increased complexity in our social organization. This does not mean that we have usually been conscious of these benefits, still less that our social organization has been planned with such benefits in mind. Quite the contrary: our conscious understanding of statistical ideas has developed slowly, usually in response to prior social developments. The formal discipline of statistics, for instance, was an outgrowth of the need of eighteenth-century nation-states to count and supervise their citizens, and to underpin their public finances by the sale of annuities whose profitability depended on understanding the patterns of mortality in their already large populations.[2] And our emotional responses to events in our lives is often more appropriate to the small hunter-gatherer bands in which we evolved than to the numberless millions to whom our fates are linked today: a television report about the abduction and murder of a child, for instance, has all the shocking power of a truly rare atrocity, yet our news media trawl in such a vast ocean that they can supply us with a diet of such stories every day, if we have the appetite for them. Our perceptions of risk are often shaped by the conspicuousness of events rather than their real frequency: far fewer Americans died in hijacked aircraft on 11 September 2001, than were to die in cars during the following week, but the events of that terrifying day have now branded themselves into our perceptions, knotting the stomachs of airline passengers and leading travelers in their millions to abandon air travel for the illusory safety of the car.

The complexity of modern society has had a radical impact on the kinds of risk we face in our lives: many of these risks are much, much smaller than anything faced by our ancestors, and some are significantly larger. Yet our ability and willingness to participate in the great experiment that has created modern society rests on a willingness to trust the strangers we meet, a willingness more emotional than reflective. What makes us willing to entrust our lives to the pilot of an aircraft, accept food from a stranger in a restaurant, enter a subway train packed full of our genetic rivals? Most of the time we do not reflect more than glancingly on these choices; when we bring them out into the open, especially in political debate, our hopes and fears can be animated by shadows — foreigners, powerful conspirators, demented scientists, child abductors, terrorists. *Homo sapiens sapiens*, equipped with emotions that have evolved to judge the dangers of hunting, the probability of finding roots and berries to eat, the risks involved in challenging dominant members of his band, whether he can commit adultery undetected, must now apply these cognitive tools to assessing genetically modified food, the returns to his private pension fund, whether to pay for an airbag in his car, whether to let his daughter cycle to the grocery store, and the increased risk of a terrorist attack if he chooses to live downtown rather than in the suburbs. Some constants remain — the risks involved in challenging dominant members of his band, whether he can commit adultery undetected — but the scale of the new challenges is vast.

In this chapter we examine the benefits that large numbers have brought us, and in chapter 3 we ask how this happened, how our hunter-gatherer psychology brought these benefits within our grasp. Though our capacity for trust is the product of our evolution, and therefore subject to powerful genetic influences, nothing implies that these genetic influences have narrowly determined how we behave — if they had done so, if we could not adapt ourselves to new challenges, the great experiment could never even have begun. The evolution of human behavior has been haphazard, and the various impulses that have been favored by natural selection at different times among our ancestors have been only imperfectly integrated into the thought and action of their descendants. Nevertheless, it is important for us to understand some of the strong personalities on the squabbling committee that is the modern human mind. We face conflicts — for instance, between our rational assessment that the probability of death in an airplane is lower than in a car and our greater emotional security when it is our own hand on the steering wheel rather than an invisible stranger's hand on the aircraft controls. Our reasoning capacities have had to survive through millions of years facing certain kinds of survival problems, and in competition with the reasoning capacities of our predators and rivals. This history has left its fingerprint indelibly on the way we reason and the way we behave.

Task-Sharing as a Way to Reduce Risk

Human beings differ from all other species in many ways, and one of particular importance for our understanding of risk is the high degree to which unrelated individuals share tasks. Task-sharing takes place to a limited degree in all species that reproduce sexually. Father and mother make different contributions to the creation and rearing of children, often highly unequal contributions in terms of the investment of time and energy they require, but both essential to the outcome. But human beings' capacity—unique in nature, as we have seen—to share tasks regularly and elaborately with others to whom they are unrelated has enabled them to exploit the presence of large numbers in a way unavailable to the other higher mammals. Creatures with large brains require high parental investment in both hardware (protein) and software (knowledge and skill). This requires long gestation and infancy periods, and a strict limit to the number of children born at each pregnancy. In addition the upright posture of human beings, by constricting the size of the female pelvis, limits the time the human fetus can spend in the womb: by ape standards, human children are systematically born premature, and all need intensive care. These facts limit the numbers of closely related individuals that can expect to be alive at any one time. Human social organization has therefore required either relatively small-sized units (like hunter-gatherer bands) or the evolution of a capacity to exchange goods and favors between unrelated individuals. The social insects have avoided running up against these constraints only because of their microscopic brain size—at a cost, therefore, of confinement to a narrow range of inflexible learned behavior patterns on the part of each individual.

What benefits have large numbers brought? Three main benefits stand out: risk-sharing, specialization, and the accumulation of knowledge. In a complex modern society the benefit of risk-sharing seems clear: the risks of the natural and social worlds do not fall simultaneously on everyone, and large numbers enable them to be shared. Not everyone's harvest fails at the same time; not everyone's house burns down on the same night; not everyone's invention fails to fulfil its promise. Sometimes the risk-sharing is accomplished explicitly, as when an insurance company uses premium income from the lucky to pay for the damage suffered by the unlucky. More often the risk-sharing is implicit, as when a bank is able to offer me a more predictable return on my investment than if I lent directly to any of its borrowing customers. Sometimes fluctuations in market conditions are themselves ways of sharing risk: when there has been widespread harvest failure in a region, prices will tend to rise, which means that buyers share in the losses that would otherwise be borne only by sellers. These high prices also act as a magnet to suppliers from elsewhere, creating a natural mechanism whereby producers of the crop who have not suffered a failure send supplies in the direction of those who have. Most generally of all, large numbers are the comfort not only of ice-cream sellers and deck-chair attendants but of all traders who face an unpredictable demand for what they sell. They are the comfort of all people who would like to go out and buy something, anything from a pizza to a pair of pants, without having to place a special order for it, and all its components and ingredients, a long time beforehand. These ways of benefiting from large numbers do not always work: banks can go bankrupt, pizzas can stay limply on the shelf, speculative frenzies can mean that rising prices attract even more buyers than sellers (as did Dutch tulips in the seventeenth century or dot.com stocks in the late twentieth). But it takes large numbers for them to work at all, and any people benefiting from them are using the laws of statistics, whether they are aware of it or not.

Our hunter-gatherer ancestors faced most of the risks of nature alone or in small bands composed primarily of close relatives. Nevertheless, there is evidence that they began to live in progressively larger groups as they evolved. The anthropologist Robin Dunbar has shown that there is a positive correlation across primate species between brain size and the average size of groups and has argued that individuals need the extra brain power to keep track of the increased complexity of social relationships in larger communities.[3] Although there is some controversy about how accurately this applies to our early human ancestors, it seems plausible that while chimpanzees live in groups of approximately 60 individuals, the Australopithecine species, who appeared about 4.5 million years ago, lived in groups averaging around 70 members, the first toolmakers (around 2 million years ago) in groups of around 80, Homo erectus in groups of around 110, and Neanderthal man in groups of around 140. It is also likely that group structures became more fluid, with subgroups coming together from time to time to cooperate on more ambitious projects.

Even though banks, insurance companies, and markets as we know them did not exist, these larger groups made possible a better sharing of risks. Those who found game could share it with the rest of the group knowing that they would likewise benefit on their own lean days from the good luck of others. Large groups also made possible larger-scale activities: hunting big animals such as mammoths, which yielded essential protein for the nourishing of large-brained infants. Part of the reason is the rewards to sheer scale in contests of force: a group twice the size of another has much more than twice the chance of killing the mammoth, so two groups that can work together have each a much better prospect of finding protein than they do when working alone. Part of the reason is insurance: a large group can afford to dedicate some of its members to an inherently risky project such as a mammoth hunt, knowing that failure in the hunt, or even the death of the hunters, will not mean starvation for the group as a whole.

TASK-SHARING AND SPECIALIZATION

The second main consequence of human beings' capacity to share tasks with those to whom they are unrelated is that large numbers enable specialization. When a large group of individuals cooperate to make their living in a hostile environment, the real benefits come precisely when they do not all behave alike, and this fact requires them to exploit the laws of conditional probability in a much more sophisticated way.

Once again, in a complex modern society this can be taken for granted. No single farmer could possibly produce all the variety of foods available in a modern supermarket, both because there are benefits to any farmer from concentrating on a few crops and because no single climate and no single soil are suitable for producing everything human beings enjoy eating. Germans are particularly fond of bananas, for example; they have one of the highest per capita rates of consumption in the world. But bananas grow badly (and expensively) in Germany, so Germans have quite reasonably concentrated on producing other things, things they can export in order to import bananas in return. In fact, the doctrine of comparative advantage, propounded in the nineteenth century by the economist David Ricardo, drew attention to the striking fact that it makes sense for individuals and countries to specialize even if they do *everything* well.[4] They should concentrate on doing what they do best of all, leaving others to do the rest. A brain surgeon should never mow her own lawn, even if she does it much better than her gardener, since the time she spends behind the mower would be much more productively spent on neurosurgery. That is good news for brain surgeons, and it is good news for gardeners, even (or especially) for not-very-good gardeners. Everyone has a *comparative* advantage even if there is nothing they do particularly well.

Something similar is true of the various contributions to the process of making a shirt. It is quite possible for an entire shirt to be made, from start to finish, by a single person, but that person must accomplish a great range of tasks, from growing cotton to spinning and weaving, to fashioning buttons out of suitable materials, to making all the tools that are used in these various operations. But in the modern world shirts are not made this way, except by extremely poor Hopis or extremely rich hippies. Instead, the different participants specialize, either because of natural advantages they possess for performing one task rather than another (the inhabitants of India have a geographical advantage over Inuits when it comes to growing cotton) or because of an acquired skill. For some tasks it may not matter what speciality you choose so long as you specialize in something.

But specializing can itself be a risky process, especially if it requires training or other kinds of investment; it may therefore depend on the presence of large numbers of potential customers to be worth undertaking. In the second half of the eighteenth century, Adam Smith described the way in which artisans, who had specialized in something more dependent on others than simply growing crops, could usually be found concentrated in towns. In towns there was less chance that the market for their products might just disappear (and they could also learn from others of their kind). There was a limit to this concentration — blacksmiths, for instance, usually remained in the villages, because they needed horses, and horses needed the land. Becoming a blacksmith was less risky in Adam Smith's time than it is today, since most villages had enough horses to support at least one smith. By contrast, it is less risky to become a biologist than a blacksmith today: in the eighteenth century most biologists had to be gentlemen of leisure, whose choice of occupation had no impact on their subsistence. But both biologists and blacksmiths need to invest their time and often their money in acquiring the skills necessary for their trades. They have to take this decision before they know who exactly is going to want their skills enough to offer them something valuable in return. The larger and richer the populations among whom they live, or among whom they can engage in exchange, the more likely it is that any degree of specialization can be undertaken at an acceptable level of risk.*

Much of the growing complexity of human societies in the last few thousand years has consisted of a self-reinforcing tendency to specialize: specialization increases prosperity so that more people are free to develop new aspirations or satisfy old ones, and thereby in turn gain the confidence necessary to specialize. And by the same logic, whole societies have sometimes been stuck in a trap in which failure to specialize has denied them the prosperity that might have made such specialization easily affordable. Examples include Japan, which closed itself to the outside world from the beginning of the seventeenth to the middle of the nineteenth centuries,[5] and many of the countries in sub-Saharan

---

* The death in April 2003 of Charlie Douglass, the inventor of canned laughter for television, was a poignant reminder that the modern world has produced a luxuriance of specialist professions that would have been utterly baffling to even our recent ancestors (see *The Independent*, 25 April 2003).

Africa that won independence from colonizing powers after the Second World War.

In fact, hunter-gatherer societies began to specialize once they had found ways to manage cooperation between people who were not related. Even hunting tasks can be divided up. Some people specialize in tracking animals, either because they are naturally good at it or because they have devoted much time and effort to mastering the skills. Others are the strategists, planning and directing the operation. Others may act as decoys, learning birdcalls and other tricks to lead the prey into a trap. Yet others do the club work at the kill. Even small bands of relatives must have divided up tasks to some degree, but as the bands grew larger, specialization, and the uses to which it could be put, became more ambitious.

Once bands were willing to make tentative peaceful contact with other bands, they could exchange with them, thereby enormously expanding the kinds of foods, tools, and resources to which they had access. We have evidence of exchange between hunter-gatherers from many thousands of years before the foundation of agriculture, although their lifestyle must have made such contacts sporadic and limited by comparison with the opportunities available to sedentary farmers in later millennia. Some of the oldest known symbolic artifacts, carved beads dating back over forty thousand years, may have played a role in facilitating such exchanges.[6] In more recent times, the Yir Yoront aboriginals of Northern Australia had stone axes even though they lived many hundreds of kilometers from the nearest stone quarries (they exchanged stingray-tipped spears for them with neighboring tribes) and even steel ones, well before their first contact with European traders at the end of the nineteenth century.[7] Trade allowed access not only to their neighbors' skills but to those of their neighbors' neighbors, and so on.

Perhaps the greatest innovation came when the bands grew large enough for some of their members to specialize entirely in activities that made no immediate contribution to the band's food supply: warfare against other human beings and the organization and transmission of knowledge. The army and the priesthood were born.

For this to happen took a great many facilitating circumstances, notably the adoption of agriculture and a settled lifestyle, without which food storage is impossible on a significant scale. But once this occurred, around ten thousand years ago, the army and the priesthood grew rapidly in both size and importance, because bands were in competition with each other. Once you have invested in an army, it pays to have a big one, since you can enslave other bands whose armies are smaller or weaker than your own and steal their food without having to grow or gather it yourself: slaves quickly became the third specialist caste. Indeed, stealing food from hunter-gatherers is usually more trouble than it is worth, since they have so little to steal. Only farmers who have stored a whole harvest are a worthwhile target for systematic plunder. The consequences of this competitive spiral are the subject of chapter 13.

Similarly, once you have a priesthood, it pays to have a literate and organized priesthood, so that this generation's specialists can draw on some of the skills of the previous generation without having to learn everything anew. Symbolic artifacts — durable records of the ideas and utterances of previous generations — become a means for sharing of tasks between generations, thereby leading to the accumulation of collective knowledge that is the third great benefit of cooperation among large numbers, a phenomenon that is examined in detail in chapter 11.

Prior to the foundation of agriculture, specialization had even fed back into human evolution by changing the stakes in the evolution of intelligence. When your band is small and everyone in it behaves more or less alike, there is little to be gained from developing a sophisticated capacity for psychological insight or a subtle sense of social hierarchy. When societies become larger and more specialized, those who can anticipate and adapt to this complexity are much more likely to prosper than those who cannot. The selective pressures in favor of social intelligence must have become significantly stronger over time (and have certainly continued since the invention of agriculture, though this time is too short for there to have been a clearly perceptible effect). It has been persuasively argued by Steven Mithen in his book *The Prehistory of the Mind* that the changed selective pressures associated with large bands and more complex task-sharing played a crucial part in the evolution of the modern human brain. They were particularly important in shaping the development of its capacities for art, culture, and a scientific approach to the natural world, of which early human beings have left us no traces older than sixty thousand years, at most.

SPECIALIZATION AND NEW KINDS OF RISK

The specialization of modern societies has increased to a degree unimaginable by our hunter-gatherer ancestors, and that would have been astonishing even to our eighteenth-century relatives. Much of this specialization has been the fruit of the greater security that larger and richer societies make possible, but its effect has not always been to reinforce that security. Quite the contrary: people specialize more than ever in activities that put them at the mercy of the disappearance of markets for their products and skills. This is no stranger than the observation

that it is usually people who own the safest cars who drive most dangerously. Such behavior is known as risk compensation; it has been documented, for example, in relation to the effect of legislation requiring the
wearing of seat belts in cars.[8] (John Adams has even argued that if we
really care about reducing car accidents we should oblige all cars to be
fitted with a sharp spike on the steering wheel pointed at the driver's
chest.[9]) Risk compensation is not pathological: it is the very behavior
that — fortunately — makes us behave more cautiously on mountainsides
than in meadows. But it has implications for the kinds of risk that modern societies face.

Until around six hundred years ago in Europe, and until a little more
recently in North America, most families ate food they had grown
themselves.[10] They were certainly not self-sufficient in the strict sense
since they usually relied on others for some things — metal for agricultural tools, for example. But changes in their links with the outside
world would rarely threaten their food supply. Today, in the same countries, most families who were prevented from exchanging with others
would starve within a few weeks. Threats to their ability to exchange
are unlikely to come from physical obstacles, except in wartime (as the
population of Leningrad — now St. Petersburg again — discovered under
siege from Hitler's army in the winter of 1941). Much more likely is a
threat to their ability to offer anything in exchange, that is, a situation
in which nobody wants to buy what they have to sell. This is the main
risk that members of highly specialized societies face today.

It is usually a mistake to think that the risks that come from depending on exchange with others are greater than the risks that come from
facing the environment alone. Most families even three hundred years
ago were far more likely to die from the failure of their own crops or
from disease than are their descendants today to die from all causes
combined. Nearly one child in five died in the first year of life, compared to less than one child in two hundred in Europe and North America today.[11] Self-sufficiency is sometimes a positive curse: without regular exchange with others you cannot get medical treatment when you
need it, you cannot borrow to cover temporary disasters, you cannot
quickly replace a broken tool. The misguided pursuit of self-sufficiency
in recent decades has cost many poor countries dearly, making them
unable, for instance, to import adequate supplies when their own domestic harvest fails. So depending on others does not necessarily create
greater risks for the citizens of today's specialized societies. But it does
create very *different* risks.

Many people in today's world have seen their livelihoods threatened
and their savings disappear, not (or not only) through any fault of their
own, not (or not only) through the hazards of a natural and therefore

impersonal environment, but through the faraway actions of many other people who in most cases have neither intended nor even been aware of that result. Coal miners for the last few decades have been squeezed between the rising costs of digging coal from the ground and the decisions of many consumers, politicians, and civil servants that coal is an expensive and dirty fuel. Those who make such a judgment did not want to put coal miners out of work, but that is what happened as a result of their decisions. Many families have lost the savings they deposited in banks that invested in the real estate booms in Texas in the 1980s or Thailand in the 1990s — savings they invested in good faith in banks that had apparently been reliable in the past. (Every time a bank goes bust, it's a break with the past; but banks go bust all the time.) The real estate investors whose loss of confidence caused the booms to collapse did not intend depositors to lose their savings as a result. They neither knew nor cared, any more than they had known or cared that depositors were benefiting from their optimism during the boom years. The reason for that collapse was a subtle misunderstanding of the laws of statistics. Each investor thought the others were making independent judgments and did not realize how correlated their behavior was. No one understood that the whole boom was nothing but a Fourth of July parade.

It would be a mistake to think that specialization and its associated risks are the consequence of the market economy alone. The market economy is one of the historical faces of specialization, but it is not the only one. Quite the contrary: some of the saddest examples of individuals and even whole communities marooned by the tides of demand for their products and skills are to be found in the countries of the former Soviet Union. Under central planning, specialization was pursued to a very high degree, with little attention to the real economic costs of the pattern adopted, which were crippling but did not become clearly visible until a system of markets was put into operation in the 1990s. Central planners combined a desire that each country in the Soviet bloc should specialize intensively, with a desire that the bloc as a whole should be self-sufficient in relation to the rest of the world economy. Many people were sent to Siberia or to Central Asia in the 1950s and 1960s to work the immense natural resources of those regions, but often wasting resources in ways that were only possible because the distorted price system treated them as free or almost free. Cotton growers in Uzbekistan benefited from "free" water, which they used in such abundance that the Aral Sea, fed from the rivers that were now dammed for irrigation, shrank to half its surface area and a third of its volume in less than thirty years. It left behind a great bowl of salt-encrusted, chemically polluted, infertile land, and from this bowl the steppe winds blow poi-

Figure 2.1. An Uzbek government poster display showing the declining levels of the Aral Sea over the last several decades. The level of the sea has fallen from 53 meters to 33 meters, its volume from 53 to 20 cubic kilometers, and the annual inflow of water from 55 to between 1 and 5 cubic kilometers per year. Photo by M. H. Glantz, taken in Nukus, Karakalpakstan, Uzbekistan, in September 1995.

son dust into the lungs of over two million inhabitants, who now suffer from one of the highest incidences of respiratory disease in the world. Here is a striking exception to the claim made in chapter 1 that shirts are comparatively free of interpersonal externalities, of the kind associated with pollution. For when the authorities treat the environment as expendable, even cotton shirts can be bad for us: decisions to grow cotton do direct damage to people's health. Uzbekistan's cotton growers also enjoyed "free" energy: as late as 1995 families were reported to be keeping their gas cookers running twenty-four hours a days because of a shortage of matches. Free or almost free energy led people to ignore energy conservation completely: even today many apartments in northern Russian cities are heated by boilers that send water across distances up to several kilometers in poorly insulated pipes laid in the frosty ground, and even today the only way to lower the temperature in many apartments is to open the window.

What was the result of such prodigality? Many towns across Russia today are in a state of paralysis: the manufacture of polluting fertilizers, drab haberdashery, unreliable tractors, bug-ridden electronic goods — many of them unsaleable at any realistic price — has ground to a halt. Those who lived by such activity were, in the main, doing their reasonable best by the standards of their time. To them it seems, not that their methods of manufacture were short-sighted but that the world that has changed its mind about what it wants.

It's hard to blame the new economic realism, any more than you can blame the funeral for the decease. After all, attempts to cover up the true costs by creative accounting still require someone to foot the bill. Fishermen in the Evenki Autonomous District of Russia's sub-Arctic, for example, still have a deal with the local Tura Aviation Enterprise. Anthropologist David Anderson explains:

> Every spring and autumn the Tura Aviation Enterprise carries a number of Russians out to isolated lakes and rivers throughout the district so that they may set nets and collect barrels of . . . whitefish and grayling. This very expensive service (costing in the order of several tens of thousands of roubles per trip) is supplied in exchange for barrels of fish which are either given to the pilots or to the enterprise (or to both) for eventual resale. Some fresh fish is realised through the [town] store. . . . Other fish is no doubt shared between the aviation community. Some fish undoubtedly finds its way to the tables of high-placed government people in Krasnoiarsk. The high tariffs charged by the aviation company for these fishing expeditions scarcely cover the paper costs of the wages, fuel, and capital costs of the aircraft. On paper, as the pilots joke, the mutual debit arrangement for transport is effected in exchange for fish which by its weight is more expensive than gold.[12]

The arrangement continues because many of the debts are never paid. How long it can continue is anyone's guess, but when it ends, the fishermen will have to find livelihoods elsewhere.

When livelihoods disappear, monetary compensation sometimes helps. But only sometimes. For younger workers a redundancy payment can provide the necessary impetus to move, to retrain, to start a second life. For workers in their forties and above, it is often too late: money may avoid starvation, but it can never restore the sense of having lived a worthwhile life. In prosperous countries those who suffer in this way are often divided, dispersed among the population, unaware of a common identity. Sometimes they become a soil for angry and vengeful political movements — usually, though not always, those of the political right. In Russia today they have found a somber identity in the mortality statistics: men's life expectancy had fallen from sixty-five years in the 1980s to 57 by the mid-1990s — a level equal to that of Zambia before the advent of AIDS, and in contrast to Zambia's, not due principally to infant mortality but to a near doubling of the death rate among men above the age of forty-five. Vodka and violence are usually implicated, often in combination, and rates of suicide have soared.

The predicament of unemployed steelworkers, coal miners, fishermen (not to mention the rich world's textile workers, secretaries, automobile assemblers — all those whose skills are less in demand than they used to be) is not at all new in history. But it has added to the risks with which our hunter-gatherer ancestors were more familiar, the risk of the natural world and its predators and the risk posed by human enemies, neither of which has disappeared. Our emotional reactions to risk are still shaped by that hunter-gatherer heritage. We treat those who suffer the hazards of life either as casualties of a blind chance that we may fear but cannot logically resent, or as victims — chosen sufferers of deliberate aggression to which the only emotional response is resentment and the only justifiable response, revenge. Even today the debate about the costs of economic change in an integrated world is polarized between those who see no casualties, only victims (like the doomed heroes who fought on picket lines to prevent the closing of British coal mines in the long and futile strike of 1984–85), and those who see no victims, only casualties (like those brisk prophets of globalization who are only concerned about reducing trade barriers and not about those who will be hurt as a result). The truth is that those who are hurt by economic change in today's world are predominantly neither casualties nor victims. They fall into a different category, one needing both an emotional and a practical response for which our history has poorly prepared us.

This brings us back to the theme with which we began. The practical intelligence that has evolved among human beings is very skilled at manipulating the natural environment and managing the interactions of small groups of individuals who see each other frequently and know each other well. It is only in the last ten thousand years — far too recently for genetic evolution to have been affected — that human beings have had to come to terms on a significant scale with the impact of strangers, and it is only in the last two hundred or so that this impact has become a dominant fact of everyday life. To manage the hazards imposed on us by the actions of distant strangers has required us to deploy a different skill bequeathed to us by evolution for quite different purposes: the capacity for abstract symbolic thought. In their response to risk no less than in their handling of conflict, modern political institutions seek to restrain by the slender threads of abstract reasoning the passions and resentments of the prehistoric tribe.

CHAPTER 3

Murder, Reciprocity, and Trust

THE MURDEROUSNESS OF MAN

Human social organization has been able, as we have seen, to exploit the advantages of large groups because of exchange between unrelated individuals. But we still need to understand how this widespread reliance on exchange has been possible. It is virtually unknown in the rest of the animal kingdom, and it involves important risks. Only rarely do two individuals make a simultaneous exchange of goods or favors of a known value. Much more commonly there is a favor extended by one in return for a compensating favor at a later date. You give me meat from your mammoth in exchange for a promise of meat in the future; you make me a loan in exchange for a promised sequence of interest payments. How can you be sure I will keep my promise? Even when exchange is simultaneous it often involves a risk: in exchange for your potatoes I have given you vodka, but the vodka may be spiked with methylated spirit; the motorbike I have given you may break down as soon as you drive it, even as I am struggling to repair the washing machine you gave me in return.*

When individuals are close relatives this element of risk does not necessarily prevent fruitful exchange. Natural selection has favored genetic mutations that encourage helping of relatives, which has two distinct advantages. First, relatives are more likely than nonrelatives to keep their promises, and secondly, it matters less if they do not. A mutation that, on balance, makes its bearer more likely to help relatives will favor the propagation of copies of itself in future generations provided enough benefit can be given to relatives for any particular cost to the giver. Indeed, although a sibling shares on average only half of an individual's genes, this still makes for as close a genetic relationship as the individual has with its own child. This does not eliminate rivalry among relatives — far from it — but it has favored, throughout the animal kingdom, valuable and sometimes complex systems of interrelative exchange.

In contrast, helping nonrelatives is valuable in evolutionary terms only when the favor is returned. But the incentives to cheat are many; and, regrettably, human beings cheat in more costly and dangerous

---

* As the old communist joke had it, "We pretend to work, and they pretend to pay us."

ways than any other species. Among the melancholy achievements of *Homo sapiens* is not only to be more intelligent than any other species but also to have slaughtered members of its own species more vigorously, systematically, and cruelly than any other in nature. In his novel *Crime and Punishment*, Dostoyevsky depicted his character Raskolnikov as haunted by the enormity of the murder he had committed,[1] and many readers have seen the novel as support for the view that human beings have a complete and instinctive repugnance for murder, a repugnance that is mysteriously absent only in a tiny minority of psychopaths. It is a moving vision, but one that is sadly incompatible with what we know of the pressures that have shaped our evolution (as well as with much of modern history). For there are good reasons to think not only that natural selection has favored a tendency to kill other members of the same species but also that the coincidence of murderousness and intelligence is not accidental. On the contrary, the selection for murderousness and the selection for intelligence are mutually reinforcing. The more murderous the species, the greater the selective benefit of intelligence to individual members, and the more intelligent the species, the greater the selective benefit of murderousness to individual members.

The first point is reasonably easy to understand. Intelligence already confers a selective advantage when the main hazards you face are the hazards of nature. But the selective advantage is even stronger when the hazards include aggression from other individuals who are on average just as intelligent as you. So any evolution toward murderousness among our ancestors would have increased the speed at which intelligence evolved.

The second point is a little more subtle. What are the selective pressures in favor of murderousness, and why should they be stronger in an intelligent species? The pressures in favor of murderousness arise from a simple fact: two unrelated individuals are rivals, both for resources and — if they are males — for the sexual favors of females. (Females are not sexual rivals in the same sense, since a male's impregnation of one female does not prevent him from impregnating another very shortly afterwards, though they may well be rivals for the resources that the male controls.) The fact that murder is much more commonly carried out by men than women, even allowing for such factors as differences in physical strength and access to weapons, suggests that sexual rivalry has been much the stronger factor of the two in the evolution of human violence.[2] Killing an unrelated member of the same sex and species eliminates a sexual rival.[3] This incidentally seems a likely explanation for the disturbing tendency of violence to be associated with a sexual thrill; it is not, regrettably, a pathological response of a sick minority but an

Figure 3.1. The spoils of war: VJ Day, Times Square. Alfred Eisenstaedt's famous photo for *Life*. Getty Images/Time Life Pictures.

evolved anticipation of the increased sexual access that comes from successful elimination of rivals. It is one that has been reinforced down the ages by a tendency on the part of females — far from universal, but sufficient to make a difference — to be drawn sexually to those who have displayed prowess in contests of force, as Shakespeare knew well when he made Henry V rally his troops before Agincourt with the cry that:

. . . gentlemen in England now abed
Shall think themselves accurs'd they were not here,
And hold their manhoods cheap while any speaks
That fought with us upon St. Crispin's Day.[4]

It is well known that once a certain characteristic becomes a basis for sexual preference, such preferences can be self-reinforcing. This is a tendency that has been adduced to explain such runaway evolutionary phenomena as the peacock's tail and the large antlers of some species of deer. The fact that females in future generations will be attracted by some characteristic, even a wholly arbitrary one, increases the adaptive benefit to any female in the current generation of seeking a mate that has that characteristic. As it happens, there is some evidence from preindustrial societies that males who kill other males tend to have larger numbers of children than males who do not—though this evidence is sketchy and controversial.[5] But even if a tendency for females to be sexually drawn to fighters had no direct adaptive benefit (say, if the greater ability of violent males to gain food from others were offset by their increased likelihood of an early death), once such a tendency had become established it could become indirectly adaptive through the greater likelihood that fighters would find mates. Even if nice guys don't finish last in the line for food, they may finish last in the line for mates. Nice guys may have other attractions (they may share more with their females, for one thing), but if they have sons who can't do well in the contest for females, that already counts against them as mates.[6]

Why, then, should the growing intelligence of the forerunners of *Homo sapiens sapiens* have increased these selective pressures in favor of murderousness? In a species where contests are decided mainly by brute force, a male can eliminate a sexual rival simply by forcing him physically to submit. But the more intelligent the rival, the more likely it is that, having submitted now, he will find a cunning way to return to his sexual pursuit later on. So eliminating permanently the rival who has been temporarily defeated is a strategy that confers much more selective benefit in an intelligent species.

Two sources of evidence reinforce this evolutionary argument that human beings, especially males, are likely to be strongly disposed to kill other, unrelated individuals in the appropriate circumstances. One source is the behavior of other primates, particularly other apes.[7] This evidence needs to be interpreted with caution, since there is great variety in primate behavior, even between such closely related species as chimpanzees and bonobos, and this variety indicates that social and ecological factors can have a strong impact on the incidence of violence. This environmental flexibility in itself should come as no surprise: indeed, it is a central argument of this book that institutional arrangements have enormously increased the ability of human beings to live without violence among those they would otherwise be disposed to fight. But careful observation in the wild has nevertheless yielded sobering discoveries. When unconstrained by fear of reprisals, many other primates systematically exploit opportunities to kill individuals who are not related to themselves. Infanticide by unrelated males, for instance, has been regularly observed among chimpanzees, gorillas, and langurs (as well as in some other mammals, such as lions). Among bonobos it is certainly less common, and no documented cases are known; but this appears to be because females work cooperatively to ensure their infants are protected against marauding males, not because the males themselves are intrinsically trustworthy. Among chimpanzees, related males regularly cooperate to launch violent, unprovoked attacks against isolated and defenseless members of other troops, even when such attacks yield no food or other resources. Such incidents were not known before the work of Jane Goodall and her collaborators (in fact, the writings of Konrad Lorenz[8] had popularized the idea that intraspecies violence was largely ritualized, a view that is now known from field studies to be mistaken). The violence among chimpanzees is particularly revealing since it occurs to a large extent between groups of males of unequal size, and without particular provocation. This kind of behavior reflects the random encounters of foraging parties and looks disturbingly similar to patterns of aggression between groups of human males. Violence, in short, is endemic among the species most closely related to man. In species where it happens less often, this is because of behaviour patterns that have evolved to deter it, and not because of instincts that would be purely peaceable without fear of reprisals. Whatever its fundamental causes, violence in primates, and especially in the great apes, cannot be described as pathological.

A second source of evidence for the innate murderousness of *Homo sapiens* consists in ethnographic accounts of contemporary nonindustrial societies, many of which (contrary to popular myth) are extremely violent.[9] Considerable controversy still surrounds these reports, and it is undeniable that levels of observed violence vary across nonindustrial societies for reasons that are still very imperfectly understood. It may be true, for instance, that simple agricultural societies are somewhat more warlike than hunter-gatherers (a reasonable conjecture, if only because they have more resources to fight over). Alternatively, this apparent tendency may reflect the fact that agricultural societies simply leave more traces of the fighting they do (in the form of torched huts and pillaged storehouses), or that they are easier for anthropologists to visit in unsettled times. But whatever the explanation for these observed variations, the idea that preindustrial societies were largely peaceful, which has had a seductive hold over human thinking since Jean-Jacques Rousseau wrote about noble savages in the eighteenth century, has now been convincingly discredited. Anthropologist Carol Ember wrote a pioneering article in 1978, "Myths about Hunter-Gatherers," which showed that nearly two-thirds of hunter-gatherer groups for which records existed waged war at least every two years.[10] Ethnographic accounts of high levels of violence, between individuals and between groups, exist for hunter-gatherers as different as the Akoa, the Bushmen, the Tasmanians, and the Yanomamo. Among preindustrial agriculturalists, regular and deadly warfare has now been documented for societies once thought to be peace-loving, such as the Pueblo Indians of the American Southwest.[11] Many such ethnographies could be cited: a striking example is the book *Blood Is Their Argument*, in which anthropologist Mervyn Meggitt records the very bloody cycles of violence among the Mae Enga people of the central highlands of Papua New Guinea.[12] Once again the message is sobering: where there are no institutional restraints on it, systematic killing of unrelated individuals is so common among human beings that, awful though it is, it cannot be described as exceptional, pathological, or disturbed.

In short, and whatever the precise evolutionary origins of such behavior, the potential costs of being cheated have become dangerously high for human beings dealing with nonrelatives. Not only may you never be repaid for the mammoth meat you gave me, but you may be murdered in return. Many itinerant traders making tentative first contacts with an unfamiliar tribe have suffered just such a fate. In the circumstances it is astonishing that systematic exchange among nonrelatives should have evolved at all, let alone that it should have become the foundation of the fantastically complex social and economic life we know today.

Remarkably, trust in nonrelatives has become an established fact of social life. When I go into a shop, a person who has never seen me before will hand over valuable goods to me in exchange for a scribble on a piece of paper. When there is a knock on the door, I am prepared to allow into my home a man I have never met, who is wearing the uniform of a local domestic appliance store. Why do I infer that his purpose is to repair the washing machine instead of to kill me and rape the women of the house? How has this degree of trust become possible? Buyers do sometimes pass bad checks; murderous rapists do sometimes pose as repairmen — but it happens rarely enough not to threaten the general trustworthiness of these social transactions. What is the explanation?

CALCULATION AND RECIPROCITY

We can be fairly confident that our ancestors evolved to trust familiar nonrelatives before they came to have trust in strangers. When two individuals expect to see each other often in the future, they have an additional incentive to keep agreements: cheating might bring a short-term benefit, but it would jeopardize the possibility of cooperation in the future. Provided the benefits of future cooperation are sufficiently large and sufficiently certain, and the future in question is not too distant, the individuals may resist the temptation to cheat for short-term gain. Such cooperative tendencies probably evolved in two main ways. First, they are a by-product of the evolution of intelligence. As human social intelligence developed, individuals could increasingly calculate that their long-term interest lay in keeping rather than breaking certain kinds of agreement, namely, those with individuals they expected to see again repeatedly in the relatively near future and from whose goodwill they expected to benefit. The second is through selection for what is sometimes called "reciprocity," namely, an instinctive inclination to do unto others as they have already done unto you. If others have treated you well, you treat them well in return, but if they have hurt you, you hurt them back. An eye for an eye, certainly, but also a gift for a gift.

Both of these motives for cooperation have been important in human evolution, and both continue to play an important part in human motivation today. At first sight the distinction between them may seem rather unimportant: what difference does it make whether the motive for cooperation is calculation or instinctive reciprocity, when most of the people with whom you deal are those whom you have dealt with in the past and whom you hope to continue to deal with in the future? And even if you knew the difference in principle, how could you tell in practice? But in fact the distinction matters, because it provides the key to how humans have evolved to trust complete strangers, those they have never seen before.

Studies of human cooperative behavior in many different contexts have clearly established that the hope of future cooperation plays an important role in reinforcing cooperation in the present. It is known that people cooperate more when they interact frequently, when they have the means of telling whether others have cheated, and when the gains from cooperation, as opposed to going it alone, are large. These factors have proved important in such diverse contexts as military engagements, care of the environment, and the effectiveness with which local political institutions respond to the needs of the population.[13] There used to be, however, much controversy about whether people also have an instinct for reciprocity (a reaction to how they have been treated in the past independently of the prospects for future collaboration). It was thought to be impossible to disentangle one motive from the other when almost all human interaction involves a seamless transition from past involvements to future anticipations.

Now a set of ingenious laboratory experiments by Ernst Fehr and colleagues at the University of Zurich has shown that individuals receiving generous treatment from others they will not meet again nevertheless respond generously to them in return.[14] For instance, in an experiment that mimicked behavior in labor markets, subjects took the part of workers or firms and were randomly and anonymously matched with each other (the participants in the experiment were students playing at computer terminals). Firms could choose to pay a minimum wage or a wage above the minimum; workers could choose to make a minimum investment (a monetary equivalent of "effort") or a level above the minimum. After each turn participants were rematched, and none knew whether the partners with whom they were matched were partners with whom they had been matched before.

It became clear as the experiment proceeded that workers who had been generously treated by their employers were likely to make high levels of investment. This investment brought them no benefit, since any firm with which they were matched in the future would not know how they had previously behaved. So their behavior must have been due to reciprocity and not to calculation. Nevertheless, firms in turn gradually learned to benefit from this, as the cost of paying high wages to workers was more than outweighed by the value of the extra investment they undertook as a result. So firms that paid high wages were more profitable than those that did not—not the conventional capitalist view.[15] There remain unresolved questions about the wider applicability of results obtained under laboratory conditions, though the findings have since been replicated so many times by other researchers that there is no longer any serious doubt about their robustness (they are not due to cheating or misunderstanding by students, for example, and real money is at stake). But these findings suggest not only that cultures of cooperation may persist through reciprocity but also that groups in which cooperative habits have developed may be more economically successful than those in which more narrowly self-interested behavior is the norm. Paradoxically, too narrow a nose for profit may be bad not only for the soul but also for the bottom line.

Similar experiments by Fehr and others have also established a systematic tendency for individuals to repay unkind behavior with unkind behavior even when this brings no benefit to themselves.[16] In one experiment with two subjects, the first was asked to propose a division of a prize between the two, while the second could simply accept or reject the proposal. In the event of rejection neither received anything. Once again subjects were randomly and anonymously matched on a one-off basis, so there could be no possible benefit from present behavior in terms of influencing future cooperation. It was clear that the second subjects would systematically reject proposals they thought gave them too small a share, even if by rejecting the proposal they would receive nothing at all. Such behavior is sometimes known as "cutting off your nose to spite your face" — a description that implies it is irrational. But rational or not, it is clearly widespread in human nature. Knowing this, the first subjects would ensure that they gave enough to the second subjects to keep the risks of rejection low, although this rarely implied equal division, especially when the sums of money at stake were substantial.

Yet another set of experiments conducted in groups suggests that the presence of reciprocators who not only respond in kind to cooperative behavior but also help to punish noncooperation in others, even at some cost to themselves, may be critical to ensuring that cooperative habits become established. Where the only motive for cooperation is the past generosity of others and there are no sanctions for cheating, an initially cooperative group culture may gradually unravel as individuals succumb to temptation; but when it is known that aggrieved parties can take revenge, and will do so even at personal cost, the incidence of cheating in the experiments shows a sharp decline.[17]

Why is reciprocity important for the ability to trust strangers? First, it explains why the complex web of trust that underlies modern social life does not unravel as soon as unscrupulous individuals test its strength. Economist Kaushik Basu describes a simple problem.[18] You take a taxi ride in a large, unfamiliar city, and when you have reached your destination you pay the driver the amount you owe. You have benefited from the ride and you will never see the driver again, so why do you bother? (This is the kind of question that sometimes gets economists a bad name.)*[19] The answer, very probably, is that you just do: you feel the instinct of reciprocity, either in the form of a wish to behave decently to a person who has just behaved decently to you, or because you believe you have a moral duty to do so (these two are not so very different, since the latter can be described as a wish to behave "correctly" toward someone who has just behaved correctly toward you). But now suppose you feel no such instinct, and instead you ask yourself, "What's in it for me?" You will probably reason that if you refused to pay, the driver would make a great fuss, at least embarrassing you in front of bystanders, possibly getting you involved in a fight, and perhaps even leading to trouble with the police. It's just not worth the bother for such a small sum. So it seems that you don't have to appeal

---

* Though not just economists: Will Durant in *The Story of Philosophy* recounts that the philosopher Schopenhauer used to leave a tip on the table at the start of a restaurant meal to encourage the waiters, but then remove it at the end.

to reciprocity as a motive: plain self-interest is enough to explain your behavior.

But wait. The driver could just as easily make a fuss even if you *had* paid, threatening you with embarrassment, a fight, and the police in order to make you pay up a second time. None of the other parties would be any the wiser. The driver will not see you ever again either, so why does he refrain from trying to wring a second payment out of you? Once again the answer might be that the driver is moved by an instinct of reciprocity — or he might just be afraid that you would react violently if he attempted to cheat you in this way. But why should he expect you to react violently? However far down the line we go to prove that your behavior or his is just the consequence of enlightened self-interest, at some point we still need to appeal to the fact that people behave differently if they feel they have been cheated than if they do not. Since nobody else observed the transaction taking place between the two of you, no third-party enforcement mechanism can explain why that transaction affects how you subsequently behave.

Even when third-party enforcement mechanisms (such as the courts) do play a role in strengthening the web of trust, reciprocity is the glue that makes these mechanisms credible. Why does the judge make any attempt to decide the case on its merits instead of simply finding in favor of the party who can pay her the most? Again, perhaps she just does. Or perhaps she is being self-interested, reasoning that if she takes a bribe she will suffer for it. But why should she think that, unless some other people (those who report her bribe-taking and her colleagues who investigate the allegations) also behave in ways that are sensitive to the intrinsic facts of the case? Every person in the web who reasons self-interestedly can do so only on the assumption that someone else, somewhere, will not be acting according to self-interest alone.

Formal mechanisms for enforcing agreements still need to draw on some instinctive and uncalculating tendency to repay kindness with kindness and unkindness with revenge. What such mechanisms can do, however, is to ensure that a little reciprocity goes a long way. Modern social life depends on a large number of ingenious arrangements for reinforcing reciprocity with self-interest. When we meet and transact with strangers, we do not always need to ask ourselves endless questions about their intrinsic trustworthiness. So long as there are enforcement mechanisms in place, and so long as there is a good enough chance that someone somewhere is intrinsically trustworthy, we may not need to worry whether the stranger at our door or at the checkout of our shop is genuinely motivated by reciprocity or merely by self-interest. Either will do for the purpose in hand.[20]

But questions that would seem paranoid in a reasonably stable and well-ordered society may be quite reasonable and even essential in a poor and violent one. Reciprocity has also mattered in the history of humanity because it has enabled hunter-gatherer bands to take the first cautious steps toward conducting exchange with strangers (such contacts occurred, as we have seen, well before the adoption of agriculture). An itinerant trader making the first contact with an isolated band whose only motivation was self-interest would almost certainly have his goods stolen and would be lucky to escape with his life. After all, the band could hardly reason that offering him goods in return would be of benefit in the long run, since it would have no reason to expect him to come back again soon or often, given that this was the first time the band had ever seen him. It has surely been reciprocity that, prehistorically, tipped the balance between hostility to strangers and a cautious willingness to deal with them. Often that reciprocity will have been betrayed, as many of the Native Americans who dealt with the first European visitors discovered to their terrible cost. But their case, though tragic, made ultimately less difference to the future of human society than the reverse — namely, the discovery that a willingness to trust others could produce important benefits to both sides. Had it not been so, modern society as we know it could never have evolved.

SMILING, LAUGHTER AND THE NEED TO SIGNAL TRUST

In short, calculation and reciprocity have complementary virtues. It is worth asking a little more precisely what these virtues are. Calculation enables an individual to trust only those others she can afford, on best evidence, to trust, and to do no more for others than is strictly in her own best interest. It's an essential ability for an individual facing a variable natural environment and a complex social environment. It is likely that the increasing size of hominid brains over the last six or seven million years reflected the selective pressures arising from a more diverse ecology and the growing size of social groups. Only individuals who could calculate well, who could judge how their behavior should be adapted to fit different circumstances, who could spot a cheat, were likely to survive to reproduce. And there is good evidence that human beings have senses very finely tuned to signals of the trustworthiness of those around them. In one famous experiment, the psychologists Leda Cosmides and John Tooby showed that subjects often had difficulty solving a logical puzzle which required them to identify playing cards that failed to conform to a rule of play. However, when the very same logical puzzle was reformulated as a problem of identifying people who had failed to conform to a rule of social behavior, the subjects performed very much better on the test. This led Cosmides and Tooby to conclude that our reasoning abilities are sensitive to context in ways that would have been beneficial for our ability to spot cheats during our evolutionary history.[21]

But calculation is not a virtue that necessarily inspires confidence in others. Suppose I know you have a shrewd nose for your own best interest, and nothing but. Then I may be cautious about cheating you, but I shall also be cautious about trusting you. I shall not make spontaneous gestures of friendship, for I know that these will make no difference to your subsequent treatment of me, which will be based solely upon calculation of your future interest. Pure calculation, in other words, exercises trust wisely but does little to inspire it.

Reciprocity, almost by definition, is less wise. It inspires individuals to be generous to others purely to repay past generosity, even when this brings no future benefit. It can also trap individuals in cycles of revenge generated by past wrongs. Based on emotion that is triggered by outside events rather than the conscious decisions of the individual, reciprocity is open to manipulation by others. But when it comes to inspiring trust in others, its insensitivity to calculation is precisely its strength.[22] If I know that my present generosity to you will incline you to help me in the future, regardless of your interests at the time, I shall be more likely to take the risk of helping you. Your disposition for reciprocity makes you a more credible partner than someone who has no such disposition. This character, in short, gives you a power of commitment beyond the reach of the most sophisticated calculation. It is a power that the calculating can appreciate even though they cannot aspire to it — calculators would rather trust reciprocators than trust other calculators like themselves.

These considerations suggest that individuals who can simultaneously exercise trust shrewdly and inspire trust in others need to have some disposition for calculation in their dealings with others — but not too much, or no one will trust them. They also need some disposition for reciprocity — but not too much, or others will exploit them, and the memory of past wrongs will cast too long a shadow on their lives. They need a way to signal to others that they have the element of reciprocity that makes them trustworthy, and they need to signal it in a way that any purely calculating person could not convincingly mimic. The psychologists Michael Owren and Jo-Anne Bachorowski have recently proposed an ingenious theory according to which smiling and laughter may have evolved in human beings as just such signals.[23] Both smiling and laughter are human capacities for which only the most rudimentary forms exist in other species. Both appear to signal emotions associated with a liking for others and a willingness to behave generously toward them—what psychologists call "positive affect." Both appear to *trigger* such feelings in others as well. Owren and Bachorowski suggest that the capacity of smiling and laughter to act as reliable signals of positive affect, and therefore of trustworthiness, would have made them highly adaptive for the individuals that could smile and laugh. Any genetic mutations favoring such capabilities would therefore have tended to spread. Given their reliability as signals of trustworthiness, evolution would also have tended to favor a tendency to respond warmly to them in turn.[24]

However, any signal that makes other people think I am trustworthy is one it would be highly useful for me to be able to fake. That way I could make people trust me, and do favors for me, without incurring the cost of doing favors for them in return unless it suited me to do so. So, Owren and Bachorowski suggest, no sooner had smiling become reasonably well established as a reliable signal of trustworthiness than it also became adaptive to be able to counterfeit smiles. Smiles that are under deliberate control are known to use a different set of neural circuitry than spontaneous smiles (the latter are also known as "Duchenne" smiles, after the nineteenth-century psychologist who first wrote about the difference). Not everyone can fake smiles successfully—indeed, politicians are predominantly drawn from among those human beings who can. Many people (myself included) are effectively barred from political careers by their inability to produce convincing smiles to order for the camera. But enough people can do so to suggest that the evolution of smile mimicry has proceeded quite far in the human species.

But almost nobody can fake laughter convincingly. Laboratory studies show that many people are unable to discriminate reliably between spontaneous smiles and those produced by good actors. But virtually everyone can tell the difference between spontaneous laughter and the deliberate laughter of even very talented actors. And deliberate laughter provokes much less positive affect in those that hear it than does spontaneous laughter. These facts lead Owren and Bachorowski to suggest that laughter probably evolved later than smiling (no doubt in response to the mimicry of the first prehistoric politicians). The fact that smiling was losing its reliability, because so many people could fake it, made it valuable to have another, better signal of positive affect. And the possibility that laughter evolved later would explain why the ability to fake convincingly has not yet had time to evolve.

A telling piece of evidence in support of the signaling theory of laughter is the way in which, across all kinds of cultures in the world, people who have made a business deal with each other tend to seal the deal by having a drink together. Drinking alcohol notoriously affects people's judgment. In fact alcohol is a depressant that not only makes people feel all stimuli less strongly but particularly diminishes people's sensitivity to pains, including future pains.[25] (The reason why alcohol provokes car accidents is not primarily that it slows down people's reaction times but that it makes them reckless, through diminished sensitivity to future dangers.) In short, if people entering into a business relationship needed to keep a clear head in order to work out carefully how much they could afford to trust their new partners, having a drink together would be the worst possible way to seal a deal.[26] But alcohol is also, famously, a disinhibitor. Most importantly, it makes many people laugh. In all cultures, many businesspeople spend evenings exchanging jokes that, to begin with, virtually nobody finds funny, but at which everyone, toward the end of the evening, is laughing uproariously. At the same time that it disables people's capacity for exercising trust wisely, alcohol is enabling people to inspire trust by stimulating an excellent signal of positive affect, namely laughter, that is not under direct voluntary control.[27]

Mimicry should not always be considered, though, as tending to weaken or undermine trust. One of the first kinds of social interaction of which babies are capable at just a few weeks of age is to return the smiles of those who have smiled at them. All of us learn at the very start of life that smiles are the sign of the love and goodwill of our relatives, particularly our parents. The first traders that successfully made contact with hunter-gatherer bands and persuaded them to exchange instead of to fight must have tried very hard to smile convincingly in order to trigger a reciprocity response. Without some degree of successful mimicry such exchanges might never have got going. Here, as in many other contexts, trusting strangers is a process of conscious and unconscious mimicry of the way in which we trust our family and friends.

So How Did Reciprocity Evolve?

Researchers are still puzzling, though, over how exactly human beings evolved the kind of reciprocity that mimicry exploits.[28] The fact that, in the laboratory, people are willing to incur personal costs to reward those who have treated them well and punish those who have treated them badly even when these people will never knowingly see them again, has led some researchers to suppose that reciprocity is an evolutionary "mistake."[29] It would have been more adaptive, according to this view, to evolve a tendency to show reciprocity only toward those you are likely to see again (we could call people with such a tendency "opportunists").[30] However, asking why reciprocity evolved may be a little like asking why human males have developed a desire to have sex with beautiful females who are currently using contraception. Obviously an evolutionary mistake (if only all mistakes were so enjoyable). But not such a surprising mistake, since what evolved was a desire to have sex with beautiful females, period. Reliable contraception arrived on the scene far too late in evolutionary history to have created any kind of adaptive pressure for a more discriminating desire, directed only toward those currently not taking contraception. Perhaps the evolution of reciprocity is no more of a puzzle than this.

Since Professor Ernst Fehr and his fellow experimenters have arrived on the scene even later in evolutionary history than the contraceptive pill, it is evident that whatever else reciprocity may be, it cannot helpfully be described as a tendency to return in kind the behavior of others whom the experimenter has ensured we shall never knowingly see again. It is a tendency to return in kind the behavior of others, period. So were our ancestors often enough exposed to people whom they had reason to believe they would never see again for there to have been some real selective pressure against reciprocity over evolutionary time? This remains a hotly debated question.[31] One possibility is that they were not, that most people who were generous to our ancestors were people they had at least some reason to expect to see again in the future. Although our ancestors were certainly highly wary of strangers, most of whom would have been hostile, if not lethal, *friendly* strangers may have been a great rarity, certainly unusual enough for there to be no great adaptive pressure in favor of cheating them. Indeed, friendly strangers can be thought of as successful mimics of our genuine friends, successful because of their comparative rarity until very recent times. A second possibility is that there was indeed some real selective pressure against reciprocity at an individual level, but that this was offset by the adaptive benefits to *groups* that displayed reciprocity (such groups might be better placed to trade with others, for instance).[32] A third possibility is that selective pressure against reciprocity and in favor of opportunism has been operating for too short a time to have become dominant in human populations—the experimental evidence suggests that a proportion of subjects display reciprocity, not that they all do.[33] In short, reciprocators and opportunists coexist. Finally, as I suggested above, opportunists may do better than reciprocators when they get a chance to cheat, but unless they can hide the fact that they are opportunists, they may be given fewer opportunities to cheat in the first place. They may even face collective ostracism from the reciprocators within their group.[34] The question remains open; all of these explanations may contain an element of truth. But we can safely agree that we owe the astonishing complexity of modern society to the presence of at least some reciprocators among our ancestors, as well as to those unrecorded heroes of prehistory who risked slaughter at the hands of strangers to explore the opportunities for mutually beneficial trade.

RECIPROCITY AND REVENGE

Reciprocity can of course be dangerous, and not just when it is manipulated. Certainly, it helps to establish cooperation and exchange. This is partly because of the tendency to repay kindness with kindness, and partly because the tendency to repay unkindness with revenge makes people more likely to keep their promises. But this second characteristic also means that once promises are broken, the participants can become trapped in a cycle of revenge. Testimonies to this from history, anthropology, and imaginative literature are legion. Modern tragedy has often located dramatic compulsion within human beings' own iron subjection to the laws of revenge, which endows the action with a sense of inevitability in works such as Shakespeare's *Romeo and Juliet* and Gabriel Garcia Marquez's *Chronicle of a Death Foretold*. The codes of honor of the Mafia culture of Sicily have come to seem strangely dysfunctional in the modern world, but they have a comprehensible rationale, as the work of sociologist Diego Gambetta has shown us.[35] Gambetta emphasizes the way in which Mafia families originally took upon themselves the role of providing some of the underpinnings of trust in a complex modern society, because the Italian state proved incapable of doing so in Sicily at the time of Italy's unification in the mid-nineteenth century. But this role came at a heavy cost: the same human motivations that can reinforce a culture of trust can also entrench a culture of distrust. In Sicily's case, trust of insiders has reinforced distrust of outsiders, a cultural handicap that has cost the region dear as it seeks to integrate itself into modern Italy and the modern world.

Fortunately, the disposition to trust in members of a certain group more than others has often been a help, not a hindrance, in widening the range of people on whom we can rely. An unknown trader coming into our village may suffer from being an outsider to our group, but he may benefit from belonging to some other group or tribe with some of whose members we have previously dealt or to a more distant branch of our own tribe; he may even come with tokens or letters of recommendation. To this day, immigrants to North America often seek out members of their own ethnic community; migrants from the countryside to Indian cities often contact members of their own caste; the stranger at my door stands a better chance of admission if he is wearing the uniform of a reputable company.

The gradual integration of local cultures of trust into larger regional, national, or even global cultures of trust, punctuated though it has been by many episodes of reversal, is at the heart of the history of modern life. It is important not to romanticize this process: when I say I can trust a stranger, I do not mean that I like him, have any curiosity about him as a person, or care in any deep sense about what happens to him. The point is that I do not need to like or care about him in order to be able to deal confidently and reliably with him. Some people have seen in this fact a chilling, even dehumanizing quality of modern societies and have yearned for the times when those who mattered to us were those we knew, people whom we might hate or love but to whom we could not feel indifferent. The economist James Buchanan has described how a purchase of fruit at a roadside stall can take place in spite of the fact that neither of the people concerned has any particular interest in the well-being of the other: they are "able to . . . transact exchanges efficiently because both parties agree on the property rights relevant to them." In reply the economist Samuel Bowles describes this as creating "a psychological environment of anonymity, indifference to others, mobility, lack of commitment, autonomy" and concludes that ".we learn to function in these environments, and in doing so we become someone we might not have become in a different setting."[36] People vary in how much this troubles them (Bowles is pointing out that anonymous markets have an important effect, though not necessarily one we should, on balance, regret). But it is absolutely clear that a warmer timbre of human interaction in all our encounters is quite incompatible with the degree of complex interaction upon which most of us now depend.

Indeed, it is precisely the most tenuous, the most anonymous, of our links to the outside world that do most to connect us to new opportunities. The powerful implications of this simple fact were drawn some years ago by the sociologist Mark Granovetter in a famous article entitled "The Strength of Weak Ties." Granovetter began by reporting a study of the social networks that helped unemployed people to find jobs. Personal contacts are often a more important means of finding work than formal institutions such as employment exchanges. Yet Granovetter found that people were much less likely to find work through close friends (their "strong ties") than through casual acquaintances (their "weak ties"), even though close friends should in principle have more reason to help them. The reason is that your close friends are likely to know many of the same people that you do; they are therefore less likely to be able to bring you genuinely new information and opportunities.[37] Casual acquaintances, in contrast, are more likely to act as a bridge between otherwise closed groups and the outside world. Granovetter's article, and other work inspired by it, have provided a welcome counterweight to the elegiac strain in sociology,[38] which has spoken of the alienation induced by modern living without noting how this is linked to the very conditions that give it energy and creativity.

Of the impersonal institutions that have enabled this gradual integration of local cultures of trust into a wider culture governing relations between strangers, none has been more central to the process than the institution of property rights. Property rights are a set of rules governing who has the right to manage the various valuable resources in our environment, to enjoy their fruits, and to dispose of them to others. Without the assurance that the resources you theoretically own now will be protected from marauders until the time comes for you to repay me, no amount of trust in your good intentions may induce me to be generous to you today. Another way to express this is that trust cannot be purely bilateral: trust between any two people rests on a web of trust between each of them and the others with whom they also deal. For this reason, as we shall see in later chapters, all societies have needed the maintenance of defense, civil order, and some degree of consensus about what the social rules decree. Some historians have even argued that the ability to establish such property rights, and the social consensus that enables them to be enforced, is the single most cogent explanation for why some countries (such as Britain and the Netherlands) were able to industrialize and grow faster than others at a critical period in early modern history.[39] As with other institutions, property rights rest on a delicate balance between reciprocity and self-interest, and different societies have placed different emphasis on the formal and the informal (or consensual) components of that balance. A growing literature on what has come to be called "social capital" examines the many subtle factors that explain why trust appears to have become more securely embedded in some societies than in others.[40] What all stable societies have in common, though, is that the balance between reciprocity and self-interest holds even when unscrupulous individuals test its strength.

It is time to look more closely at some of the social institutions that have been responsible for this extraordinary spread of the willingness to trust strangers. The hallmark of the most successful of these institutions is their ability to entrench a culture of trust with a minimum of explicit enforcement. For instance, what distinguishes safe cities from dangerous, crime-ridden ones? Jane Jacobs has written that "the public peace — the street peace and sidewalk peace — of cities is not kept primarily by the police, necessary as police are. It is kept primarily by an intricate, almost unconscious, network of voluntary controls and standards among the people themselves, and enforced by the people themselves." Indeed, she argued, "once a street is well equipped to handle strangers, once it has both a good, effective demarcation between private and public spaces and has a basic supply of activity and eyes, the more strangers the merrier."[41] In other words, cities need an institution of peace-keeping, doubtless backed by formal sanctions but largely informal in its day-to-day activity. And that institution has to be stable, in the sense that people react to its presence by behaving more, not less, cooperatively.

We shall look in more detail at cities in chapter 7. But first we shall look at one of the most remarkable trust-creating institutions of all, one that no sane person would take seriously for a moment were it not for the fact that everyone else in society is normally quite willing to do so. It is money.

CHAPTER 4

Money and Human Relationships

MONEY AND BARTER

In northwestern Russia a man and a woman are bartering goods, each offering something they have made against something they want. This is the way goods have been exchanged for most of the human past, and it epitomizes the traditional culture of face-to-face interactions. What are they exchanging? Animal skins, it turns out, against rather simple shoes. You could be forgiven for imagining the scene as taking place in a forest clearing, or at the side of a muddy track, with horses occasionally stamping their feet and launching clouds of breath into the winter air. In fact, the woman is sitting in a heated office, and the man is nowhere to be seen. They are talking on the telephone.

It is February 1992. The consignments whose exchange they are negotiating are far too large to fit on a horse and must be sent for several hundred miles across the frozen landscape by container truck. Almost everything about the transaction speaks of the industrial age: the animal skins have been scalded with chemicals, the shoes have been cut and stitched by machine, the goods will be accompanied by invoices and bills of lading, the man and the woman are dressed in machine-made clothes and work by the glare of strip-lights. Only one thing is preindustrial: they refuse to use money. Inflation is currently running at 2,000 per cent per year, and the money would lose its value faster than they could pass it on.

Now travel forward to 2001. Throughout the decade that has elapsed since the end of communism, barter has taken the place of money for a remarkable proportion of transactions in a society that in most other respects has been seeking to model itself on the market economies of the industrialized West. These are not just deals between individuals trading household goods or personal services (a well-known phenomenon under communism). Firms are trading commodities with each other instead of trading them for money, and doing so at all stages and all scales of production. No goods are too large or too sophisticated to be part of a barter exchange; tanks, airplane engines, and oil and gas refinery equipment have all featured in such deals.

Understanding how a modern society can function without money

tells us a great deal about the role money plays in more normal times. For make no mistake: living without money has cost Russian society very dear.[1] There are some obvious costs: the man who receives shoes in exchange for his animal skins cannot possibly use so many shoes, not even by distributing some of them to his workers (who would probably have preferred other things, though they are in no position to complain). He has to exchange them in turn, and that means storing them till he can find someone who wants them. Building a warehouse could cost him his entire annual investment budget; if it could have held its value, money would have been much cheaper to store.

Sometimes the arrangements required to make barter work are even more complex. The woman receiving animal hides had set aside a portion of her firm's annual investment budget to set up a plant making sausage skins. Why? The supplier of hides was getting restive, for good hides could be sold for American dollars abroad, and he was wondering whether to stop supplying them to Russian buyers. But the supplier had his own problem, which was that he also produced meat, and to dispose of the meat he needed good-quality sausage skins. So the woman had an idea, which was to make her company indispensable to him by producing the elusive skins. That way she had a hostage she could use to secure the supply of his hides. She and her colleagues might know nothing about making sausage skins, but these were extraordinary times.

Her case was not at all unusual, except in being observed by a visiting British economist. At a shoe factory I visited three years later in Tashkent in Central Asia, even more complex deals were in the making. The finance director had tried in vain to persuade his suppliers to take shoes in payment, so now he was setting up as a supplier of general consumer goods. His senior management colleagues spent their time scouring local markets and telephoning their friends in other firms. Tomato paste, porcelain, and pasta were particularly prized, for they could be used to pay not only suppliers but the workforce as well.

I visited a plastics factory and tried to talk to the director about his restructuring plans, but he had other things on his mind. "We've found a reliable source of potatoes," he told me, with evident pleasure. "The workforce will be very glad; the arrears in their wages had been building up. There's not much else to pay them with. Though to tell the truth, we tend to turn a bit of a blind eye these days to pilfering from the company stores."

Figure 4.1. During Germany's high inflation in the 1920s a shopkeeper uses a tea chest to store money that won't fit into the cash register. Getty Images/ Hulton Archive.

In Kiev in 1995 I met an energetic young man who had set up a dairy-processing plant on the land beside a coal-fired power station. The collective farms in the region were all hopelessly in arrears for their electricity, and besides useless Ukrainian currency all they had to offer in exchange was milk. The power station was not interested in milk payment, unless some means could be found to process and market it — which was where the entrepreneur came in. It didn't sound very ecological, and it would doubtless be redundant in a few years' time, but in the meantime it was working so well that plans were afoot to build a pasta factory and a brewery on the same site.

It has often been fashionable to claim that more than seven decades of communism have completely atrophied the Russian people's entrepreneurial spirit. Nobody seeing the ingenuity devoted to these complex barter deals could believe this facile insult for a moment. But like the creativity with which ordinary Russians evade taxes, navigate among gangsters, outwit shortages, and care for their families when health and education services are collapsing, this ingenuity makes one wonder what Russian society could achieve if it were harnessed to a more fruitful and less mutually destructive end. Money is one of the great human inventions precisely because it helps to narrow the gulf between the ingenuity of each individual and the interest of others; it helps our inventiveness to serve purposes other than mutual theft. Not the least of its benefits is that it frees shoe manufacturers to do what they are good at (making shoes), instead of obliging them to become porcelain merchants, sausage-skin manufacturers, or stockists of potatoes simply in order to keep their shoemaking business afloat.

We shall probably never know when the first forms of money came into existence. As James Buchan points out in his book *Frozen Desire: An Enquiry into the Meaning of Money*, "money may be older than writing but we will never know: an archaeologist may think an object he finds is old money, but he cannot know it is without an inscription to tell him so."[2] So we are even less likely to know whether money came about as a conscious invention of some local ruler or came haphazardly into existence as individuals engaging in barter found they were willing to accept as payment certain kinds of objects whose durability was more important than their immediate usefulness. Indeed, every time someone thinks, "I've no real use for it now, but I can keep it till I pass it on to someone else later," they are participating in the invention of money. The untidiness of this second explanation makes it seem more plausible than the first, but the truth may be that money came into existence many times, with more conscious forethought in some circumstances than in others. What we do know is that once money has acquired certain characteristics, its use becomes self-enforcing: people are willing to accept it in exchange for their goods because they genuinely prefer to do so, and not because the law says they must. This self-enforcing character is what enables money to be the kind of institution that makes trust in strangers possible: we accept it in exchange for valuable goods in spite of the fact that we may know nothing about the individuals who are offering it to us.

What are the characteristics that make the use of money self-enforcing? Any form of payment people accept for their own goods and services with the intention of later trading it for other goods and services we can call a medium of exchange. In principle a society can try to enforce legal tender for any medium of exchange (shopkeepers can be fined if they refuse to accept it), but in practice legal tender is enforceable only when the medium has considerable acceptability in its own right. For a medium of exchange to be attractive it has to have a number of characteristics:

- It has to be reasonably easy to store and to transport. Water is a poor medium of exchange even in the desert, where it has considerable value.
- It has to be sure not to lose its value before it is resold — through decay, through theft, or simply through people's inability to tell the difference between good quality and bad. Bread is too perishable. Clothing, even valuable clothing, is too easy to steal. Diamonds, though highly valued, fantastically durable, and easy to hide from thieves, have rarely been used as a medium of exchange because too much expertise is required to tell the difference between gemstones and fakes. The only circumstances in which diamonds have functioned temporarily as a medium of exchange is in transactions between experts and during civil wars in diamond-producing countries, where, paradoxically, it may be harder to get hold of convincing fakes than of the real thing.
- It must be scarce, either naturally (like gold) or artificially through the restricted printing of banknotes that are difficult to forge. If it were not, there would be easier ways to obtain money than by offering valuable goods in exchange. If acorns functioned as money, for instance, people would stop producing other goods and start collecting acorns instead.
- It has to be more widely acceptable by other people than the goods in exchange for which it is offered. If it were not, then there would be no point in accepting the money; the seller could just hold stocks of her own products until the time came to exchange them.

So the acceptability of money rests in part upon what people believe about its probable acceptability in the future. There are some factors that make acceptability more likely, such as anonymity, which ensures that potentially interested trading partners will not be arbitrarily excluded from using it. It seems obvious today that money is anonymous;

this is what gives it a quality at once clean and a little sinister, like a room so exaggeratedly scrubbed as to make one wonder what might have happened there just before it was cleaned. But historically some kinds of money have been restricted to transactions in certain classes of society, like the shell currencies of the Solomon Islands, which until the late nineteenth century (as the anthropologist Denis Monnerie reports) had separate denominations for use by chiefs and commoners.[3] This had the incidental consequence that a commoner who had sexual inter-course with the wife of a chief could incur the death penalty. This was not because it was a capital offense: it was, on the contrary, considered an offense against property, and like most offenses against property at-tracted only a fine. However, the fine could only be paid in the currency of the aristocracy, so the offending commoner would be executed for nonpayment of the fine rather than for the original offense.[4]

Not surprisingly, these shell currencies were soon driven out by com-petition from the currencies brought by foreign traders (most obviously by the U.S. dollar), once such traders arrived in significant numbers in the late nineteenth century. Why accept shell currencies that not every-one else will accept when there is a universal and anonymous alterna-tive readily available? And the story of the shell currencies has very nearly been imitated in the 1990s by the Russian rouble.

It is certain that many billions of American dollars are circulating inside Russia today, although nobody knows exactly how many since their owners are understandably reticent about revealing their holdings. This foreign currency has cost the Russian economy dearly: it represents many billions of dollars' worth of American goods that could have been bought and shipped to Russia at a time when many of its people have been suffering extreme poverty. It would be much better if the Russian authorities could persuade people to hold roubles instead of these dol-lars, for the cost of roubles to the country as a whole is only the cost of printing them. But the loss of confidence in a currency is cumulative; once some people are reluctant to hold it, others will become reluctant as well. And the very attractiveness of roubles to the authorities—the fact that they cost so much less to produce than they are worth in ex-change—is exactly why confidence may be lost in the first place. For much of the early 1990s roubles were like acorns. The ease with which the authorities could make them made it irresistible to simply print more roubles to pay for the government's spending on everything from the army to old-age pensions, instead of doing hard work to persuade citizens to pay their taxes in full and on time. But if roubles are just printed on demand, their scarcity value—the very quality that makes them valuable as money—will be irresistibly undermined.

As it happens, the Russian authorities were able to restore the scarcity value of roubles by the mid-1990s, since the rate of price inflation (and therefore the decline in the value of roubles over time) fell to very modest levels by around 1995. But the incidence of barter went on rising for at least another three years. What was wrong now was not the ease of making money but the ease of transferring it — the very anonymity that makes money in most circumstances such a useful component of modern life. For during the wrenching conditions after the fall of communism, many Russian firms had run up extremely large debts, and large debts create long queues of creditors. If you lend money to a firm which owes money to many other people, the chances are high that your loan will not be used to do anything productive or new, but instead will be used merely to pay off creditors further up the queue. In fact, the creditors further up the queue have a legal right to insist on it, and if these creditors include the tax authorities, they even have a legal right to impound the money from the firm's bank account. In these conditions it is hardly surprising that lenders will lose all willingness to provide finance for business. And without finance it is impossible for Russian business to begin the task of adapting its products and processes to the modern world.

In an economy based on money, then, the queue is long, and the creditors are stern. If the queue becomes too long, barter may provide a way to jump it.[5] If I deliver goods to you in exchange for a promise to pay me back in money, then the money you have earmarked to pay me may be seized by any one of your creditors, and the law will uphold their right to do so. But if you have promised to pay me back in goods, then I count as one of your customers, not one of your creditors. Your other creditors are less likely to want to seize your goods anyway, and even if they do, they cannot invoke the law to help them, so my chances of being repaid are much higher.

Systematic queue-jumping is at best a quick fix, not a permanent answer to the problems of Russia's chronically overindebted firms. Not least of its costs is that everyone ends up settling for second best. You may not want the shoes your trading partner offers you: they may not be the quality or the style you would have chosen, but you accept them because it is better than not being paid at all. Even the government is doing it: a firm manufacturing buses claims the only way it can pay its local taxes is to deliver buses to the local authority instead of cash. The buses don't work very well; indeed, they break down rather often, leaving passengers stranded in the snow. But the local tax office is not concerned, so long as it can place a tick against the bus company in its records.

Russia's firms have in fact found things easier in the last few years, thanks largely to higher prices for Russia's exports (especially oil) that have enabled more of the creditors in the queue to be paid off than anyone realistically imagined. Barter is declining as a result — fortunately, for those who have tried barter know how much it hurts.

MONEY, ANONYMITY, AND UNEASE

At the same time that Russia's citizens have been feeling the pain of barter, the attraction of barter is growing in some parts of the industrialized West. The International Reciprocal Trade Association (www. irta.net) is an enthusiastic ambassador for the benefits of barter trade in the modern world. It claims that "Over 7.5 billion dollars in sales is transacted each year by the commercial barter industry. This figure is growing at an estimated rate of 8 percent a year." It points to the role of computers and the internet in matching the demands of different customers and achieving the "double coincidence of wants" that has been such a challenge for barter transactions in the past — the enormous effort that has to be put by suppliers of one good into finding buyers who not only want the good in question but have a desirable good to offer in return.

Small-scale barter networks (often known as local exchange trading systems, or LETS)[6] have also been growing in a number of towns. They allow individuals to trade goods and services on a small scale and to build up credit in points or some other artificial currency for exchange against other goods and services at a later date. Their attractiveness may depend to some extent on the greater ease with which their transactions escape taxation and to some extent on a yearning to decouple one's community from the monetary economy, but for whatever reason, their popularity is unquestionably on the rise.

Many claims are made for barter by its enthusiasts: that it is more efficient, that it is more fun, even that it is more ethical. Many people have felt that there is something a little sinister about the ubiquity and anonymity of monetary transactions in the modern world. "Money has no smell," said the emperor Vespasian, and it is precisely this that makes some people shudder (Vespasian was referring, somewhat smugly, to the fact that he had succeeded in imposing a tax on public lavatories). A lyrical, even purple, expression of this point of view appears in the closing paragraph of James Buchan's book *Frozen Desire*, in which he holds out the dream of a world free of money:

> One day, who knows, the human race might stir. My heroes and heroines wake from their sleep and rub their eyes. Honour pushes credit away with an indescribable grimace of disgust, charity runs shrieking from the Charity Ball and virtue and solvency discuss a separation, which becomes permanent. Lib-

erty puts down her shopping bag and rests her bunioned feet. The Owl of Minerva opens one eye, then the other, and extends her tattered wings for flight. And as these dreams dissolve, the Age of Money, which came after the Age of Faith, will itself draw, as all things under the sun, to an end.[7]

But whatever else may be claimed for it, barter is never an efficient system for society as a whole, though taxes and other regulations, or the absence of trustworthy money, may make it an understandable refuge for many individuals. Even with sophisticated computer- and internet-based systems for bringing about a double coincidence of wants, barter will always run up against a fundamental problem: when searching for someone who wants to buy what I have to sell, how can I be sure that what he has to offer in return is of the quality I require? The attraction of money is precisely that I can be more confident of its quality than I can of almost anything else a buyer can offer. Barter will always survive where participants have already overcome the problem of trust in other ways: in small communities where people know each other well, and even on a larger scale where the goods exchanged are sufficiently standardized for their quality to be quickly verifiable without much effort. But as a means of mediating the exchange of inscrutables between strangers, on which more and more of modern life is based, no realistic alternative to money has ever yet been found.

What about the ethical appeal of barter? What is the foundation for this widespread unease about the Age of Money? It doubtless has many roots, and it would take another book than this to explore them all. Disdain for money is sometimes just a shorthand way of expressing disdain for wealth (money is, after all, a shorthand for all the many things it can be used to acquire). More subtly, disdain for money has often been a coded expression of the insecurity of aristocrats and those who lived on *inherited* wealth in the face of wealth acquired through economic activity and — especially — trade. This insecurity may have had important social and economic consequences, through the way it shaped attitudes toward economic activity in many societies, from ancient Athens to modern Britain. The historian Martin Wiener has argued that the "decline of the industrial spirit" in Britain was due to exactly such unresolved insecurities among the dominant figures in British culture, from the landed aristocracy of the nineteenth century to the literary and artistic influences on so important a figure as John Maynard Keynes.[8] More complicatedly still, disdain for money has often played on a deliberate ambiguity between "money" in the sense of wealth and "money" in the sense of an anonymous medium of exchange whose very anonymity and superficiality makes it somehow suspect. As a rhetorical device it becomes a term of disparagement by a hinted association that would rarely stand up to examination if it were presented as an explicit argument. Many writers who bemoan the spread of the market in the modern world have expressed their complaint in terms of the influence of a money mentality,[9] a complaint that might be less rhetorically persuasive if it were directed simply at the division of labor and the spread of social exchange.

Even a cursory glance at the place of money in poetry and prose literature reveals how closely this unease is tied up with ambivalence about the human body, and particularly with the ambiguities of our sexuality. This does not mean that the ambiguities of our sexuality cause us to feel this way about money, but it is likely that we use terms that convey our unease about sexuality in order to express the unease we feel — perhaps for other reasons — about money and its pervasive social influence. The word "luxury" used to mean "lechery" as recently as the seventeenth century, and to this day the French for lechery is "la luxure." The Jacobean dramatist Cyril Tourneur has the duke in *The Revenger's Tragedy* described by an onlooker as "a parch'd and juiceless luxur."[10] The word "expense" (as in Shakespeare's sonnet that begins "the expense of spirit in a waste of shame") used to stand for orgasm, and until the late nineteenth century the colloquial term for having an orgasm was not "to come" but "to spend." Perhaps this analogy is due to the similarity between the tiredness that follows in the wake of sexual pleasure and the financial depletion that succeeds the pleasure of spending money (both kinds of exhaustion frequently occasioning, and perhaps being confused with, feelings of guilt). Partly it may be due to the sense that money as an accounting mechanism submits pleasures to an unforgiving scrutiny, like that of traditional morality. Most of all it has to do with money's anonymity, the sense that the trust it buys is somehow fraudulently acquired, being based on impersonal rules rather than personal understanding. Sexuality is the area of human life most permeated by the ideal of willing and autonomous exchange between partners motivated by convergent desire, and yet it is also the one most poisoned by the suspicion that the appearance of desire is but simulation, cloaking a more indirect and mercenary motive. The indirect masquerading as the direct is likewise at money's very heart.

Money tantalizes us by the disparity between what it looks like on the surface and what it hints at underneath. As James Buchan puts it: "Money, to use an old-fashioned mechanical metaphor, has become a sort of railway shunting-yard which is for ever receiving the wishes and dreams of countless people and despatching them to unimagined destinations."[11] This sense of limitless possibility also undermines the comfort of familiar categories, leading to an impression that people with money can buy their way out of confinement by the social and moral judgments that constrain the rest of us. Balzac puts this complaint in the mouth of Esther, the rather innocent heroine of his novel *Splendors and Miseries of the Courtesans*:

> A girl with no income finds herself in the mud, as I was before I entered the convent. Men find her beautiful, they make her serve their pleasure without according her the smallest respect, they come for her in a carriage and then send her away on foot. If they never quite spit in her face, it is only her beauty that spares her this outrage. But let her inherit five or six million, and she will be sought out by princes, saluted as she passes in her carriage; she can choose from the most ancient coats of arms of France and Navarre. This world, which would have sneered at us [her and her impoverished lover] for being two handsome creatures, united and content, has constantly honoured Madame de Staël with her bohemian life, because she had an income of two hundred thousand *livres*. The world, which bows before Money and Glory, has no wish to honour happiness or virtue.[12]

A later writer, Martin Amis, uses the same device in a back-to-front way by making his narrator play with the idea of money as protection: "Money," he writes, "I must put money round me, more money, soon. I must be safe."[13] The deceptive promise of safety has become one of the most enduring themes in our contemporary attitude toward money, and one that has become more insistent the safer money has historically become. It is an intriguing feature of modern life that as sexual morality has increasingly been privatized, the ethics of financial probity have become the growing object of collective regulation. This is both inevitable and desirable, but that does not stop it from feeling strange. Even the AIDS crisis has not reversed the growing belief that in prosperous societies financial behavior has more seamless links to the fate of the rest of society than does sexual behavior. Sex may be the subject of endless curiosity but in the end creates smaller ripples in the pond (though the tragic exception of Africa, now ravaged by AIDS, reminds us that in the very poorest societies the reverse may now be true).

The fact that money is safer now in most prosperous societies than it has ever been makes its remaining hazards all the more troubling. It symbolizes the way in which we are connected to strangers as never before. Our response to these connections, and our attempts through political institutions to reassert control over the financial structure of our economies, have led to edifices of regulation as striking in their complexity as the financial institutions they seek to dominate. These are the subject of chapter 5.

CHAPTER 5

Honor among Thieves: Hoarding and Stealing

STORAGE, LENDING, AND PANIC

A wide range of animals hoard food outside their own bodies, from the *Sphex* wasp (which paralyzes insects for its own larvae to feed on) to dogs, bees, and squirrels. It is something that becomes harder to do the larger and more sophisticated the animal. Big animals are big eaters and big excreters, often too much so for their immediate environment to support them for long, so they are obliged periodically to move on. But the gypsy life limits how much you can store, for it must all be carried with you.

When our ancestors first began to settle down to a farming lifestyle some ten thousand years ago, the burden of carrying stores of food was soon replaced by the burden of protecting them. How many times must a family have stared in dismay at the cracked clay vessel, the scattered stones, the trail of grain marking theft by rats or men and whispering the prospect of starvation, before it occurred to them that sometimes the best protection is not the closest to home?

The division of labor long ago proved its value for the hoarding of food as well as for its production. Indeed, one of the best ways to hoard the food you have produced is to sell it, to a merchant whose solid warehouses give him an advantage in protecting his stores while the coins or banknotes he gives you in return are more suitable for the limited protection you can provide. But even before money was invented, families probably deposited their stocks of grain at the sturdier houses of others whom they believed they could trust. Later they would do the same with money too. The first banks were no more than places of safekeeping.

Borrowing and lending are as old as communal living, as deeply embedded in social life as the sharing of meat from a kill. But banks are a remarkable and much more recent innovation; no records can tell us when they first began, but a plausible guess is that it was after the invention of agriculture and before, not after, the invention of money. They may have begun simply as storehouses (certainly that was true of the first *recorded* banks).[1] Their subsequent transformation into proper banks may even have been the fruit of deceit, the ingenuity of a warehouse owner who realized that he could lend out some of the grain he was storing on others' behalf without the knowledge of its owners.[2] If he was a prosperous enough farmer in his own right, he might hope to keep secret for a while the fact that not all the grain he lent out was his own, but in small communities the secret would soon be out. In towns of some size, the operation might keep going for longer: what was needed was enough owners of grain, with diverse enough requirements, for the fledgling banker to feel confident he could always meet the demands of any one owner who came to reclaim his stock, by drawing on the unclaimed stock of others.

It must still have been difficult, winning the trust of suspicious peasants who wanted to know why the grain they reclaimed came from other vessels than those in which they had first seen it stored, and who must have wondered whether it was of quality as good as their own. The gradual arrival of money must have made that task easier, since its obvious anonymity makes irrelevant the question "But is it really mine?" To the peasant too poor to afford secure storage, the arrival of money meant that grain could be sold instead of lent, while money could be hoarded at home, deposited for safekeeping elsewhere, or lent out explicitly for use by others.

But lending money is risky in its own way. Its anonymity and the ease with which it can be concealed make fraud all the more tempting. So banks have not completely displaced that old standby of peasant societies, the storeroom in a corner of your house. Over a billion peasants around the world still store food at the end of the harvest for as long as the supply holds out. Even those who sell the produce often feel the money is less safe in a bank than under the mattress. In rich industrial societies it *is* safer in the bank — most of the time. For banks have flourished because of their ingenious capacities for helping people to live with risk. Like many of the human institutions that do so, they have reduced everyday risks to levels low enough to make us forget that risk exists at all, sometimes leaving us startlingly unprepared for the more unusual hazards, whose impact can be very large.

If you want to hoard what you value — food, money, objects of beauty — but don't trust the safety of your own home, you have to find someone who not only is capable of storing it for you but can also be relied upon to return it to you afterward. The storage is a service performed on your behalf. It will therefore usually cost you something (a portion of the value preserved), unless your valuables can be made to perform a service of their own in the meantime. So instead of asking your neighbor to store grain for you, you could try asking him to plant it. By planting it he will reap a harvest that may substantially exceed what he needs to return your grain to you at the end of the season.

Now you are doing him a service, one for which he may be prepared to pay you. Your hoard of grain is no longer idle, but it is not instantly accessible. In order to allow it to perform a useful service you have had to forgo the right to call it back whenever you want it. And in the meantime it is vulnerable to all the usual hazards of the harvest.

The ingenuity of banks rests on their using the law of large numbers to create the illusion that anyone's hoard is accessible even while most people's hoards are being made to perform a useful service. It is an illusion, though no more dishonest than the illusion that anyone may visit the U.S. Senate or the Houses of Parliament even though it would clearly be impossible for everyone to do so at the same time. Or the illusion that I can go to the bus-stop without a reservation and expect to find a space on the bus. Or the illusion that I can always make a telephone call without a prior appointment, or switch on the kettle to make myself coffee without overloading the capacity of the electricity grid. Or the thousands of other daily illusions that keep modern societies in motion. There are frequent rents in the fabric of such illusions: sometimes the bus is completely full; a commercial break in the television coverage of a British royal wedding has been known to cause chaos on the electric grid as millions of kettles switch on within seconds; and simultaneous toilet use during the breaks in the Super Bowl imposes heavy strain on the drains. And once in a while there is a run on a bank.

Bank runs are dangerous, and not just because people's life savings may be involved. Some broken illusions lead to a stabilizing reaction: if the bus is full, I wait for the next one; if the telephone network is busy, I make my call later. But if I hear a rumor that there is a run on my bank, do I stay home until the panic has subsided? Not if I know what is good for me. When a bank run is threatened, the only sensible thing to do is to run faster than the others, and that in turn means that it may take only an unsubstantiated rumor for a bank's customers to run to it in panic. In a matter of days or even hours, the illusion that their savings are all simultaneously accessible can unravel.[3]

This vulnerability of banks to panic runs is what makes the financial system a peculiarly fragile part of the network of institutions that make up modern social life. A panic run can damage a healthy and well-

Figure 5.1. President Andrew Jackson (1767–1845) refuses in 1832 to renew the charter of the Bank of the United States on the grounds that it is a tool of the rich, choosing to remove all government funds from the bank and to deposit them in state banks around the country. Pandemonium ensues amid "The Downfall of Mother Bank." Newspaper editor Seba Smith (1792–1868), who wrote under the pseudonym of Major Jack Downing, cheers from the sidelines. Getty Images/Hulton Archive.

managed bank no less than an incompetent or corrupt one, for even a healthy bank will have used its deposits to make loans that cannot all be instantly called back (indeed, if banks did not make such loans, investments could never be undertaken by people who have ideas but not enough funds to back them). So the fate of different banks may be linked, and the risks of banking may propagate themselves across a whole society with alarming speed. In some ways the dangers are harder to avoid than many of the other risks that people transmit to each other. Viruses (physical or informational) can be transmitted rapidly across the world, but once people realize the dangers, they adjust their behavior to compensate: they are more scrupulous about practicing safe sex, for example, more cautious about opening email attachments. With bank runs, by contrast, the greater the danger, the more people's behavior multiplies it as everyone tries to avoid being the last in line.

In most industrial societies, governments have responded to these dangers by setting up systems of deposit insurance, in which all depositors are subject to a small tax in order to pay compensation to those who lose their savings through incompetence or fraud. The result has been to calm the panics — but not to avoid all the crashes. For if too much nervousness can unravel the delicate system of illusion on which the banking system depends, too little nervousness can lead to lethargy and gullibility, thus issuing an open invitation to fantasists and charlatans. Most days my incoming email contains messages urging me to make a fortune for almost no effort by sending money to an address somewhere in cyberspace. It is a safe bet that the few such invitations that are not downright dishonest are wholly unrealistic, relying on the chain letter principle to make money for early participants at the expense of later ones. If I were insured against loss every time I sent off money in response to an email solicitation, I would have no need to be careful, and the number of people trying to make money out of others in this simple way would explode. Why do any productive work if you can make money from people who will be bailed out by the government for every penny they send to you?

So when governments offer deposit insurance they do so at a price: only institutions that hold a deposit-taking license may qualify, and as quid pro quo they must subject themselves to detailed and intrusive supervision. For if depositors no longer have an incentive to monitor the activities of banks, the government must do so, on behalf of the taxpayers whose money is now at risk. Supervision is not infallible; both incompetence and fraud can and do slip through the net. Even if runs occur much more rarely than they once did, they are not unknown. In January 1991 the newly elected governor of Rhode Island closed forty-five of the state's banks within three hours of taking office, thereby freezing the accounts of some three hundred thousand people. He did this because their deposits had been insured by a private insurer that became insolvent, and there were signs of an incipient bank run. The next day the announcement of losses at the Bank of New England led in turn to a run on that bank and its subsequent seizure by the government. Without the atmosphere of panic caused by the Rhode Island action, there would probably not have been a run on the Bank of New England. Without the insolvency of the Rhode Island Share and Deposit Indemnity Corporation, there would have been no closure of Rhode Island banks. And without losses the previous November by Heritage Loan and Investment, a tiny, two-branch bank in Providence, Rhode Island, there would have been no insolvency on the part of the insurer. The president of that bank, one Joseph Mollicone, was subsequently convicted on five counts of embezzlement, nineteen counts of false bank entries, and two counts of conspiracy and was given a long prison sentence.[4]

If the failure of a two-branch bank can cause a widespread run, how much more threatening is the failure of a large bank? Among the main depositors with banks are other banks, and in any case deposit insurance is usually less than perfect, and the contagion of panic undiscriminating, so other banks may suffer by association even when they have no direct links with the failing bank. Deposit insurance and supervision are not enough, therefore, to prevent either bank failure or the threat of a run on an otherwise healthy bank. Instead, the authorities find themselves from time to time playing the role of "lender of last resort." The authorities stand ready to do what the markets by themselves will not: they allow banks to borrow, usually on easy terms, to cover the costs of their exposure to the bank that has failed. In return they usually insist on the closure of the failing bank. Its managers are rarely punished, except in the most egregious cases of fraud, but most of them lose their jobs and fritter away their golden parachutes in a retirement of complaint at their unreliable customers and overzealous regulators. Their fate is hardly one to strike terror into the heart of their surviving colleagues in other banks, but the authorities in most industrialized societies think the damage done by complacent bankers who lend too easily is less severe than the damage unwittingly done by bankers who are too nervous to lend at all.

Most of the time the authorities are right, but once in a while the sheer scale of incompetence and fraud can catch everyone by surprise. After the great American banking crises of the 1930s, in which some ten thousand banks failed, and which led to the creation of the Federal Deposit Insurance Corporation (FDIC), American banking enjoyed thirty-five postwar years without runs or panics of any kind and with very few bank failures at all. But at the beginning of the 1980s, looser regulation of banks allowed them (and particularly the savings and loan institutions specializing in mortgage finance) to offer higher interest rates to depositors while investing speculatively in real estate. Bust followed boom in a vertiginous cycle. There was a startling increase in bank failures, which by 1988 were running at over two hundred a year. By 1991 the FDIC was spectacularly insolvent, ending the year with a deficit of $7 billion even though it had received an injection of $30 billion from the U.S. Treasury earlier in the year (as one U.S. senator put it, in a different context, "A billion here, a billion there, and soon you're talking real money"). Regulation has since been overhauled, but if the bank failures have slowed to a trickle, it has been largely thanks to the American economy's remarkable subsequent growth. The same has not been true in Japan, where banking weakness and slow economic growth have been locked in a crippling embrace.

BUYING TRUST

The banking system builds great Gothic structures of interdependent transactions upon a slender foundation of trust, but there are more modest edifices all around us, for trust is the mortar for most of the encounters between strangers in a modern society. Even something as simple as a trip to buy fruit at a street market involves the buyer in a careful evaluation of the quality of the produce on offer. In theory most legal systems pay homage to the principle of "caveat emptor" — let the buyer beware — meaning that it is the buyer's responsibility to ensure she is not cheated. There is sense in this, for buyers have the keenest interest in looking out for defective goods and are usually the best placed to spot them. But in practice very few legal systems ever place complete responsibility on the buyer. The fruit I buy may go rotten as soon as I take it home, and I shall have nobody but myself to blame. But if it contains a proscribed chemical, then the law may become involved.

The limits of the caveat emptor principle are usually drawn according to an uneasy compromise between the wish to encourage care and skepticism on the part of buyers and the fact that many of the greatest dangers are too subtle and invisible for buyers to check. In most industrialized countries, the law intervenes in everyday transactions in many thousands of arenas: safety at work, the chemical content of food and medicines, the technical specification of electrical equipment, the terms of financial services, the training of teachers and doctors, the content of advertisements, the emission of exhaust gases on cars, the takeovers and mergers of firms. Not all of these interventions are justified by an appeal to the protection of the buyer, but a large number of them are.

But the law is a clumsy and unreliable ally of the buyer, and its interventions are inevitably limited to correcting those breaches of trust that are clear and precise enough to be established in front of a court, or at least by a formalized administrative procedure. Many of the other familiar institutions of social life can be seen as a way for buyers to seek allies from among themselves, and even — strange paradox — for buyers to seek allies from among sellers, the very people whose unreliability such alliances seek to prevent. The explanation is that unreliability harms many sellers too: everyone who has a good car to sell but cannot persuade a buyer of its merits, good, fresh food to trade that cannot be made to stand out from the mediocre produce on neighboring stalls, a medicine that promises a real cure but looks too much like the remedies of a thousand mountebanks. So: trade associations, money-back guarantees, the Hippocratic oath, the *appellation contrôlée*, inspectors of weights and measures, the convention that "my word is my bond," trademarks and brand names, the salesman's uniform, the training certificate hanging on the office wall, the opulence of a professional waiting room that soothes the visitor's anxiety about how much it is all going to cost with the subliminal assurance that nobody who makes this much money can be peddling unsound advice — all of these are signals, more or less subtle, that what the seller has to offer is the best anyone could reasonably expect. Sometimes the signals have to be subtle in order to make them difficult to fake: comparing television advertisements from the 1950s with those made half a century later is intriguing because it makes us realize how unpersuasive were direct boasts about the quality of a laundry detergent once viewers woke up to the fact that makers of low-quality laundry detergent could make the very same boasts. So the race to be persuasive has taken ever more baroque forms, much as the peacock's tail evolved toward an efflorescence further and further removed from the original signal of health and strength to which it must have owed its origin. Nowadays television advertisements are increasingly a parade of dandyish preening and ironic self-reference, as makers of even the most humble domestic products strive to project that indefinable quality (panache? flair?) that makes us think we have found the rare genuine article in a world of dross.

To put the matter slightly differently, the peasant virtues in all societies have included never taking anything on trust but always checking for yourself the quality of what you are offered. But checking for yourself is impossible once you are involved in more than a few transactions a day. So modern societies have resorted to a division of labor in the verification of authenticity, just as they have resorted to a division of labor in almost everything else. The creation of brands—now a multi-billion dollar activity in its own right—represents an investment in trustworthiness. It is both a signal to customers (our products must be good if we can afford to spend so much money telling you about them) and a commitment mechanism that in fact keeps firms up to the mark (if we let standards fall, we shall destroy the value of our brand).

Banks in particular have come a long way from their simple origins as places of safekeeping. The best bank is no longer the place with the most secure vault, since the money you entrust to your bank will not simply be stored; it will be invested elsewhere. The best bank is now the one with the shrewdest eye for sound investments. It is therefore the most convincing purveyor of trust in the many claims made by would-be borrowers for the quality of their business propositions.

Modern man buys his trust as he buys his food and his clothes and his house. Sometimes the ultimate guarantor of his trust is the state, but more often, in many thousands of everyday ways that are so familiar as to be quite invisible unless we open our eyes to them, it is his fellow citizens who are the guarantors—the very people whose trustworthiness is in question. The idea of "honor among thieves," though coined as a paradox, is in fact one of transparent simplicity, for only in a world of thieves is honor necessary. It is no accident that the strictest codes of honor in any society are those that govern relations among its criminals, for honor is one of the most effective ways to organize relations in the shadows where the law does not reach. But even in the daylight, the law is at most a background presence. The honor, reputation, and trustworthiness of those with whom you deal—qualities in which they may have invested mightily, but which you accept on possibly the slenderest of objective evidence—are the foundation of your willingness even to step outside your house in the morning. When the whole structure of a modern society rests on such a foundation, it is not surprising that the collapse of trust that can follow a banking scandal, a political upheaval, or the exposure of corruption among trusted public figures can take on the dimensions of a major social earthquake.

CHAPTER 6

Professionalism and Fulfilment in Work and War

SOLDIERS AND PHILOSOPHERS

[T]en thousand Greek mercenaries are hired under false pretences by a Persian prince, Cyrus the younger, for an expedition into the hinterland of Asia Minor, whose real aim was to oust Cyrus's brother Artaxerxes II; but they are defeated at the battle of Cunaxa, and now leaderless and far from their native land, they have to find a way back home amidst very hostile peoples. All they want is to go back home, but everything they do constitutes a public menace: there are ten thousand of them, armed, but without food, so wherever they go they ravage and destroy the land like a swarm of locusts, and carry in their wake a huge following of women.

Thus Italo Calvino describes the predicament of a meandering army in the fifth century B.C., one similar to many thousands of others through the course of history and unusual only in that one of its officers, Xenophon, recorded its passage in a book that has survived for us and is called *The Anabasis*. After comparing Xenophon with the later writer T. E. Lawrence, and noting — with some approval that in contrast to Lawrence's aestheticizing vision, "with the Greek there is nothing beneath the exactness and dryness of the narration," Calvino goes on to say:

Of course there is a kind of pathos in the *Anabasis*: it is the anxiety of the soldiers to return home, the bewilderment of being in a foreign land, the anxiety not to get separated, because as long as they are still together they carry their own country within them. . . . In these memoirs of a general from the fifth century BC, the contrast is between the role of locust-like parasites to which the Greek army of mercenaries had been reduced and the exercise of the classical virtues — philosophical, civic, military virtues — which Xenophon and his men try to adapt to these new circumstances. . . . Man can be reduced to a locust but can apply to this condition of locust a code of discipline and decorum — in a word, "style" — and consider himself satisfied; man is capable of not even discussing for a minute the fact that he is a locust but only the best way of being one. In Xenophon we find already delineated, with all its limitations, the modern ethic of perfect technical efficiency, of being "up to the job," of "doing your job well" quite independently of what value is put on one's actions in terms of universal morals. . . . In this attempt to give a certain "style" or rule to this parasitical movement of greedy and violent men amidst the mountains and plains of Anatolia resides all his dignity: not tragic dignity but rather a limited dignity, fundamentally a bourgeois dignity . . . the Greek army, creeping through the mountain heights and fjords amidst constant ambushes and attacks, no longer able to distinguish just to what extent it is a victim or an oppressor, and surrounded even in the most chilling massacres of its men by the supreme hostility or indifference of fortune, inspires in the reader an almost symbolic anguish which perhaps only we today can understand.[1]

Nowhere more than in an army does the health of the whole depend so totally upon the absolute reliability of the parts. Armies everywhere seek through the rigor of their training to impart adherence to a code, a set of procedures and what can also be called an ethic, which together aim to ensure loyalty even in the face of overwhelming individual temptations to betrayal. This code is transmitted through the procedures of training, everything from the mindless repetition of parade-ground drill to the complex task mastery of the military engineer. It is also transmitted through the atmosphere of the military institution, whether this be the high-mindedness of the academy, the clubby vulgarity of the mess, or the intensity of the shared bivouac or the night exercise. This code, once it has been mastered to the point of second nature, can be called tunnel vision in its starkest form, one that not only ignores speculation about the wider consequences of adherence but seeks deliberately to exclude such speculation. At the Nuremberg war-crimes trial of 1945 to 1946, this code came up against the onslaught of a different, more universalizing conception of human duty.[2]

Rudolf Höss, the former commandant of the Auschwitz concentration camp, though not himself on trial, was among those called to give evidence at Nuremberg. His testimony included heartrending details of the gassing of prisoners, after which he was asked, "Did you yourself ever feel pity with the victims, thinking of your own family and children?" He replied, "Yes." The examination continued: "How was it possible for you to carry out these actions in spite of this?" Höss replied, "In view of all these doubts which I had, the one and only decisive argument was the strict order and the reason given for it by the Reichsführer Himmler."

The defendants in the trial also resorted to what has since become known as the Nuremberg defense, namely, that they were only following orders. Few of them gave it a rationale, but Franz von Papen, who had been chancellor of the Reich in 1932 and later Hitler's representative in Vienna and then Ankara, was one who did. Sir David Maxwell-Fyfe asked: "Why didn't you after this series of murders [of his close friends and associates] which had gone on over a period of 4 years, why didn't you break with these people and stand up like General Yorck or any other people that you may think of from history, stand up for your own views and oppose these murderers? Why didn't you do it?"

Von Papen replied:

> If you ask me, Sir David, why despite everything I remained in the service of the Reich, then I can only say that . . . I did my duty — my duty to Germany, if you wish to know. I can understand very well, Sir David, that after all the things we know today, after the millions of murders which have taken place, you consider the German people a nation of criminals, and that you cannot understand that this nation has its patriots as well. I did these things in order to serve my country, and I should like to add, Sir David, that up to the time of the Munich Agreement, and even up to the time of the Polish campaign, even the major powers tried, although they knew everything that was going on in Germany, to work with Germany. Why do you wish to reproach a patriotic German with acting likewise, and with hoping likewise, for the same thing for which all the major powers hoped?

Hermann Göring, the most articulate of all those on trial, was adamant about the unrealistic nature of the standard to which the defendants were being held. He was scathing about the impracticability of applying the Hague Convention of 1907 to the conditions of a modern war, and when questioned about the possibility of disobedience to Hitler's will, asked the court:

> How does one imagine that a state can be led if, during a war, or before a war, which the political leaders have decided upon, whether wrongly or rightly, the individual general could vote whether he was going to fight or not, whether his army corps was going to stay at home or not, or could say "I must first ask my division"?

As von Papen and Göring knew only too well — and as many of the judges and prosecutors uncomfortably realized — ethical considerations are a fragile restraint against the overwhelming sense of urgency that warfare demands from its participants. The Nuremberg process was riddled with contradictions in any case: the senior Soviet tribunal member I. T. Nikitchenko had been one of the three prosecutors at the first of Stalin's show trials in 1936 and was so unused to the concept of a dissenting opinion that he had to ask his Western colleagues how to formulate one when — on orders from Moscow — he objected to the leniency of their sentencing.[3] Nevertheless, though the Nuremberg trials brought out these tensions explicitly and in a starker form than ever before or since, the sense that the life of a complex society encourages a single-mindedness essential to our success, while simultaneously provoking deep unease at the effects of this single-mindedness on the quality of our lives, has been with us for many centuries.

THE SEARCH FOR NARRATIVES

The ability to see the limitations of particular individual perspectives, and their proper place in some overall scheme of things, is a remarkable human capacity for whose evolution we have still only a partial explanation.[4] It is all the more remarkable since societies with the leisure to develop and reward this ability among their citizens have usually had to call upon considerable single-mindedness, both military and commercial, in order to achieve so great a degree of material success. The historian Peter Hall has noted that the civilization of ancient Athens, to which we owe just that concern with the right way to live and the capacity for inquiry into human nature that can be described as the foundation of the Nuremberg vision, expressed an attitude to trade and the division of labor so ambivalent as to amount almost to institutionalized denial: "From the sea the Greeks got trade, and from trade came ideas, and then empire; but from empire came wealth, and with wealth leisure and the opportunity to create new ideas and new art. . . . [But] there was an emerging contradiction: the old aristocratic value system said it was honourable to earn one's living in agriculture, or even in the higher forms of business and banking; but retail trade and manual labour, even craftsmanship, were ignoble."[5] He quotes an earlier historian, H. Michell, as saying that "the citizen was an aristocrat who disliked manual labour; lounging in the market place and gossiping, or occupying himself with the endless political intrigues of the state was much more to his taste, if he could afford it."

In much less dramatic ways than the army, almost all occupations in a modern society embody an ethic, a code. For trust requires an assurance of reliability, and some of the most effective policemen are internal, lodged in the surveillance mechanisms of the individual personality. The fiercest external vigilance will rarely be enough to ensure the honesty of a really determined cheat, so what better than to deal with people whose character, training, or upbringing leads them not to want to cheat even when they have the chance? Those who can convince others of their intrinsic honesty may thereby prosper, and it may be easier for the genuinely honest to be thus convincing—the more so if honesty, or at least the true and honorable performance of a certain trade or skill, requires a degree of style, confidence, even grace, built up over a long period of commitment to the task, that are hard for an opportunist to feign. Even so-called unskilled work involves people in learning how to fit into a team, on the construction site, on the fruit farm, in the workshop, at the checkout counter. And most kinds of professional training, whether apprenticeship as a mechanic or studying for the bar or attending an off-site course as a chef, involve learning not just how to accomplish particular tasks but how to project yourself as a certain kind of person.[6] One consequence is that many people have a training that appears disproportionate to the tasks they subsequently need to undertake (or to put it another way, many people are challenged less by the work they do than they are led to expect during their training). Another consequence is that people need to find within them the commitment to persevere with the process of learning how to project themselves in this way. At the very least, for someone to have this commitment, she needs to be able to explain to herself the purpose for which her commitment is made. In a word, she needs a narrative of her life and her work.

For a long period in recorded history, that narrative was supplied to individual members of society by their social order and its public relations officers, that is to say, its poets, philosophers, and priests. The Indian caste system can be understood as an elaborate social expression of what was originally a division of labor; soldiers, priests, merchants, farmers, potters, leather workers, and other occupational groups were assigned to castes that were not allowed to intermarry, nor even to live in the same neighbourhood.[7] The citizens of modern India have developed a sophisticated division of labor to which these categories are now wildly inappropriate, and yet the narrative retains a startling power to govern the behavior of individuals, as a glance at the matrimonial columns of any Indian newspaper will confirm. Intercaste marriages remain rare, and for reasons that are self-reinforcing. In all societies, even if the conventions underlying social compatibility are arbitrary ones, marriages based on social compatibility can last longer and weather crises better than ones that set social and erotic bonds in conflict with each other, as countless unsung Romeos and Juliets of the suburbs have found to their cost. Shakespeare killed his young lovers because he could not bear to imagine them in resentful middle age.

The European feudal system similarly furnished its members with a narrative, one that was still being celebrated hundreds of years after the system had begun to crumble: "The rich man in his castle, / The poor man at his gate, / He made them high or lowly, / And ordered their estate," as the Victorian hymnal tells us.

Finer poets and more farsighted priests had seen the shifting of the sands long before, however. They knew that the social order was too fragile to have been ordained by God for all eternity. In a sermon delivered in 1622 John Donne, the dean of St. Paul's, reminded his audience of the transiency of social distinctions:

> [Death] comes equally to us all, and makes us all equal when it comes. The ashes of an Oak in the Chimney, are no epitaph of that Oak, to tell me how high or how large that was; It tells me not what flocks it sheltered while it stood, nor what men it hurt when it fell. The dust of great persons' graves is speechless too, it says nothing, it distinguishes nothing: As soon the dust of a wretch whom thou wouldest not, as of a Prince whom thou couldest not look upon, will trouble thine eyes, if the wind blow it thither; and when a whirlwind hath blown the dust of the Churchyard into the Church, and the man sweeps out the dust of the Church into the Churchyard, who will undertake to sift those dusts again, and to pronounce, This is the Patrician, this is the noble flower, and this the yeomanly, this the Plebeian bran?[8]

Donne knew that the apparently eternal verities of status and social position were all dissolved in death. But in truth they had long been threatened by the more mundane solvent of economic change. As late medieval society saw the old categories shift, a trickle of sons began to ask themselves whether they should aspire only to do the same work as their fathers (daughters were to find it hard for centuries to ask analogous questions about their mothers). The question became inevitable not only because the division of labor was accelerating and new opportunities were opening up but also because those new opportunities required aptitudes that were specific to the individual and could not simply be handed down from father to son. Workers moved to the cities, guilds were challenged by new forms of production, workshops and depots set up in chaotic competition against one another. And the narratives they told were in competition too. An individual no longer had a single public identity as the occupant of a place in a known order but rather had multiple public identities: apprentice, brother, friend, citizen, warrior, competitor. Hamlet is an intellectual, a lover, a prince: but he is also a son, a fatherless son, and he is tormented because he can neither deny this identity nor make its demands compatible with the demands of these other identities.

It is one of the recurring refrains of modern life that as the individual comes to rely more and more upon others to supply the necessities of his daily existence, he can no longer simply borrow from others the narrative that is to make sense of his life but must fashion his own. The division of labor in production requires a stern self-sufficiency in respect to the story of our own lives. In one of the most famous and melancholy accounts of the consequences of modernization, Emile Durkheim argued that some individuals would fail to create a narrative to compensate for the rootlessness of life in the modern city, and the most desolate among them would turn to suicide. In effect, the war between multiple identities within a person can destroy them all, leading to no identity at all. It represents the same danger for the individual personality as the danger we have already noted for the individual's occupation: to survive in the modern division of labor, each individual must acquire some capacity, some skill. But some individuals will find that the skills they have are inadequate to the demands the world makes of them, just as some individuals will find that the narrative they have constructed out of their multiple identities is inadequate to make sense of the demands these identities impose upon them.

Durkheim's theory of suicide has been much debated and criticized, notably for being almost impossible to test.[9] It may or may not turn out to be useful for scientific understanding or social diagnosis, but it is a very intuitive and reasonable conjecture about what happens to some of the people who build an identity for themselves in a world shot through with risk. This conjecture follows from three observations. The first is that in order to exchange with strangers people need a way to signal their trustworthiness. The second is that one of the most effective ways to do this is to create an identity for yourself, a set of internal rules in which you yourself believe and by which you live, and which will make you unhappy if you fail to honor them. The third is that dealing with multiple strangers creates conflicts between different components of this identity. Although we should expect evolution to have endowed most of us with the psychological resources to manage these conflicts, the sheer randomness of modern life — the accidental nature of so many of our encounters, projects, and challenges — will make some of them very difficult for some people to bear.

Even in contexts less dramatic than among the suicidal, the capacity of people to find satisfaction in their work and in their lives may depend as much on their ability to reconcile the conflicting demands of their multiple identities as on the objective conditions of their lives. The sociologist Frank Furedi has written (in his book *Paranoid Parenting*)[10] about the widespread perception that children in modern society get too little attention from parents obsessed with jobs and careers. He claims that recent decades have seen a dramatic increase, not in the time parents spend at work, but in the time they spend with their children. "Even full-time employed women with children devoted more time to childcare in 1995 than non-employed mothers did in 1961." Whether or not this startling claim is true (and it's hard to document such changes rigorously), it is clear that society now has very different expectations about the parenting role: "today's parents must pay attention to every moment of their child's day — ensuring that their lives are filled with stimulating and appropriate activities." It is quite possible, then, for parents to be fulfilling their role more faithfully, and simultaneously feeling worse about it, than ever before.

More optimistically than Durkheim, the American oral historian Studs Terkel set out in his book *Working* to recount the many ways in which people tell the story of their everyday lives. Such a book might simply have been a collage of stories of how people live and work, but it is much more than this. His subjects talk not only of what they do but of the shape this activity gives to their lives (the book's subtitle is "People Talk about What They Do All Day and How They Feel about What They Do"). His much-quoted story of the parking lot attendant is a masterpiece of Zen concentration:

> After twenty-five, thirty years I could drive any car like a baby, like a woman change her baby's diaper. I could handle that car with one hand. I had a lot of customers would say "How you do this? The way you go around this way?" I'd say "Just the way you bake a cake, miss, I can handle this car." A lotta ladies come to you and a lot of gentlemen come to you, say "Wow! You can drive!" I say "Thank you ma'am." They say, "How long you been doin' it?" I say, "Thirty years. I started when I was sixteen and I'm still doin' it." . . . I was so good when I was nineteen, twenty. A guy bet me five dollars that when a certain car came in I wouldn't make a hole. I had one hand and I whipped it into that hole, and I did it three times for him. Another guy said, "You're too short to reach the gas pedal." I said, "No, I can even push the seat back and I can sit and swing that car in with one swing" — when I was younger I had one customer, he was a good six feet seven and I'm only five feet three. He said, "You better pull the seat up." It looked like I was sittin' in the back seat and I was barely touchin' the brake. I whipped his car in the hole. He said, "You mean to tell me, short as you are, you put the car in that hole there?" I said "I never move anybody's seat." I may pull myself up and brace from the wheel, but I never miss that hole. I make that one swing, with one hand, no two hands. And never use the door open, never park a car with the door open. Always I have my head inside the car, lookin' from the back-view mirror. That's why they call me Lovin' Al the Wizard, One-Swing Al.[11]

Notable in this and many other extracts is a sense that the activity, however humble it may seem, has a wider significance, often barely articulated. Without such a sense it is hard to see how anyone could devote himself so single-mindedly to mastering the necessary skills, nor apply himself so faithfully to performing them with rigor and with love every working day for years on end.

For all the extravagance of recent claims that the world of work is under threat of dissolution from new technology, the workplace remains one of the most important means through which the values of society are transmitted between individuals. It is as important as families and schools, whose influence, though formative, is exerted for a much shorter time. Most individuals cannot survive outside a working environment — genuinely lone artists are very rare. They depend for their economic viability on the skills and capacities of their colleagues, in ways whose consequences for the structure of businesses will be explored in a later chapter. This very dependence makes them particularly prone to give a privileged place to the needs and demands of their workplace in the narrative they construct of their own lives.

Yet the very distance imposed by a narrative framework — a step back from immersion in the detail of our working lives — can for some people create a vertiginous sense of the futility of the whole endeavor. The concerns that seem so urgent to us because of the demands of tunnel vision shrink to insignificance from a more objective perspective. The variety that is part of the buzz of modern living and a part of what makes for challenging work,[12] can come to seem like mindless dissipation. The effect can be tragic, or comic, or both. Here, from Georges Perec's *Life: A User's Manual*, is a description of the working life of a television producer, one of the characters in the novel:

> Rorschash lived out his career entirely in office buildings. Under the vague title of "Project Manager" or "Director of Restructuring and Associated Initiatives," his only activities consisted of daily attendance at meetings, conferences, committees, preparatory workshops, AGMs, interdisciplinary consultations, plenary sessions, working groups and the other such gatherings that represent, at this level of the hierarchy, the essence of the life of such an organization, with their telephone calls, conversations in corridors, business lunches, screenings of rushes and business trips abroad. Nothing stops us from imagining that, during one such meeting, he could have launched the idea of a Franco-British opera or a historical series inspired by Suetonius, but it is more likely that he spent his time preparing or commenting upon audience figures, picking at budgets, writing reports about the booking levels of editing studios, dictating memos, or rushing from meeting-room to meeting-room, taking care to make himself always indispensable in at least two places at once so that, barely seated, he would be called to the telephone and obliged immediately to depart.[13]

In the quarter-century since Perec wrote, computers, electronic mail, and portable telephones have done nothing to diminish the satirical energy of his vision.

PROFESSIONAL CODES AND TUNNEL VISION

More worryingly, though, some narratives of our working lives, far from unsettling and depressing us, may not unsettle us enough. They

may reinforce our tunnel vision precisely when its more distant consequences are most disturbing. Why?

A narrative may serve to give the individual a kind of equilibrium
amid the conflicting demands of the modern world. But does what
serves the individual's equilibrium also serve the interests of the wider
world? What we have seen of the narrowness of tunnel vision gives us
reason to pause. Let us start with an extreme example. A report issued
by Amnesty International in February 2001 claimed that over 150 companies around the world manufacture electroshock stun equipment,
whose use is almost exclusively confined to the torture chamber.[14] There
are some restrictions on trade in such equipment, but not many, and
such restrictions as there are serve only to underline the nature of its
most probable application: for instance, the German government does
not allow the weapons to be used in German prisons or by German
police on German residents but allows German companies to market
and sell them for use abroad. The great majority of the companies making such equipment are not criminal organizations but ordinary businesses, with offices where people who have families and careers meet,
talk, cluster from time to time around the coffee machine, and share a
sense of collective endeavor.

A Studs Terkel who arrived with a tape recorder in hand would doubtless find as much humor, philosophy, and even Zen-like concentration in
such a business as in many of the others whose employees he interviewed.
The anthropologist Hugh Gusterson has documented the subtle way in
which young, often politically liberal men with doctorates in physics
turned into convinced and professional designers of nuclear weapons at
the Lawrence Livermore Laboratory in California.[15] Indeed, the dislocation between the emotions and qualities fostered in people by their immediate environment and the more distant consequences of their activities
was a central theme in a later book by Studs Terkel, *The Good War*. It
was inspired by the paradox that for many veterans, the Second World
War was the finest moment of their lives, "a moment in history . . . when
buddies felt they were more important, were better men who amounted to
more than they do now. It's a precious memory."[16] The preciousness of the
memory appears to have been unrelated to the ostensible aim of the war
(to rid the world of the Nazi regime) and undiminished by the fact that
many individual soldiers even on the Allied side were involved in atrocities for which there was no conceivable military justification. It was a
product of local bonding, of a relationship between soldiers and their
service units that bore close structural similarities to the hunting groups
of our male ancestors. Effective armies are often those that have known
exactly how to exploit these similarities, as anthropologists Peter Richerson and Robert Boyd have argued.[17]

The division of labor between soldiers and other citizens is only an imperfect analogy for the division of labor among civilian members of society, and — fortunately — no one can plausibly claim that tunnel vision typically takes as intense a form outside the army as within it. The overwhelming majority of businesses do not manufacture torture equipment, and the degree of dislocation required to dissociate oneself from the consequences of one's actions is much less striking in most of the ordinary world of work. But conscientious managers can still drive their employees to stress and misery in an honorable quest to run their businesses well; conscientious trade unionists can still inflict workplace disruption that harms those whose cause they wish to serve; conscientious scientists can still devise chemicals that pollute the earth, and conscientious political activists can still inflict harm on people thousands of miles away in whose name they believe themselves to be acting. The consequences of their actions can never be corrected purely by an appeal to their honor or their professionalism, because it is precisely to their honor and professionalism that the consequences are due. To put it another way, it is the task of politics more than of ethics to provide tunnel vision with its appropriate countervailing power.

Warfare is also a terrible reminder of how hard it can sometimes be to reconcile the conflicting visions to which tunnel vision gives rise. We have no books written by Xenophon's victims, but later wars have more than compensated for this deficiency.[18] A mother sees her son return at the end of a war, during which she had no idea whether or when she would ever see him again. She senses in him an echo of her frightened little boy, let loose in a strange and violent world, negotiating hazards he can scarcely imagine and that she can picture only by giving them dim and terrible shapes. She knows that he has aged, in body and in spirit, and her relief that he has survived this test, when so many of his friends did not, makes her reluctant to question her sense of deliverance. What can she say to another mother, a thousand miles away, whose daughter's corpse lies in an unmarked grave, abandoned after her rape and torture by a platoon of advancing soldiers drunk with lust and fear? The bewildered boys who light up their mothers' eyes at the end of a war are the same as the marauding monsters who formerly darkened the land over which they moved. The difference is one of geography and timing.

We may be shocked by evidence that brings home to us the unswerving fierceness of a military training, though the atrocities of war — of all war — are by now so well documented that none of us who votes to send soldiers to war has any excuse for innocence about the consequences. But we all avert our gaze to some degree from the more distant repercussions of the ways we work and live and cultivate a systematic deafness to their more disturbing echoes. We could not navigate in the bewildering complexity of our social world if it were not so—if we did not have rules of loyalty, of doing as others expect of us, of conforming to a code that betrays our three-dimensional sense of ourselves but is the only code simple enough for us to convey reliably to others. And we need others to follow their codes too: we may be hurt by those who are fierce, but we could not trust those who were never unswerving. Still, in our moments of reflection we need to understand the unintended consequences of our tunnel vision for the world as a whole. This is the task of part 3.

Epilogue to Parts I and II

Part 1 described how a surprising degree of coordination can be achieved by a system of decentralized activity of production and exchange in which individuals are concerned about nothing more than what is happening in the markets for the things they buy and sell. Modern economic analysis has made this claim very precise.[1] Specifically, markets that satisfy a number of key conditions achieve *Pareto-efficiency*, in which all opportunities for making individuals better off without harming others have been exhausted. The most important of these conditions are:

- There are large numbers of buyers and sellers (so that no one party has the ability to manipulate the market).
- There are no direct interdependencies (known as *externalities*) between individuals other than through their all being participants in the market; one individual's actions do not directly affect the welfare of another.
- There is complete information available to all relevant parties about the quality of the goods being traded.

In reality, no markets precisely satisfy all these conditions, but markets where the conditions are not too flagrantly violated are likely to behave with a reasonable degree of efficiency.[2] Economic analysis also tells us where to look for signs that markets may be failing to coordinate activity efficiently: look out for monopoly, or for externalities like pollution, or for circumstances where some participants know much more than others about the quality of the goods being traded (as in the used car market). The theory also suggests ways to begin to tackle these problems: try to foster more competition where possible; try to make sure that polluters bear the true costs of the damage they cause; and try to ensure that sellers have an incentive (through regulation, for instance) not to deceive buyers.

More recently, economic theorists have systematically compared the merits of imperfect decentralized markets to those of (also imperfect) centralized administrative structures in tackling different kinds of task. So, for instance, where the costs of coordination failure are very high, and the costs of squandering resources to achieve coordination are comparatively low (as in directing an airplane safely to its destination), markets subject to information frictions may pose unacceptable risks of sys-

tem failure.[3] Such considerations explain why so many advanced industrialized countries have opted for centralized government intervention
and planning in wartime — a choice that has often left them shackled
with bureacratic structures unsuited for responding to the challenges of
peacetime. Economists have also explored the risks of globalization in a
world in which markets for risk-sharing are imperfectly developed.[4]

Impressive as it is, the theory of competitive and efficient markets has
two major gaps. The first is that Pareto-efficiency says nothing about
equality: if the poor cannot be made better off without harming the
rich, competitive markets will not help them. In fact, the history of
recent economic development suggests that the poor and the rich *can*
have a mutual interest in exchange,[5] but it's important to remember that
competitive markets are about exploring avenues of mutual interest, not
about redressing preexisting imbalances of power and wealth.

The second gap is that the theory says nothing about what makes it
reasonable for individuals to trust those with whom they have to deal.
It takes for granted that when people make deals and write contracts
with each other, the deals will be respected and the contracts carried
out. The fact that the people in modern market societies do seem to
trust each other enough, most of the time, at least to do business together is one important reason why these societies can achieve such
feats of decentralized coordination. But it is a fact that requires in turn
an explanation of its own. Why do we believe that strangers can usually
be trusted? This was the subject of part 2.

The divorce between an interest in the psychological and cultural
foundations of economic life and an interest in the consequences of economic interaction has been a peculiar feature of professional economics
during the second half of the twentieth century, rather than an intrinsic
character of the subject. Indeed, Adam Smith famously wrote about
both "The Moral Sentiments" and "The Wealth of Nations,"[6] and the
economics profession has been recently rediscovering the intimate links
between these themes, as a recent book by Peter Dougherty describes.[7]
Part 2 focused on a subset of the many questions that have been explored in this literature, namely, why people are willing to trust strangers, and what happens when this trust becomes fragile. The difficulty
people face in trusting the quality of the goods offered by their trading
partners has been the subject of a vast literature in the field that has
come to be known as "the economics of information."[8] The fact that
this might prevent some markets from functioning well, or even from
existing at all, was the subject of a famous article on the used car market ("The Market for Lemons") by George Akerlof.[9] Akerlof's point
was that when some traders sell low-quality goods, buyers will be so

cautious that even sellers of high-quality goods cannot get a reasonable price unless they can find some credible way to signal the quality of what they are selling.

There has also been a great deal written on the question of whether people might be more willing to trust one another if they deal with each other repeatedly, so that cooperation today takes place in the hope of inducing cooperation in the future. This literature has concluded that repeated interaction can indeed help to build trust if it is reasonably frequent (that is, provided the future matters enough relative to the present), if individuals can observe reliably enough how others have behaved, and if the cost of forgoing the cooperation of others is high enough relative to the rewards of cheating.[10] Interestingly, some uncertainty about people's character and motives can actually help (in the right circumstances). Even unscrupulous people have an incentive to behave well if they want to make others believe that they are not really unscrupulous after all. They have an incentive, in other words, to "build a reputation," even if this reputation is created rather than intrinsic to their character.[11] By contrast, those who are known for certain to be untrustworthy have no such incentive. We now have a clearer understanding of when competition for customers can encourage trustworthy behavior through the need for reputation, and when formal regulation is likely to be needed.[12]

This research has drawn attention to the importance of the expectations of others for inducing trustworthy behavior. In short, cultures of trust and distrust can come to be self-reinforcing.[13] Such ideas have been explored both theoretically and empirically in recent years, and a large literature on "social capital" has tried to explain the political and economic performance of whole societies in terms of the presence or absence of cultures of trust.[14]

More recently, work analyzing survey evidence as well as experimental findings has established that human motivation differs systematically from the simple calculating self-interest that has been the dominant working hypothesis of most research in economics. First, experiments by Ernst Fehr and others have shown clearly that reciprocity can be a powerful influence on behavior even when people do not expect to deal with each other in the future.[15] Secondly, careful comparative analysis of families with stepparents and biological parents has shown that people behave systematically less selfishly toward those with whom they share close genetic ties.[16] Such research attempts to control carefully for other variables in order to isolate the effect of individuals' motivations, but other studies look at variability of behavior between societies, in which individual motivations and expectations about the likely behavior of others play roles that are difficult to distinguish. There seems to be a good deal of variation between societies in the extent to which they succeed in inducing a willingness to trust in the reliability of others.[17] This underscores the way in which societies can take on a character that emerges from innumerable individual interactions, without any individual having intended that result.[18]

Prologue to Part III

Economists of the seventeenth and eighteenth centuries, like moralists of the ancient world, were fond of drawing parallels between human societies and the colonies of social insects such as ants and bees. Mandeville's *Fable of the Bees* was in a tradition stretching back to Aesop, carried on by his contemporaries such as La Fontaine in the fable of the grasshopper and the ant, and inspiring the likes of Woody Allen even today. In fact those parallels are seriously misleading: modern human societies are not like colonies of ants, bees, or termites. As we have seen, human societies involve the interactions of unrelated strangers instead of close relatives. Nevertheless, the social insects hold a different lesson for us, for they provide striking examples of complex systems behaving in ways that are no part of the intention (or even the awareness) of any of their participants. Here is a description of the way termites build a nest:

> When they start to build a nest, termites modify their local environment by making little mud balls and placing them on the substrate; each mud ball is impregnated with a minute quantity of a particular pheromone. Termites deposit their mud balls probabilistically, initially at random. However, the probability of depositing a mud ball at a given location increases with the sensed presence of other mud balls and the sensed concentration of pheromone. The first few random placements increase the other termites' probability of putting their loads at the same place. By this blind and random game little columns are formed; the pheromone drifting across from neighbouring columns causes the tops of the columns to be built with a bias towards the neighbouring columns, and eventually the tops meet to form arches, the basic building units.[1]

Termites are not architects, in other words, for all that their handiwork may look like architecture. They are merely breeze-sniffing mud carters. Architecture emerges from the combination of all their separate endeavors. Over two centuries ago, Adam Smith had a similarly unelevated view of the motivations of merchants, and a nevertheless upbeat assessment of what they might achieve in combination:

> As every individual, therefore, endeavours as much as he can both to employ his capital in the support of domestic industry, and so to direct that industry

that its produce may be of the greatest value, every individual necessarily labours to render the annual revenue of the society as great as he can. He generally, indeed, neither intends to promote the public interest, nor knows how much he is promoting it. By preferring the support of domestic to that of foreign industry, he intends only his own security; and by directing that industry in such a manner as its produce may be of the greatest value, he intends only his own gain, and he is in this, as in many other cases, led by an invisible hand to promote an end which was no part of his intention. Nor is it always the worse for the society that it was no part of it. By pursuing his own interest he frequently promotes that of the society more effectually than when he really intends to promote it. I have never known much good done by those who affected to trade for the public good. It is an affectation, indeed, not very common among merchants, and very few words need be employed in dissuading them from it.[2]

Although many writers and politicians in later times have tried to recruit Adam Smith as a drumbeater for various right-wing causes, he certainly did not think the unintended social consequences of private greed were invariably beneficial. He famously inveighed against cabals of merchants whose main purpose in meeting together was to raise prices to the detriment of the public. Emma Rothschild has even suggested that his use of the metaphor of the "invisible hand" was a sardonic echo of the "bloody and invisible hand" apostrophized by Shakespeare's Macbeth to cover up the crimes he is about to commit.[3] But although we shall never know what Smith would have thought of modern political alignments, we can be sure that he was fascinated by society's capacity to display patterns that had never been consciously designed by any of its members. Some of these patterns might provoke admiration, some might provoke alarm. Smith constantly cautions his readers against thinking we can use our admiration or disapproval for someone's *motives* as a touchstone for deciding whether their actions in society should be encouraged or controlled.

Part 2 of this book asked how cooperation among strangers is possible in human society—both how it may have come about and on what psychological and institutional foundations its credibility rests. Part 3 now looks at some of the wider consequences of the human behavior described in part 2, often drawing on historical accounts of the results of human interactions. Chapter 7 looks at cities, which have been the crucible of prosperity and creativity in society as well as sinks of pollution, violence, and disease—often all of these things simultaneously. Great cities are never consciously designed in their entirety, but reflect a mysterious tango between conscious planning and happenstance, with myriad unplanned interactions between individual city-dwellers. These interactions are known to economists as "externalities," and are the key to understanding that elusive spark that differentiates great cities from the rest. But externalities, especially those of pollution and disease, are a major challenge to our capacity for cooperation. Cities have often overcome their own pollution by collective action, usually with the result that the pollution is exported to the surrounding countryside. But the world as a whole cannot do so, for it has no surrounding countryside. It must find ways to care for its own environment by accounting properly for the costs imposed on that environment by the mass of human activity of which no one is in overall charge. Chapter 8 looks at one particular kind of environmental problem, the use of water, as an example of both the challenges faced by humanity and the way in which our response to such challenges has historically evolved. Successful responses have typically involved creating property rights—allocations of responsibility—in which priorities are ranked by systems of prices, yet it is mysterious how prices can come to embody all the complex information they would need to play this role. Chapter 9 therefore looks at price systems and how they evolve through a process of interaction in markets. Though their participants do not intend this, markets can often extract and summarize information about what their buyers and sellers believe and want, information that tells us something very important about how to manage resources in a world of scarcity.

Yet many important interactions between human beings are not mediated by markets at all, taking place instead in institutions whose component activities are more consciously coordinated, notably in firms. Chapter 10 asks what explains the growth and character of the modern firm and what are the relative roles of markets and firms in the division of labor. Firms have flourished to a considerable extent as vehicles for the propagation of knowledge, but also as mechanisms for its control. So chapter 11 considers how the growth of knowledge in society has arisen as another manifestation of unplanned interaction between strangers—a division of labor between generations, in effect. Finally, chapter 12 looks at those excluded from many of the benefits of modern society: the poor and the sick, notably the mentally ill and depressed. Is the division of labor partly to blame, and if so could greater conscious coordination improve their lot? This forms a natural bridge to part 4, which will consider the nature of collective action—planned responses to the more alarming unplanned consequences of exchange between strangers.

Unintended Consequences: From Family Bands to Industrial Cities

CHAPTER 7

The City, from Ancient Athens to Modern Manhattan

THE FLAIR OF GREAT CITIES

What makes a great city? And in particular, what gives certain cities at certain periods a burst of creativity, an innovative flair, an ability to attract and stimulate people with talent and ideas? Here, too, geography and timing are everything; it is as simple and as mysterious as that. The questions "Why here? why now? Why not there? why not then?" have probably been asked more often about cities than about any other human phenomenon. While the detailed answers differ, there is something the most convincing answers all have in common. They point to a quality in all great cities that transcends the particular intentions of any of the individual people within them, even the most powerful of such people. This quality has been given many names: the atmosphere, the buzz, the networks, the opportunities, the pulse. Whatever else people may try to plan in a city (from its boulevards to its sewage system), nobody can realistically hope to plan *that*. The *citta ideale* painted by Piero della Francesca has the most harmonious proportions imaginable but an eery absence of life. The most famous planned cities in the world — Brasilia, Chandigarh, Canberra, Milton Keynes — are bywords for worthiness and lack of spark, and even St. Petersburg has acquired a faintly exotic reputation only with the patina of time (which is the sole perspective from which the intrigues of bored aristocrats can appear creative).[1]

The historian Peter Hall has tried to understand what the golden ages of a number of cities have in common — whether these are artistic golden ages such as those of Athens under Pericles, Renaissance Florence, or Hapsburg Vienna, or ages of great industrial innovation such as those of Victorian Manchester or Glasgow or postwar Los Angeles. What he writes of Athens rings true of many other such golden ages:

> Athens in the fourth century BC gained enormously from the personal and social tensions brought forth by a unique moment of social evolution: a movement from a static, conservative, aristocratic landowning society to an urban, trading one open to talent. The old society gave way in face of the new, but at the same time bequeathed to it many if its values. We find that

kind of transitional society at other particular moments in urban history, and nearly always it is highly creative; it is the society of Elizabethan London, of nineteenth century Paris, of Weimar Berlin. . . . However . . . creativity of that order is never stable; it carries within it the seeds of its own destruction . . . the tension between the principle of order and the principle of freedom brings something uniquely wonderful, but it does not last beyond a few golden years, for the tension will result in victory — usually, though not invariably, for the forces of change — and with that the wellspring of creativity will dry up.[2]

More mundanely, the common ingredients of such creativity are (1) enough wealth to give those with ideas some hope of finding patrons, (2) a substantial immigrant population eager to challenge the established order, and (3) a total population large enough to contain a critical mass of talent, but with enough focus in its geography to allow for effective networking. These are as true of ancient Athens as of today's Silicon Valley. Again and again Hall stresses the importance of networks that bring people of talent together, and bring them to the attention of financial backers (be they art dealers or venture capitalists), but at the same time allow them enough stimulation by variety, by the unexpected. He writes, for instance, of fin-de-siècle Paris: "Since the artists were concentrated geographically in Montmartre and Montparnasse, since they interchanged between these centres, since they spent so much time in the cafés and the cabarets, since they lived and worked together on the river, this was clearly a highly networked society."[3] But it was just as important that painters did not only mix with painters; Montmartre "was a rendezvous of the entire avant-garde of the city: an extraordinary crowd of artists, poets and writers."[4] The fact that networks mix people together matters critically, and paradoxically the most sophisticated networks may not mix people up enough. Networks that are too primitive and inefficient keep people with ideas from ever meeting each other; but networks that are too predictable and efficient mean that like may spend too much time with like, the official rules may be too solemnly respected, and nobody is quite open enough to surprise. After all, the most effective social networks in French society of the time were the academies and salons against whose formalism and lack of creativity the impressionists and their successors had rebelled.

For the fact is that creativity is almost impossible to aim at directly. As Hall says, some Marxist theories "go wrong in attributing a quite unnatural degree of deliberate knowingness to the artists [of this period], in ascribing to them a deep — perhaps even unconscious — desire to undermine the foundations of the bourgeois order. The artists did no such thing: they painted what they found, and interpreted it in order to solve problems of a purely artistic nature, problems that obsessed them. They painted people, and they painted groups of people together in society, but that was because they were interested in the play of light on them, or the problems of rendering their three-dimensionality on a flat piece of canvas."[5]

Just as nobody can plan an artistic revolution, nobody quite plans the networks that make them possible. They are the outcome of the various affinities that move ordinary people in their choices of where to live and work. Every time someone moves, she changes the environment she leaves and gives a new character to the environment she joins, without intending or necessarily even being aware of it. And the most innovative people have always been footloose, restlessly seeking out opportunities over time and space. Over two centuries ago Adam Smith described the tendency for artisans and innovators to seek each other out, to congregate in towns and cities. Although proximity forced them to compete, it also enabled them to learn from each other, and their gains from learning usually outweighed their losses from competition. But in a predominantly agrarian society, there was a natural limit to this clustering process, because the bulk of people's work was tied to the land, which cannot move. Even restless entrepreneurs cannot move too far from other people and their activities. Blacksmiths may have needed other blacksmiths, but they needed horses even more.

When people did move to cities, the free play of their elective affinities shaped their whole physical space, as the historian Robert Hughes describes in his account of medieval Barcelona:

> All work was done by hand until the end of the eighteenth century, and all workshops were small. Sometimes they were half on the street. They consisted, typically, of one skilled man, the *mestre*, and an apprentice or two, the *aprenents*. These little cells agglomerated. The natural sympathy among workers in the same trade created the intricate, durable *esprit de quartier* of Barcelona, as of other medieval cities. Like hangs out with like; tools need to be shared; if you need to buy a plank of chestnut or a roll of ribbon, and fast, it makes sense to be near other carpenters or upholsterers. Dyers had to be near running water; shoemakers tended to set up shop near tanners, and vice versa. A client wanted to be able to comparison shop among various craftsmen in the same place, rather than zigzag all over the city. It was said, with some truth, that a blind man could find his way around the Barri Gòtic by smell and sound, knowing where he was by the rasp of saws or the clink of hammers on the cooper's bands, the stink of tanning leather, or the fresh-hay smell of drying esparto grass in the espadrille makers', or the fumes of forges. These sounds and smells were street signs, and the concentration of similar workers in the same places also enabled them to keep out the competition.[6]

No one in medieval Barcelona set out to create an *esprit de quartier*, still less to set up so poetic and sensual a system of street signs: they did other things, notably to try and make a living, and the *esprit de quartier* emerged as a result of their uncoordinated decisions. Each person who set up a workshop changed the landscape for others, sometimes for good, sometimes for ill. Economists have given a name to the usually unintended effects that individuals have upon each other, and which give rise to some of the most intriguing, exhilarating, and sometimes disturbing aspects of modern life in mass societies. They are called "externalities," and they are what tunnel vision leaves out.

Some externalities are ignored by tunnel vision because we don't care enough about them, even though we can foresee them. It is absolutely predictable that traffic will become gridlocked at the entrance to large cities in the morning and evening rush. Each driver knows that she is holding up the cars behind her, but she does not see why she should leave her car at home in order to clear the lanes a fraction for the benefit of everyone else. She cares about the delays others impose on her, but not enough about those she imposes on others. It is quite certain that if every factory is given the freedom to pump smoke into the air, the atmosphere of the city will become unfit to breathe, for no one factory owner will wish to exercise forbearance entirely for the sake of the others. Foreseeing and curbing such externalities, through cajolery or coercion or both, is the daily task of political life. It is a task that depends (as we shall see in later chapters) on making the vision of our political institutions comprehend what the tunnel vision of each individual citizen neglects.

But there are other kinds of externalities which are neglected because they are extremely hard for us even to foresee, depending as they do on the idiosyncrasies and serendipities of the way in which individuals interact and the mutual spark they provoke. The history of urban planning is full of examples of cities that have worked hard to remove some of the most obvious causes of physical blight but have proved incapable of alleviating boredom, delinquency, and violence. In her book *The Death and Life of Great American Cities*, Jane Jacobs described how even such matters as physical safety on the streets were less the result of formal policing than the unintended by-product of the "seeming disorder" of the sidewalk, which she likened to a dance:

> The stretch of Hudson Street [her home in New York's Greenwich Village] is each day the scene of an intricate sidewalk ballet. I make my own first entrance into it a little after eight when I put out the garbage can, surely a prosaic occupation, but I enjoy my part, my little clang, as the droves of

junior high school students walk by the centre of the stage dropping candy wrappers. (How do they eat so much candy so early in the morning?)

While I sweep up the wrappers I watch the other rituals of morning: Mr. Halpert unlocking the laundry's handcart from its mooring to a cellar door, Joe Cornacchia's son-in-law stacking out the empty crates from the delicatessen, the barber bringing out his sidewalk folding chair, Mr. Goldstein arranging the coils of wire which proclaim his hardware store is open, the wife of the tenement's superintendent depositing her chunky three-year-old with a toy mandolin on the stoop, the vantage point from which he is learning the English his mother cannot speak. Now the primary children, heading for St. Luke's, dribble through to the south; the children for St. Veronica's cross, heading to the west, and the children for P.S. 41, heading toward the east. Two new entrances are being made from the wings: well-dressed and even elegant women and men with briefcases emerge from doorways and side streets. Most of these are heading for the buses and subways, but some hover on the curbs, stopping taxis which have miraculously appeared at the right moment, for the taxis are part of a wider morning ritual: having dropped passengers from midtown in the downtown financial district, they are now bringing downtowners up to midtown. Simultaneously, numbers of women in housedresses have emerged and as they crisscross with one another they pause for quick conversations that sound with either laughter or joint indignation, never, it seems, anything between. It is time for me to hurry to work too, and I exchange my ritual farewell with Mr. Lofaro, the short, thick-bodied, white-aproned fruit man who stands outside his doorway a little up the street, his arms folded, his feet planted, looking solid as earth itself. We nod, we each glance quickly up and down the street, then look back to each other and smile. We have done this many a morning for more than ten years, and we both know what it means: All is well.[7]

Though the rhythms of her description might hint otherwise, Jacobs's account is not some re-creation of mythical village life transplanted to an urban context, complete with urban counterparts to the blacksmith and the priest. No: cities are different from villages and small towns precisely because the streets are mostly full of strangers. But even among strangers there can be trust, and even people who know each other need trust to help them deal with the many strangers who surround them. And, as Jacobs reminds us:

the trust of a city street is formed over time from many, many little public sidewalk contacts. It grows out of people stopping by at the bar for a beer, getting advice from the grocer and giving advice to the newsstand man, comparing opinions with other customers at the bakery and nodding hello to the two boys drinking pop on the stoop, eyeing the girls while waiting to be called for dinner, admonishing the children, hearing about a job from the hardware man and borrowing a dollar from the druggist, admiring the new baby and sympathizing over the way a coat faded. Customs vary: in some neighbourhoods people compare notes on their dogs; in others they compare notes on their landlords. Most of it is ostensibly utterly trivial, but the sum is not trivial at all.[8]

STENCH AND WASTE

Cities are full of externalities, and they are not all so stimulating to creativity, nor so poetic, as the street signs in the form of sounds and smells described by Robert Hughes. Medieval Barcelona, like all large cities of the period, was periodically racked by epidemics of cholera or plague. Quattrocento Florence at its most spectacular had just endured an attack of plague that reduced its population by over a third.[9] Nobody intended to pass the bacillus on to others. No one even knew what caused such epidemics until well into the nineteenth century. One of the most famous maps of London is that drawn by the physician Dr. John Snow in the cholera epidemic of 1854, who noted the way cases of infection were geographically clustered around a particular water pump in Soho. His findings led the authorities to close the pump, thereby perhaps hastening the end of the epidemic, though not until it had claimed over five hundred lives.[10]

The disposal of sewage has been a problem for humanity ever since the beginning of agriculture and a settled lifestyle some ten thousand years ago. Inadequate solutions to the problem meant that large cities became sinks of disease, even though they were also the crucible of creativity in their societies. In early eighteenth-century London between 35 and 40 percent of infants died in the first year of life, a rate well above that of the surrounding countryside and one that would be utterly intolerable to us today.[11] Stench and filth were facts of life in large cities, and it was not until the nineteenth century and the first large-scale sewage works that a clean urban environment came to be considered something to which citizens could reasonably aspire. Ancient Athens was remarkable for the contrast between the grandeur of the Acropolis and the squalor of its residential streets, but only by a very modern eye would the squalor even have been noticed.

Jorge Luis Borges, in his essay The *Argentine Writer and Tradition*, quoted Edward Gibbon to the effect that "in the Arab book par excellence, the Koran, there are no camels; I believe that if there were ever any doubt as to the authenticity of the Koran, this lack of camels would suffice to prove that it is Arab. It was written by Mohammed, and Mohammed, as an Arab, had no reason to know that camels were particularly Arab; they were, for him, a part of reality, and he had no reason to single them out, while the first thing a forger, or tourist, or an Arab nationalist would do is bring on the camels."[12] As it happens, Borges (and Gibbon) were wrong about camels, which appear frequently in the Koran. But it is certainly rare when reading Balzac or Dickens or any of the other contemporary fictional chroniclers of life in the great filthy cities of the past to find any reference to their revolting smell. This is not because smell was unimportant to city-dwellers; it was an object of everyday comment and interest, fascination, even scientific inquiry (as Alain Corbin's book *The Foul and the Fragrant* has evocatively described).[13] But when novelists wanted to open their readers' sensibilities, they would focus on aspects of city life people did not notice or properly appreciate, rather than those aspects everyone knew about. To feel the full stench of eighteenth-century Paris invade our nostrils, we must turn to a modern writer, Patrick Susskind:

> In the period of which we speak, there reigned in the cities a stench barely conceivable to us modern men and women. The streets stank of manure, the courtyards of urine, the stairwells stank of moldering wood and rat droppings, the kitchens of spoiled cabbage and mutton fat; the unaired parlors stank of stale dust, the bedrooms of greasy sheets, damp featherbeds, and the pungently sweet aroma of chamber pots. The stench of sulfur rose from the chimneys, the stench of caustic lyes from the tanneries, and from the slaughterhouses came the stench of congealed blood. People stank of sweat and unwashed clothes; from their mouths came the stench of rotting teeth, from their bellies that of onions, and from their bodies, if they were no longer very young, came the stench of rancid cheese and sour milk and tumorous disease. The rivers stank, the marketplaces stank, the churches stank, it stank beneath the bridges and in the palaces. The peasant stank as did the priest, the apprentice stank as did his master's wife, the whole of the aristocracy stank, even the king himself stank, stank as a rank lion, and the queen like an old goat, summer and winter. For in the eighteenth century there was nothing to hinder the bacteria busy at decomposition, and so there was no human activity, either constructive or destructive, no manifestation of germinating or decaying life that was not accompanied by stench. And of course the stench was foulest in Paris, for Paris was the largest city of France.[14]

Smell, like some kinds of disease, traveled on the air, and thereby narrowed the distance between rich and poor, a distance that by more conventional measures, such as income, was much larger than it is today. Until the late eighteenth century, the children of the rich were as vulnerable to disease as the children of the poor: externalities were no respecters of wealth or class.[15] In the modern world, the rich are much less vulnerable to disease than the poor, virtually everywhere on the planet. The reason for this change is that there is a better understanding of the nature of disease transmission and in most societies a greater political willingness to organize city life to take this understanding into account. Using this knowledge, the rich have found ways to distance themselves from the detritus of their lifestyle, whether this involves sending the garbage away or removing themselves to the suburbs. In every city in the world, the rich export their waste to a safe distance while the poor remain surrounded by it. As one environmental writer has pointed out, "in poor cities and especially their poor neighborhoods, environmental problems tend to stay close to home. Inadequate household water supplies are typically more critical to people's well-being than contaminated waterways. Air pollution in the kitchen is often far worse than outdoors."[16]

In the process of cleaning up their cities, the world's affluent have nevertheless, on the whole, improved the environment of the poor. They have done so largely out of self-interest, but the achievement is no less valuable for that. Even in some of the world's poorest countries, newborn children have a much better chance of surviving the first year of life than did any children anywhere a century ago. Italy on the eve of the Second World War had a rate of infant mortality that was as high as Uganda's is today, even though by any other standard Italy was much more prosperous than Uganda has yet become.[17] This worldwide improvement has been due partly to the spread of knowledge about what individuals can do to avoid disease: boiling water, using rehydration solution in cases of diarrhea, and so on. Partly it has been due to immunization and public health campaigns against such diseases as smallpox, malaria, and tuberculosis, though we are starting to realize that our spectacular early victories against these diseases will not be permanent. Organisms that survive complete extinction evolve resistance to the drugs we use against them. We shall need to go on finding more and more sophisticated drugs against the bacteria and viruses of the natural world, in an evolutionary guerrilla war that we can hope to contain but never to win.

To a considerable extent, though, the improvement in children's survival prospects has been due to initiatives in the removal and treatment of urban waste. The affluent and politically well-connected have realized that their urban environment need not be as dirty and dangerous as was universally accepted in the past. They have organized to demand the construction of sewage systems so that human excreta are no longer dumped straight into the river. They have found various ways to dispose of ordinary household waste, particularly the skins and packages, organic and inorganic, in which their food and other consumables are wrapped. Nowadays all cities of any size undergo a nightly transformation that begins no later than the hour before dawn, but different cities across the world have different methods. Where there is poverty of resources or public organization, as in Calcutta, the transformation is brought about by the initiative of individual rag-pickers, tinkers, dung-gatherers, paper-collectors, dogs, cows, and recyclers of anything and everything, who emerge as soon as the twilight permits to sort through last night's discards of the reveling rich. You might think from this example that one man's externalities are always another man's opportunities, so that the eternal opportunism of someone's tunnel vision might be relied upon to clear up what another person's tunnel vision ignores. But as we know from our own history, such opportunism was the fruit of misery: only a society with desperately poor and marginalized people could leave its waste disposal entirely to individual initiative. In Victorian London, the gatherers of "pure," dog shit sold for curing leather, were forced by increasing competition to search earlier and harder each morning, until the weakest and oldest among them dropped out of the contest altogether. In his classic study *London Labour and the London Poor*, published in 1861, Henry Mayhew distinguished them from "bone-grubbers and rag-gatherers, who are, indeed, the same individuals . . . the cigar-end and old wood collectors . . . the dredgermen, the mud-larks and the sewer-hunters . . . the dustmen and nightmen, the sweeps and the scavengers."[18] As his classification suggests, there were respects in which the division of labor in Victorian Britain was much more elaborate than it is today, and Mayhew was its ideal chronicler (he was nothing if not meticulous, spending several pages discussing the merits of rival calculations before concluding that the amount of horse dung dropped in the whole of London must lie between seven hundred and a thousand tons per day). Mayhew interviewed "a poor old woman resembling a bundle of rags and filth stretched on some dirty straw in the corner of [her] apartment." He noted that "to my astonishment I found this wretched creature to be, to a certain extent, a 'superior' woman; she could read and write well, spoke correctly, and appeared to have been a person of natural good sense, though broken up with age, want and infirmity." She described to him the trials of "pure" gathering in terms that show a very precise grasp of the laws of supply and demand:

> If we only gathered a pail-full in the day, we could live very well; but we could do much more than that, for there wasn't near so many at the business then, and the Pure was easier to be had. For my part I can't tell where all the creatures have come from of late years; the world seems growing worse and worse every day. They have pulled down the price of Pure, that's certain; but the poor things must do something, they can't starve while there's anything to be got. Why, no later than six or seven years ago, it was as high as 3s.6d. and

4s. a pail-full, and a ready sale for as much of it as you could get; but now you can only get 1s. and in some places 1s.2d. a pail-full; and, as I said before, there are so many at it, that there is not much left for a poor old creature like me to find.[19]

Cities that relied on individual initiative alone to dispose of waste have paid a large human cost.

CIVIC ACTION AND THE URBAN ENVIRONMENT

Today in rich societies, fortunately, not everything is left to individual initiative. There is teamwork, usually organized by the state but often employing immigrants who are glad of the work. A sight modern visitors to Florence rarely encounter is the teams of silent sweepers—mainly Ethiopian or Somali—who clean away the Renaissance extravagance of the filth that has accumulated in the city's streets by about 4 A.M. (I myself have seen them only through a travel-planning failure that left me without a hotel.) In Mexico City the neighborhoods are divided up among private, often criminal gangs, who defend their territory with fierce and sometimes violent determination, since amid the garbage there are many dispersed items of value, individually unremarkable but together amounting to gold. Waste disposal can be a profitable business. Mayhew himself commented of Victorian London that "Were the collection of mud and dust carried on by a number of distinct individuals—that is to say, were each individual dustman and scavenger to collect on his own account, there is no doubt that no *one man* could amass a fortune by such means—while if the collection of bones and rags and even dogs'-dung were carried on 'in the large way,' that is to say, by a number of individual collectors working for one 'head man,' even the picking up of the most abject refuse of the metropolis might become the source of great riches."

But it is also a business that thrives by storing up trouble for the future. It is characteristic of increasing prosperity that people export their pollution to more distant places. The distances to which these effects can be displaced are limited by the size of the earth, so the policy, adopted by today's prosperous countries, of exporting pollution will no longer be feasible for the more prosperous world of tomorrow.

The inescapable fact is that the comfortable lifestyle to which modern citizens rightly aspire creates waste. And there are only two things that can be done with waste. One is to transform it into something harmless or even beneficial, as happens when we ask our allies among the bacteria to break down our excreta into compounds that add to the fertility of the soil, or when scavengers devote their energies to finding those discarded items that have alternative uses. The other solution is to send the waste away to a place where we hope to be able to ignore it for the foreseeable future (ecologists call such places "sinks"). But as humanity's exploitation of the planet and its resources has expanded during the course of the last century, we have come to realize that there are fewer and fewer places in which our waste may be safely ignored. Until the 1950s and the great urban smogs of London and other large industrial cities we had treated the atmosphere as a sink, and the discovery that soot particles did not travel far but clung to the city's mantle produced a systematic and largely successful political reaction: the air of London, Paris, and New York really is much cleaner today than it was forty years ago. We have since come to realize that carbon dioxide and chlorofluorocarbons (the emissions that cause global warming and deplete the ozone layer) are no less toxic for acting much more slowly and much further away. Sometimes our efforts at recycling even add to the pressure on our atmospheric sinks, as when we use energy to melt glass bottles and thereby preserve our backyards at the price of adding yet more carbon dioxide to the air.

As an alternative to the organization of collective life to make our waste less dangerous (either by breaking it down organically or by removing it to a "safe" distance), the history of humanity has shown us only one solution. This is a solution from biology, and a drastic one at that, namely, the evolution of resistance. As human beings crowded together into villages, towns, and cities, only those who had some resistance to the toxic environment would survive into fertile adulthood and transmit that resistance to the next generation. In his book *Guns, Germs and Steel*, Jared Diamond has sought to explain one of the most striking features of the encounter between European settlers and Native Americans in the sixteenth and seventeenth centuries: brutal as the Europeans were, the numbers of Native Americans they killed were dwarfed by the number who died of European diseases to which they had no prior immunity.[20] Europeans in turn faced some new American diseases, but far fewer of them died as a result. The reason, suggests Diamond, is that livestock rearing was much more common in the agriculture of Europe, so that Europeans had been used for several millennia to living among cattle, sheep, pigs, and horses, and to sharing their germs (as Americans had not). Something similar must have been true of the germs human beings received from each other, and from rats. The terrible death toll of medieval cities was part of a process that for millennia had been making European citizens the hardy carriers of germs that would prove more fatal to Native Americans than any deliberate weaponry.

As Diamond's evidence about livestock has shown us, it is not only in cities that human beings transmit externalities to each other. Some of the world's great man-made environmental crises have taken place in rural areas many miles from the cities, like the drying up of the Aral Sea described in chapter 2. The environmental economists Gary Libecap and Zeynep Hansen have written about another man-made disaster, the Dust Bowl crisis of the 1930s in the American Great Plains, described vividly by John Steinbeck in *The Grapes of Wrath*: "In the morning the dust hung like fog, and the sun was as red as ripe new blood. All day the dust sifted down from the sky, and the next day it sifted down. An even blanket covered the earth. It settled on the corn, piled up on the tops of the fence posts, piled up on the wires; it settled on roofs, blanketed the weeds and trees."[21] Libecap and Hansen have shown how the crisis came about as a result of the division of land on the plains into plots that were too small to be economically viable. The result was that farmers used intensive cultivation practices that contributed to severe wind erosion, failed to place land into fallow, and could not afford to diversify into pasture. Over two hundred thousand farms in the Great Plains states had done what they reasonably could to survive. None of them had wanted to contribute to soil erosion, and none of them individually could have halted the plowing up of native grasses and the reduction in the size of soil particles from intensive cultivation that made the land so vulnerable to the wind once drought set in during the early 1930s. But the result was devastating: "one dust storm in May 1934 started in Montana and spread south, carrying some 350 million tons of soil towards the east Coast. During a storm of February 7, 1937, 34.2 tons of soil fell per square mile at Ames, Iowa, 14.9 tons at Marquette, Michigan, and 10 tons across the continent in New Hampshire. [It was] estimated that in 1935 alone 850 million tons of topsoil had blown away from 4.3 million acres in the southern plains." The one thing which could have helped, a consolidation of farms into larger units that could afford to use more sound ecological practices, was resisted by local politicians out of a combined sentimental attachment to the idea of the small family farm and fear of the likely loss of voting population. When such consolidation did eventually occur, the plains went through successive droughts in the 1950s and 1970s without anything like the same catastrophic environmental consequences.

These episodes, like the terrible epidemics in medieval Europe, show us what happens when our political institutions fail to meet the toxic challenge of our increasingly affluent lifestyle. From one point of view, our history is encouraging, because those political institutions have eventually risen to each new environmental challenge: the continuously falling toll of infant mortality throughout the world is a convincing response to those pessimists who believe that there is never any progress in history. Even ancient Athens, with its poky houses and smelly streets, could offer its (adult, male, free) inhabitants the inspiration of the Acropolis, constructed at enormous expense by concerted political action. In the late nineteenth century, cities such as London, Paris, and Berlin could systematically build subways, sewers, and water systems that allowed vaster populations than ever before to live together without choking on their own waste.

From another point of view, though, our history is full of warnings: our political institutions have always responded sluggishly, under pressure from terrible catastrophes, and with a bias toward threats that are immediate, visible, and close to home. As the rich and politically powerful become better informed and more organized, those threats have been gradually better managed. The foreseeable externalities have been progressively tamed. But threats that are yet to come, invisible, unpredictable, and faraway remain un-addressed. And a larger, more affluent, and industrially more inventive world population may well create such threats faster than the tunnel vision of its individual members will allow them to respond.

Governing Cities

Raymond Chandler once commented on the power and reach of criminal organizations by writing that in the modern world "gangsters can rule nations and can almost rule cities."[22] His remark is an acknowledgment that even those with apparently great power—derived from their ability to inflict unchallenged violence—find the sheer complexity of cities impossible to organize to their satisfaction. The inhabitants of cities interact with each other in ways that no one has foreseen, not even themselves. Conservative authorities—aristocracies, churches, guilds—have always been wary of cities, seeing them as decadent places not only because decadent people choose to live there but also because people's behavior changes when they arrive in the city. In the city, individuals experiment and invent; they refashion everything from their political ideologies, their relationships with their parents, their sexuality, and the music that moves them, to the industrial processes with which they work. Others have admired cities for just that reason, and for writers such as Balzac the corruption and cynicism of the city—the ease with which people can change their skin—are the very features that give it energy and life.

If the world as a whole were really becoming a vast city, the history of existing cities would be a cause for great optimism about the future of mankind. Cities have often been violent, pestilential, polluted, and physically repulsive, but they have also seen some of the most spectacular capacities for human ingenuity, not only in technological invention but also in political and social organization. Unlike some nation-states and some civilizations, cities have not destroyed themselves. But that is because cities have a safety valve in the natural environment that surrounds them. Cities have been able to live off the resources of their hinterland — its food, its water, its energy — and export their waste to it in turn. But for all the talk of information technology bringing the whole of humanity face to face in one vast neighborhood, the world as a whole is not a city, for the simple reason that it has no hinterland. It must find its own resources, and it must dispose of its own waste. In order to do so, it must start to account properly for them both. For much of human history, cities have undervalued the resources they used and trivialized the cost of the waste they created. They have benefited from tunnel vision much more than they have been harmed. So chapter 8 looks at one such resource and explores what would be meant by accounting properly for its use. The resource is one that many people in affluent urban societies think of as free. It is water.

CHAPTER 8

Water: Commodity or Social Institution?

THE MANY MEANINGS OF WATER

What would it mean to account properly for water as a valuable resource? To answer that question we need first to understand why we value water and what we value about it. Answers to this question are many, varied, and paradoxical. The government of Mexico spends around 400 million dollars per year providing drinking water to its population, of whom nearly half in rural areas still have no access to safe sources of supply. This is one-fifth of what consumers in France (which has a population three-quarters the size of Mexico's) spend per year on bottled mineral and spring water, which (as magazine or television advertisements confirm) is primarily marketed as beneficial to health.[1] However, French tap water is of excellent quality and universally available, so the principal benefit to health from drinking bottled water is that it may induce people to drink less alcohol. This difference can hardly mean that Mexicans are less concerned with health: a child born in Mexico City is more likely to receive immunization than a similar child in a large American city. Yet although water from a standpipe in Mexico City is for most purposes chemically identical to water from a spring in the Massif Central, and although both answer to a deep human concern for health, as economic commodities they could hardly be more different.

There is widespread agreement that the world in the twenty-first century will face major health, security, or economic crises[2] if nations are not willing to undertake what the Dublin International Conference on Water and the Environment called the management of water "as an economic good," a concept that is also at the heart of the policies now advocated by the World Bank. But what does this mean? What kind of economic good *is* water? The more we examine the evidence the more we see that water is not one kind of good, but many. These goods differ along physical and biological dimensions, but not only along these: they differ also in the way that human societies construct and evaluate them.

What we shall see in this chapter is that water means such widely different things to different people in different circumstances—a life-giver to some, a threat to others, an inspiration for poetry to some, a reason for concentrating political power to yet others—that it seems the last thing in the world one could ever realistically value by something as apparently simple and one-dimensional as a price. And yet, *precisely for that reason*, water needs to be properly accounted for as a scarce resource—in a word, "priced." For the very complexity of water's appeal to different users will make it impossible for them to agree how to share it, unless they focus on the one thing that prevents them from having as much of it as they would like: its scarcity. And accounting for water means measuring not how important, beautiful, or poetic it is, but simply how scarce it is in the places that people need it.

Scarcity is the most fundamental economic characteristic of any good; indeed, the canonical definition of economics itself is "the study of the allocation of scarce resources among competing ends."[3] Water is scarce in many parts of the world, relative to the physiological needs of the inhabitants of those regions. Around 1,250 cubic meters of water per person are required every year for the supply of habitats and the production of subsistence crops, without counting the amounts necessary for industry or cash crops. Over 200 million people in Africa are in a position known as water stress, where more than 600 people share every million cubic meters of water available annually,[4] and the proportion of the world's population living in conditions of water stress or worse has been predicted to grow from 8 percent in the year 2000 to 38 percent in 2025.[5] In other circumstances and in other parts of the world, water can be in excess: floods in Bangladesh or in China regularly claim more lives than do droughts. There are also regions of the world in a happily intermediate position, with water in abundance, neither scarce nor in excess. Our entire attitude toward water changes with its scarcity: water in conditions of scarcity is life-giving, but in excess it is life-threatening, one of the most terrifying of natural forces. The consciousness of having escaped from the threat of the sea was so central to the thought of the citizens of the early Dutch Republic that they invented a gruesome punishment, the "drowning cell," for those convicted of unwillingness to work: "They are tethered like asses and are put in a cellar that is filled with water so that they must partly empty it by pumping if they do not wish to drown."[6]

The value of water depends, in other words, on whether it is physically located where we want it to be, and in the right quantity. Royce Hanson has written that "taken as a whole, the United States has plenty of water, now and for the future. The problem is, of course, that no-one lives in the United States as a whole."[7] This is no less true for the world as a whole: there are on average far more freshwater resources per head of the world's population than the most profligate use could ever require, but they are not where they are needed. Entire empires have been founded on the need to organize the movement of water from where it is naturally found to where it is required for human life—from where it is abundant to where it is scarce. This is the consequence of an important technological fact: the cost of water to its users is dominated by the cost of transporting, storing, and delivering it. The technology of doing so is subject to major economies of scale, meaning that the costs of transporting any given amount of water are lower if it is being transported in large quantities. This means that the control of water has historically tended to be a major monopoly—indeed, as the jargon has it, a "natural" monopoly (one due to the inherent character of technology rather than to artificial restrictions on trade). Water has always been controlled by the politically and militarily powerful rather than by merchants, and in our day that makes it almost everywhere the prerogative of states more than of private markets.

Water's value depends also, and more subtly, upon its quality. Water is virtually never pure, and its biological or chemical contents can destroy us. Diarrhea from water-borne diseases alone was estimated in the late 1980s to kill 4.5 million people per year in developing countries excluding China, equivalent to thirty jumbo-jet crashes per day. Six million cases of malaria (spread by mosquitoes that breed in stagnant water) were reported worldwide in 1987, almost certainly a major underestimate of the true incidence. Onchocerciasis, or river blindness, infected over 18 million people worldwide in 1983. There were six hundred thousand reported cases of cholera in 1991, a similar prevalence to that of guinea worm, which is also water-borne.[8] Fortunately, guinea worm, a serious, painful, and disabling parasite, has been on the retreat in the last decade, with a decline in cases to below one hundred thousand by the year 2000.[9]

For millions of the world's inhabitants, therefore, even when water is in abundant quantity, water quality is scarce. Yet organic contents are in the long run less to be feared as pollutants of water than inorganic chemicals. There is a natural hydrological cycle, in which the organic contents of water are broken down by the processes of biological decay and an equilibrium established in which the stock of water is renewed. But chemical pollutants threaten this cycle, since many of them are stable over very long periods of time. Indeed, stability is in many respects a highly desirable quality of industrial and agricultural chemicals, since otherwise they would degrade into inert components and cease to perform the functions for which they have been synthesized. Much effort, therefore, is devoted in the world's laboratories to building longevity into chemical design, an effort typical of tunnel vision, since it takes no account of the consequences of this longevity for the natural environment.

When threatened by sufficiently persistent chemicals, water ceases to be a renewable resource and becomes a non-renewable one. It is possible to make a comeback from the destruction of water quality by inorganic chemicals only in certain environments, such as rivers (from which today's stock of pollutants can be washed out to sea, where they become someone else's problem). And even here the cost can be great, as shown by the many billions of dollars spent on cleaning up the Rhine. The Rhine Action Plan, agreed to in the mid-1980s, set as its main goal the return of salmon and other higher aquatic species to the Rhine; since the annual salmon catch was around a quarter of a million fish in the late nineteenth century, this implies that the more than half a billion dollars spent by one firm (BASF) alone in 1991 was equivalent to an implicit valuation of over two thousand dollars per fish.[10] But the impressive technical success of the plan shows at least that rivers can recover from chemical pollution. Groundwater sources are more vulnerable to pollution and much harder to decontaminate. There is growing evidence that the quality of groundwater in the United States is deteriorating due to both toxic materials and salination: in 1983 the U.S. Office of Technology Assessment estimated that 29 percent of the groundwater supplies of 954 towns and cities with populations over ten thousand were contaminated, and the situation has certainly worsened since then.

Another of the highly variable physical characteristics of water is the extent to which it impedes or facilitates movement. Water can be a barrier: the English Channel preserved the British Isles from invasion during the Second World War (as during many earlier conflicts), and even today many political frontiers are marked by rivers. This explains why so many river basins (which are natural economic units) have to be managed by negotiations between a number of sovereign political authorities. But water can also be a carrier, of good things or bad. Rivers, canals, and seas have supported the world's most efficient long-distance trade routes, and the great overland routes, such as the Silk Road, flourished only where waterborne alternatives were too lengthy or dangerous. Inland seas such as the Mediterranean and the Black Sea have been the hub of the world's most dynamic civilizations.[11] But the same water that brought prosperity has also brought disease: rats bearing the Black Death traveled by ship to Europe, and the great cholera epidemics were transmitted by contaminated drinking water.

The very invisibility of the dangers transmitted by water means that our perception of them is prone to powerful cultural manipulation. The ideological foundation of the Hindu caste system is the fear of pollution transmitted by members of lower castes, and water is the most potent symbol of such transmission: even today millions of Hindus will not accept water unless offered by members of their own caste.[12] In the Northeast and far West of the United States, recreational activities involving bodily contact with the water have traditionally been forbidden on domestic water supply reservoirs (in spite of the absence of any objective health risk), because water managers and public opinion view such activities as contaminating; in the remainder of the country, such activities are not only allowed but encouraged.[13] Nuclear and industrial pollution affecting our water has a peculiarly intimate and threatening contact with us, as the old protest song reminds us: "What have they done to the rain?"

It is precisely this intimacy that explains our ambivalence toward water. The change in sexual behavior and conventions in industrialized countries since the Second World War may have been accelerated by the Pill, but enhanced opportunities for personal hygiene have also been a major factor: aristocracies have always treated sex as a recreation and an art, with or without contraception, but only with widespread indoor plumbing has sexuality been democratized. The spread of AIDS means water has come to seem menacing as well as liberating: bodily fluids are the vector, and the San Francisco bathhouses are the symbol of the epidemic's arrival. But water as the universal solvent has always had powerful and ambivalent poetic force. W. H. Auden begins his melancholy tribute "In Praise of Limestone" with the words

> If it form the one landscape that we the inconstant ones
> Are consistently homesick for, this is chiefly
> Because it dissolves in water. Mark these rounded slopes
> With their surface fragrance of thyme and beneath
> A secret system of caves and conduits.[14]

Water in the poem comes to symbolize balance and familiarity (for it creates landscapes "of short distances and definite places"), but also the mysterious (like music it "can be made anywhere, is invisible and does not smell"). And of course it stands as well for death, the dissolution of life. Its omnipresence gives it a multitude of symbolic properties.

In some ways our awareness of water has increased as societies have grown richer, partly because of its greater domestic availability but also because education brings us knowledge of its invisible properties. Water has always had ambivalent chemical functions—sometimes as a catalyst, sometimes as an extinguisher—but we have long known about the latter, whereas we are learning ever more about the former. Opinion poll evidence suggests a systematic difference in perception of water issues in rich and poor countries.[15] Not only are environmental issues generally ranked as much more important in relation to other matters of political concern in rich countries, but water *quality* typically ranks as one of the top two environmental issues cited there by poll respondents. In poorer countries, water quality often appears far down the list: in a 1990 opinion poll in Lima (Peru), pollution of drinking water and pollution of rivers and seas were each cited by a mere 1 percent of respondents as the main environmental problem facing the country, well behind "rubbish in streets and public places" (42 percent), air pollution from vehicle exhausts (30 percent) and "air pollution from power plants and industry" (12 percent). Paradoxically, access to adequate *quantities* of water is the concrete concern of the poor, even though water quality is a much greater objective threat to the poor than to the rich. Only the literal invisibility of water quality can explain this.

So, to sum up, water has a vast range of meanings, uses, and values — in the abstract or ethical sense of the term "values." Fortunately, though, two strangers who exchange water do not need to engage with the meanings, uses, and values each imputes to the good they are exchanging. All they need to do is agree on a price: how much water against how much of something else. In this lies the simplicity of market exchange: what matters is the scarcity of water for each party, relative to the scarcity of anything else they may want.

SCARCITY AND PROPERTY RIGHTS

But the scarcity of water is not determined just by its physical geography. It depends also on the kinds of property rights that can be vested in it. For water that someone can drink but is not allowed to pump through a pipe will, effectively, be more scarce than water that people are allowed to transport. To put it another way, the right to transport water to where it is needed can relax to some degree the constraint imposed on us by water's natural scarcity in the place where it is needed, and that is why the property right is valuable. Property rights are, above all, rules that determine how water may be used, and water use is a social institution whose rules we collectively invent. Throughout the world, we create such rules in many ways, constrained both by the physical scarcity of the water and by the direction and nature of the interactions between its different users. Rules are worth making only if we can afford the expense of enforcing them. So water is sometimes a purely private good, as when it is bottled for drinking. What it means for it to be a private good is that its owner must be able to prevent others from having access to it. Its high weight and volume relative to its value make this unusual: only when users are willing to pay enough to make it worth the expense of physically sealing it from the outside world, and when nobody else benefits or suffers from the use made of it, is water strictly a private good. At the other extreme, some water resources are available to all users, like the world's oceans, where the prohibitive cost of enforcing rules of access beyond territorial waters means there are, effectively, no rules. Such resources are sometimes called public goods, and they have two defining characteristics: first, that no one can be excluded from access to them, and second, that one person's access to them does not appreciably diminish the use that others can make of them.

In between the extreme cases of private and public goods lie two types of property that include most of the interesting cases. Water is sometimes common property, when a whole community has collective jurisdiction over its use. Each member of the community is potentially in a position to inflict externalities on the others, whether by polluting the resource or simply by failing to take account of the reduced amounts left for other users. Communal irrigation systems, inshore fisheries, and many aquifers are of this kind. Alternatively, water use may be characterized by externalities that go in only one direction, such as when one group of users has control, while another group is affected significantly by the first group's use but has no formal rights it could exercise to restrain that use and must rely on persuasion. The relationship between upstream and downstream countries along an international river is the most striking example of such a system. It is now becoming fashionable to see the greatest threats to the world's security in the twenty-first century as coming from "water wars," triggered by the tensions between such upstream and downstream users and by the inadequacy of international legal and arbitration mechanisms to deal with them.[16]

The nature of property rights in water will be influenced by how easily some users are able to exclude others from access. But exclusion is not an all-or-nothing matter: someone who can be prevented physically from withdrawing water from an aquifer for use may still be capable of polluting the source. And again, even if private rights to the water itself cannot be established, somebody may have clearly defined rights to something *in* the water, such as fish or mineral deposits. This means that we should expect rules that adequately govern all the uses we may make of water to be extremely sophisticated, continuously evolving as technological and other circumstances change, and highly sensitive to the particular natural context in which the water is found.

There is much historical evidence that our social institutions have adapted in remarkably flexible ways to the physical circumstances influencing our need and capacity to control water use. One telling example is the difference in the forms of law relating to surface water use in the eastern part of the United States and the corresponding forms in the West.[17] Broadly speaking, the Eastern states have laws based on the doc-

trine of "riparian rights," which give no absolute right of ownership of
water resources to any party but a circumscribed right of use to parties
located on the bank of a river or lake. The western states, by contrast,
have laws based on the doctrine of "prior appropriation," which essentially grants a more or less unqualified right to the first established user
of a water resource. (There exist also some hybrid legal variants in a
number of central states.) The difference between the two systems is
that riparian rights emphasize the community of water users and restrict
what any one member of the community may do with a source of water
because of possible external effects on other members. Currently, the
cost of this closer regulation of water use is to restrict incentives for the
direction of water resources toward their most productive applications.
Prior appropriation, however, leaves the interactions between different
users of a water resource more open to resolution by collective negotiation but also frees an individual user to adapt applications (for example,
by transporting water to a different place) if it is profitable to do so.
Neither system is perfect, but the former is one whose virtues will be
more apparent when there are significant community interactions and
difficulties in coordinating a community-level response to these. The
system of prior appropriation will be better suited to situations where
community interactions are less important than a real need to direct
scarce water resources to productive uses. Indeed, in the American
West, where nineteen states employ a version of the prior appropriation
doctrine (nine of them strictly), water is much scarcer than in the East,
and the law evolved originally to deal with the high water-intensity of
hydraulic mining techniques in places that were remote from rivers —
and at a time when the impact of inorganic pollutants on water quality
had yet to provoke public concern. The picture is somewhat more complex with respect to groundwater rights, where issues of users' interdependence are more likely to arise, but a similar East-West division is
visible here too.

The notion that the physical characteristics of water might influence
the evolution of the social and legal practices that define it as a commodity was taken to an extreme and ambitious conclusion by the historian Karl Wittfogel in his book *Oriental Despotism*.[18] He used the nature of water to explain not just parts of a legal system but an entire
structure of centralized social and political authority. Wittfogel sought
to explain the fact that earlier historians, "contemplating the civilizations of the Near East, India and China . . . found significant in all of
them a combination of institutional features which existed neither in
classical antiquity nor in medieval and modern Europe . . . the common
substance in the various Oriental societies appeared most significantly
in the despotic strength of their political authority." Wittfogel argued

that all of these societies were created in response to the need to organize what he called "hydraulic agriculture" — large-scale irrigation works transporting water from its natural location to where it could most enhance the fertility of the soil. In contrast to the opportunistic exploitation of rainwater resources ("small-scale irrigation farming"), which could be achieved by merely local forms of cooperative organization, hydraulic agriculture "involves a specific type of division of labor. It intensifies cultivation. And it necessitates cooperation on a large scale." The division of labor required to build large irrigation works required a degree of political authoritarianism unnecessary for self-sufficient city-states. It also provided the political authorities with the human resources to build palaces, temples, and other public works and to maintain that control over the population which had been necessitated by the requirement for forced labor in the first place. In other words, from an analysis of specific physical attributes of water ("Water is heavier than most plants. It can nevertheless be much more conveniently managed . . ."), Wittfogel went on to derive a complex and ambitious thesis about the differences between societies that happened to find themselves in a different relation to this vital natural resource. He did not claim that these differences were inevitable and cited numerous cases where the tendency implied by the underlying physical relationship to water was outweighed by other factors. But whether or not the substance of his thesis is ultimately convincing, the underlying idea remains a powerful one: that water as a resource takes many forms, some of which are due to its varying physical characteristics and some to the varying rules and customs governing its use. These rules and customs can be so central to the organization of society that they come in turn to influence many of society's other features.

Certainly, more modest analogues to Wittfogel's argument have been amply documented. There is considerable evidence that local communities have been able to evolve sophisticated informal systems of collective management of irrigation resources, systems that can overcome incentives for the individual to "free ride." One study of South India by Robert Wade showed that "villages located towards the tail-end of irrigation systems and with soils fertile enough to support a high density of livestock show a larger amount of corporate organization than villages elsewhere," because these features create a higher risk of crop loss if water is poorly managed.[19] There is therefore a greater incentive to manage the economic interdependencies between farmers through a system of rules, collectively determined and collectively enforced. The fact that these communities are local is not accidental. It's easier to evolve systems that govern the interdependencies between farmers when farms are close enough together for monitoring and enforcement to be rela-

132 • Chapter 8

tively easy. Wittfogel claimed that the sheer scale and geographical extent of the water systems he described necessitated correspondingly grander solutions.

Over the course of history, our social institutions have adapted remarkably well to the resource constraints imposed by water availability. But this is hardly a ground for optimism about our immediate future: just as nobody lives in the United States as a whole, nobody lives through the course of history as a whole. There are several reasons why the social institutions that have adapted well to past constraints may prove cumbersome and ineffectual in the face of future challenges. Partly this is just because success in the past is no guarantee of success in the future. For example, one impressive by-product of the hydraulic civilizations described by Wittfogel was the development of water clocks, which were probably far more accurate than the early mechanical clocks developed in Europe. Yet the historian David Landes has described this technology as "a magnificent dead end," because the rival mechanical clock developed in Europe, "aside from its usability in all times and weather . . . was susceptible of miniaturization, to the point of eventual portability." This allowed people, he claims, to apply notions of efficiency in the use of time to the bustle of their everyday lives rather than having to rely on timekeeping by the public authorities. "The clock made possible, therefore, private as against public, general as against hieratic or royal time." The result in his (admittedly speculative) view was a notion of productivity and its enhancement that was to underlie much subsequent technological advance. "That the mechanical clock did appear in the West, and with it a civilization organized around the measurement and knowledge of time, is a critical factor in the differentiation of the West from the Rest and the rise of Europe to technological and economic hegemony."[20]

A second reason for concern has to do with the direction of water flow and the asymmetries this creates among users. Upstream users of a watercourse have a capacity to affect the welfare of downstream users without being subject to a reciprocal dependency. True, some optimists believe that informal bargaining between the affected parties can overcome the effects of environmental externalities: a renowned example is the economist Ronald Coase, who pointed to the fact that many lighthouses, generating many beneficial externalities, were built by private individuals rather than by state institutions.[21] Indeed, the famous "Coase theorem" argues that if negotiations can be costlessly undertaken between all affected parties, all problems of externalities can be resolved. The polluter may not care about the damage she inflicts on the pollutee, but the pollutee can offer her enough inducements to make her care.[22]

The optimistic expectation that downstream users can negotiate efficient water management solutions with those upstream—that they will, in other words, be able to offer inducements to upstream users that cost less than the benefits gained from the arrangement—ignores the fact that such bargains, even if desirable, may not be credible. Promises made today (even in good faith) may be impossible to resist breaking tomorrow, especially given the long time-spans needed for planning water use and especially given that political regimes cannot bind their successors.

If every individual living along a trade route were empowered to extract a toll from commercial traffic, such traffic would soon dry up. Agreements between individuals about efficient levels of tolls would crumble in the face of the incentive to raise tolls unilaterally. Because such agreements are hard to monitor, and the individual benefits of breaking them exceed any likely cost imposed by a retaliation on the part of those who suffer further along the route, each individual would be tempted to cheat and raise the toll. So just as the great land routes through Central Asia became economically important only once the Mongol emperors established a centralized monopoly of force along the way, a formal centralized control of water systems has proved the only credible solution once water systems extend over a wide enough area. The presence of some sixty independent tolls along the river Rhine at the beginning of the fifteenth century was a major obstacle to continental European trade; in England, where there were no such river tolls, trade flourished.[23] The multiple depredations of warlords in contemporary Afghanistan may be an instance of the same phenomenon. Centralized control does not, however, guarantee efficient outcomes, as the sometimes disastrous environmental record of Soviet central planning should remind us.

The evolution of centralized systems may indeed respond in part to ecological and economic imperatives. But it is dependent upon so much else—the stability of political structures, the balance of military power between rival contenders for control—that it would be foolish optimism to put great faith in our capacity to resolve conflicts over water resources in the twenty-first century. Some of the most important international interdependencies in water management (to be increased by future developments in damming and irrigation) occur in the basin of the river Jordan and in the Tigris and Euphrates system, two of the world's most politically volatile regions. The institutions of international law are weak and of disputed legitimacy; there is no mechanism of centralized control and no agreed-upon criterion of fairness. One of the lessons of successful collective management, where it occurs, is that it needs stable norms, supported by consensus: individual incentives to break an agreement are hard enough to overcome even within a generally accepted and legitimate system. Where there is no legitimacy, no agreed-upon norm, efficiency and equity in the use of water resources may be almost impossible to attain.

The variety of the social institutions that have evolved to deal with water, testament though it is to the flexibility and adaptiveness of human society, implies also that the norms and values that characterize our attitudes toward water will be many and conflicting. Some people reject the very idea of treating water as an economic commodity, perhaps because they think (mistakenly) that if water is an economic commodity it cannot at the same time be anything else, such as an object of veneration. Whatever the reason, metering water use and charging for consumption has been strongly opposed in many countries where water has traditionally been treated as a "basic good" that should be, and often is, provided free by the state. But such arguments make sense only when water is plentiful. Once it becomes scarce, as in more and more parts of the world today, failing to charge for its consumption will only make it even more scarce in the future. Some people argue that charging prices for water is futile because household water consumption is relatively insensitive to both price and income: a study of the city of Austin, Texas, showed that per capita water consumption has changed little since the 1950s and not at all since 1970, although the city and its consumption habits have changed dramatically in every other imaginable respect.[24] But though direct household consumption may be relatively insensitive to circumstances, *indirect* consumption through agriculture and industry has large effects on water use and is extremely sensitive to prices. The "green revolution" in agricultural technology in poor countries since the 1960s has dramatically increased the water intensity of agriculture, and alternative methods of producing everything from cotton to cars may consume very different amounts of this scarce resource.

There is no serious alternative to treating water as an economic commodity. It is scarce in many locales even if it is not globally scarce, and its local scarcity may eventually prove globally threatening. But calling it an economic commodity begins rather than ends the argument. What would it mean to treat it as such? First, water's scarcity requires users to be given incentives to use it efficiently. These need not always be price incentives, but we know that price incentives often have desirable features that other kinds do not. In particular, they make possible the decentralization of decisions, when we lack the detailed knowledge and mutual trust required for direct regulation or moral persuasion. The great merit of charging a price for water is that we no longer need to argue who deserves it more: if people are poor they may deserve our help, but if water can be priced to reflect its scarcity relative to other goods, we no longer need to argue the case for helping them separately when we consider food, housing, water, clothes, and all the other aspects of their lives. Proper pricing *strengthens* rather than weakens the case for helping the poor.

A second implication of treating water as an economic commodity would be to abandon trying to manage water in similar ways across the whole range of circumstances in which it is found in the world. It is quite natural that arid zones and humid zones should have different systems of law, different institutional arrangements, even different attitudes toward pricing and regulation. Thirdly, treating water as an economic commodity would mean accepting different solutions under different technological constraints. For example, the scale economies involved in transmission and storage of water make a degree of monopoly almost inevitable. Water purification technologies, on the other hand, are less dependent on large scale (indeed, it often makes sense to treat water contamination close to the point of discharge rather than wait until water has collected in large quantities). The result is that decentralized solutions may be more appropriate to water purification than to water distribution. Fourthly, treating water as an economic commodity means acknowledging trade-offs: different uses of water involve different costs and benefits, and different distributions of these costs and benefits across the population. Potentially explosive international conflicts over water resources may be made less dangerous by being brought explicitly into the kind of horse-trading arena that is the daily currency of relations between states when it comes to other resources.

We saw at the start of this chapter, in the comparison of Mexican piped water with French bottled water, that cultural perceptions may make two quite different economic commodities out of chemically interchangeable substances. Systems of law, criteria of fairness, structures of political authority have for centuries shaped the institutions that govern the management and distribution of water. These differences are explicable in terms of the conditions to which they were a response. They will need increasingly to be reconciled if conflicts over the world's water resources are to be avoided in the coming century.

Is there a realistic way to reconcile these differences, given the capacity for tunnel vision that characterizes our species? In chapter 1 we looked at the remarkable coordination of international activity that takes place in the manufacture of shirts. This is achieved without any overall plan, simply through the reaction of individual participants to the possibilities offered by customers and suppliers, possibilities represented to them by prices at which they expect to be able to buy and sell.

Perhaps the hope for escaping conflicts over water, as for escaping conflicts over other resources, lies in ensuring that prices more accurately reflect costs, the costs to everyone and not just to the immediate user. To see what this would mean, we must first look at how systems of prices get established in the first place, and their strengths and limitations in coordinating reciprocal exchange. This is the task of chapter 9.

CHAPTER 9

Prices for Everything?

PRICES AS COORDINATORS

Traders in shares around the world sit in front of computer screens displaying dozens, sometimes hundreds, of numbers at a time. These numbers are prices, and they represent the amounts of money at which other traders (known as "market makers") are willing to exchange what are literally shares in the control of firms — rights to participate with others in deciding how these firms should be run, and of course to be paid some fraction of the profits that result from doing so. Sometimes nothing much happens for a long time: the numbers rarely change, and the faces in front of the screens express a trancelike state. Sometimes news spreads across the world like an electronic spasm: one company reports that its profits are unexpectedly low; another announces successful trials of a miracle drug; the chairman of the U.S. Federal Reserve makes a few enigmatic remarks. The clicks of thousands of computer mice transmit orders from the people who hear the news first: buy, sell. The prices change, and others who haven't yet heard the news realize something is going on. The adrenalin surge is powerful: a subtler form of entertainment than bullfights or public gladiatorial contests but — for those who like that sort of thing — apparently no less compulsive. And it is very public indeed: traders in Tokyo and in Tierra del Fuego may be sitting in very distant rooms, possibly alone, but the chances are that the numbers they are looking at are the same, even if they are not connected to the same website. Two quotations for the price of Microsoft shares cannot differ by more than a tiny margin; if they do, the Lone Rangers who patrol cyberspace will quickly eliminate the difference by buying cheap and selling dear.

Not all prices are so public. Visit the souks in Marrakech, and let your eye linger for a fraction of a second over a carpet. Instantly you will be invited to discuss the matter, confidentially, perhaps over a glass of mint tea. You will always be offered a "special price." There is no deception here, so long as you do not presume that your special price will always be especially low. It will be tailored to what the seller guesses to be your motivation, your expertise, and your budget. Sometimes that means the price will be higher than others might pay; sometimes it will be lower, particularly if you can convincingly signal that your expertise is high or your motivation and budget are low. But it will be your price, and yours alone, because no one else has observed what you and your interlocutor have negotiated.

The prices people pay for apparently similar items can display a startling variety, one that modern innovations such as computerization and the internet are not necessarily acting to diminish. Next time you take an airplane, try asking the two people in the seats next to yours how much they paid for their tickets. You may easily find differences of up to ten times: one bought a ticket months in advance, another is returning without staying a weekend, yet another is traveling standby. Airlines use sophisticated software to differentiate their fares by route, by ticket type, by the day of travel or the day of sale. Their customers in turn use sophisticated software to compare fares between one airline and another. Every seller wants to seduce each individual buyer into paying as much as she can, and each buyer wants to play the field of different sellers so as to pay no more than she must. It is a continual tango, constrained only by the mysteries of each buyer's individuality and the fact that rival sellers are always somewhere else, while the present opportunity is here, is now.

Both sellers and buyers increasingly call technology to their aid: my computer has been spied upon by little programs ("cookies") copied on to my hard disk by sellers whose websites I have visited. Now, when I return to Amazon, I am greeted with lists of recommendations supposedly tailored to my unique tastes in reading and viewing matter by a particularly empathic computer. Car manufacturers use ever more elaborate strategies to target people who are likely to have a higher desire to buy a car than most: General Motors has links with "life event" sites that offer information and support to people who have recently married, become parents, gotten divorced or suffered a bereavement, since market research has shown that 80 percent of such people buy a new car within a year. ("Mrs. Smith, we were so sorry to hear about your husband. We wonder whether now might be an opportune time to consider switching to a smaller car.") But customers can respond with technology in turn: they visit different sites to check prices—doing their research more thoroughly the more expensive their intended purchase. And they remain stubbornly individual: far from trading sensibly down, Mrs. Smith may be planning to splash out on that convertible she never dared to buy while the old curmudgeon was alive.

How can systems of prices—set in this apparently chaotic way—perform the remarkable feat of coordinating all the different activities that contribute to modern economic life? Even something as comparatively simple as making a shirt involves many stages, as we saw in chapter 1, and nobody is in overall charge of making sure that the different stages connect with each other. Prices are the terms on which the links between each stage in the chain are forged: the farmer sells his cotton to the merchant at one price, the merchant sells on to the factory for spinning and weaving at another. The bargaining at each stage will doubtless be hard, and one party may walk away with most of the benefits of the deal, but both will be convinced that they are doing better, if only fractionally, than they might do by dealing with someone else. The more alternative opportunities they have, the stronger their bargaining position: the merchant may sell to the factory for a much higher price than he paid the farmer, but he is less likely to be able to do so if the farmer can negotiate with other rival merchants. That is one reason why so much of the world's poverty is concentrated in rural areas, where farmers have few alternative outlets for what they produce.

The fact that increased opportunities strengthen your bargaining position explains how prices respond to supply and demand. Are there too many potatoes on the market today? Customers can shop around more keenly and offer lower prices, knowing that if any one seller refuses, there are always others who may accept. Is there a shortage of fresh fruit? Now it is sellers who have the upper hand, since there are many willing buyers and a seller can always try to edge the prices upward. These price movements are not just about transferring cash from buyers to sellers or vice versa, as though the market were one continuous lottery. For they also signal to those who hold supplies where those supplies can best be sent. When the harvest has failed in one region, the high prices act as a magnet to outsiders, dampening the price rise but — most importantly — moving supplies to where the shortages are.

Such a healthy stabilizing reaction depends, of course, on outsiders having access to where the opportunities are. Not all markets are so open. When instead access is limited and the markets are controlled by a monopolist or by a few insiders (perhaps acting together in what is known as a cartel), then the ability of prices to play a beneficial coordinating role may be seriously compromised. A monopolist will typically take advantage of the absence of any alternative supplier to raise prices. He will not raise them without limit, because eventually he would lose all his customers, who would decide to forgo what he has to sell. But he will be prepared to sacrifice some customers in order to make more money out of those who remain. The fact that he does so leaves the lost customers without access to these goods. They would have been willing to buy them at a price that reflected what it cost the monopolist to produce or procure them, but his unwillingness to supply them at such a price leads to a lost opportunity for mutually beneficial trade. This is an example of what economists term a "market failure," a case where the prices established by markets no longer send the signals that make efficient exchange between strangers possible. Pathologies such as these — even more common in the fragmented markets of the developing world than in rich, industrialized societies — provide the intellectual foundation for policies to restrain monopolies, open markets, and encourage trade. Such policies are highly unpopular with would-be monopolists and are often difficult to devise and enforce, but almost all countries now at least claim to be giving them serious attention.

It is when there is competition between rival buyers and sellers (so each has a choice of partners with whom to deal), when buyers and sellers are reasonably well informed about the opportunities they face, and when transactions between two people have no serious effects on anybody else, that tunnel vision is at its most impressive and effective. The whole complex process of coordinating international shirt production is fitted together by nothing more sophisticated than the restless opportunism of buyers and sellers, each seeking out chances to make a slightly better deal. When consumers decide they like a particular design better than another, sellers take the chance to shade the prices upward. In turn they seek out more supplies so as to take advantage of the more favorable prices, leading the makers of cloth, thread, and buttons to steer their efforts in the direction of the more popular design. Nobody is trying to make the system as a whole respond to demand, but that is exactly what it does. And anyone who is contemplating a career in shirt-making can make a shrewd assessment of the prospects by looking at the prices of shirts, and the prices of all the things that are needed to make shirts, and calculating whether the margin between the two offers any space to breathe. If shirt prices rise by more than the prices of the cloth, the thread, and the buttons, a few more would-be shirt-makers may decide to try and fill that space. A career in shirt-making remains a gamble — but it is a gamble whose odds are better described by the prices of shirts and their components than by any other information anyone could reasonably demand.

The idea that prices summarize important information about the future in an accessible and easily interpretable way is the key to understanding how they can play their extraordinary coordinating role. Shirt prices tell us something about how much buyers value the chance to own shirts. The prices of cloth, thread, and buttons tell us something about how much the producers of these items mind the trouble, expense, and sheer hard work of creating them. If there is a margin between the two, this tells us there's room for shirt-owners and shirt-makers to come to an arrangement that is in the interests of both sides. Tunnel vision works, when it does, by putting together a vast jigsaw of bilateral arrangements that, step by uninspiring step, make all of us dramatically better off than we would be if we had to put together all the components of our lives alone.

PRICES AS OPINION POLLS

What may seem mysterious is how prices can come to summarize information in this way. What is the process by which a price, changing in response to the vagaries of many individual decisions to buy and sell, can come to embody information about anything interesting at all?

To see how, make a visit to Iowa Electronic Markets (www.biz. uiowa.edu/iem) in the weeks leading up to an American presidential election. This is a site run by the Henry B. Tippie College of Business at the University of Iowa for the purpose of trading in financial contracts ("stocks"). But unlike most financial contracts, such as those traded on the New York Stock Exchange, many of the contracts here make cash payments that depend on something other than the performance of firms. Here you can buy a contract that pays a dollar if the Republican candidate wins the presidential election, and nothing otherwise (similar contracts are available for the Democratic candidate, and for any independents who may stand). This is known as a "winner-takes-all" contract, in contrast to other contracts that may pay a range of different amounts for different outcomes. As the election approaches, watch the price at which the stock trades. It rises as traders' estimates of the candidate's probability of victory improve and falls as they decline. Why? Suppose the current price is fifty cents. Any trader who thinks the Republican has a better than even chance of victory will buy, while one who thinks the chance is worse than even will sell. If there are more of the former than the latter, the price will rise until the optimists and pessimists just balance each other out. If news comes in making it more likely that the Republican will win, the price at which they balance will rise. The price of the stock therefore represents the center of the traders' estimates (actually what statisticians call a median)[1] of the probability of victory. The price was correctly predicting a Democratic victory two months before the election of November 2000 — I say correctly, because "victory" was defined as gaining the largest number of votes cast, a feat achieved by candidate Al Gore even if this did not suffice to take him to the White House.

As well as a "winner-takes-all" contract, whose price represents an estimate of the probability of victory, you can also trade contracts that pay a number of cents equal to the candidate's share of the popular vote. These contracts will therefore trade at a price equal to the traders' collective best guess about the share of the vote. This is exactly the same information that traditional opinion polls have sought to discover, and the Iowa Electronic Markets have a track record in prediction that most opinion pollsters would envy. (Three months before the elections of both 1992 and 1996 the markets were predicting Bill Clinton's share of the popular vote to within two percentage points of the eventual outcome.) It's not surprising, really: an opinion poll gathers together information about the voting intentions of one or two thousand people, who have no particular incentive to tell the pollsters the truth about their intentions. The electronic markets gather together information about the predictions of as many traders as want to get involved, and they have a financial incentive not only to tell the truth but to gather information from as many other sources as they possibly can.

Other websites offer an even more varied array of future events on which to speculate. Newsfutures (www.newsfutures.com) is a French/ American site that has run bets on various stages in the war on terrorism, the progress of corruption investigations into the affairs of President Jacques Chirac, the outcomes of the Tour de France and the Super Bowl, the likelihood that the SETI project will discover messages from extraterrestrial beings, the state of human cloning research, and the love lives of the celebrities Jennifer Lopez and Britney Spears, among other issues of more or less cosmic significance. In each case there are winner-takes-all contracts, defined around a specified event, and by tracking the price of the contract, you can plot precisely the rise and fall in traders' confidence that the event will happen as described. The Hollywood Stock Exchange (www.hsx.com) offers contracts of a slightly different kind: they are essentially bets on the box-office takings of particular movies, and the value of one contract in dollars is the number of millions of dollars that the movie in question grossed in its first month of release. If the movie grossed 50 million dollars the contract is redeemed for fifty dollars. Anyone who has information suggesting the current price is an underestimate can expect to make money by buying contracts; anyone who thinks it is an overestimate is well advised to sell. When the optimists and the pessimists just balance each other out, the price will remain steady. So, just as in the other markets, the price at any time represents a collective best guess, in the sense that the number of people thinking it an underestimate just matches the number of people believing it to be an overestimate.

These markets are purely financial, in the sense that they involve transfers of money between participants under certain carefully defined circumstances, but no real goods change hands. A great number of markets, of course, do involve the transfer of real goods or the performance of real services. Here what prices do is to represent information about the value that the goods or services have to the traders. And sometimes the whole purpose of the markets is to elicit this information so as to ensure that the goods or services pass to the traders that value them most. In recent years the role of prices in revealing information has been particularly visible in the case of auctions.

Auctions

Auctions have been used for a long time and to sell many things: we know that slaves were auctioned in Roman times and tulips in seventeenth-century Holland, while the list of categories on the eBay website runs all the way from "Antiques and Art" to "Yo-yos." Edward Gibbon recounts how the entire Roman Empire was offered for auction by the Praetorian Guard after their murder of the Emperor Pertinax in A.D. 193, since they feared that from the expected successor, Sulpicianus, "they might not receive a just price for so valuable a commodity":

> This infamous offer . . . reached at length the ears of Didius Julianus, a wealthy senator. . . . The vain old man hastened to the Praetorian camp, where Sulpicianus was still in treaty with the guards, and began to bid against him from the foot of the rampart. The unworthy negotiation was transacted by faithful emissaries, who passed alternately from one candidate to the other, and acquainted each of them with the offers of his rival. Sulpicianus had already promised a donative of five thousand drachms (above one hundred and sixty pounds) to each soldier; when Julian, eager for the prize, rose at once to the sum of six thousand two hundred and fifty drachms, or upwards of two hundred pounds sterling. The gates of the camp were instantly thrown open to the purchaser; he was declared emperor, and received an oath of allegiance from the soldiers, who retained humanity enough to stipulate that he should pardon and forget the competition of Sulpicianus.[2]

An auction works by asking people to state their own prices, or at least to indicate their willingness to pay prices announced by an auctioneer, or by some other mechanism such as a clock. They can do so openly, or in a sealed envelope, or in various other ways. People are often cautious about what they say, at least more so than Didius Julianus seems to have been (though Gibbon records that after he was carried in procession to the imperial palace, he "passed a sleepless night").[3] They fear, often correctly, that the keener they are seen to be to buy something, the more they will have to pay (in auctions, unlike ordinary markets, the price at which people actually trade is not determined until after they have revealed their willingness to pay but adjusts according to the bids received). So bidders have potentially strong reasons to dissemble. Nonetheless, well-designed auctions succeed in finding out

Figure 9.1. Down through the ages auctions have been used to sell almost anything, including people. Here are two kinds of human auction. *Above*, a slave auction at Richmond, Virginia (from the *Illustrated London News* of 1856). *Below*, the dance troupe Pan's People sold at Sotheby's in 1980 to an anonymous buyer for £3,000. Stanley Devon/Getty Images/Hulton Archive.

enough about how much people really value the goods to allocate them to those who value them most—an insight the Praetorian Guard put to profitable use. They may do so through a range of devices. One is to make the winner pay the price of the second-highest bidder (so that people know the price they pay will not depend on what they themselves say). Another is simply to encourage bidders to continue until all but one has dropped out of the race. The last one left does not have to declare the true value he places on the object, so long as he declares one that is higher than anyone else is prepared to declare.

Of course, we may doubt whether auctions can really compare the true value different people place on the objects for sale. I may tell myself that the wealthy bidder who buys the old-master painting does not really value it more than I do. He's just richer; money means less to him. But the fact that he's richer means he can afford more of *everything* than I can. It's still true that, compared to me, he values spending his money on the old master more than on some rival purchase. And it's in that limited sense that the auction has allocated the painting to the right person. It wasn't the auction's purpose to redress the imbalance that makes him richer than I am, merely to ensure that, given the existing imbalance that gives some people more money than others, the painting goes to the person who most wants to spend his money on that particular object.

In the last few years, auctions have been used increasingly to make a number of decisions that used to be made by government committees without the involvement of any kind of price mechanism at all. An auction of radio spectrum licenses for third-generation mobile telephony in the U.K. in March and April 2000 raised the remarkable sum of 22.5 billion pounds—and this for a privilege (the right to broadcast on a particular part of the electromagnetic spectrum) that used to be awarded free to broadcasters and telecom companies alike. In principle that sounds like good news: the licenses go to those companies who can make best use of them, and public assets yield revenue to the state instead of unearned profits to company shareholders. In practice, though, the good news has been tempered by an increasing concern that the companies concerned may have paid too much, may have suffered from a problem that is known as "the winner's curse." In the example of the painting discussed above, we assumed that buyers wanted a painting only for their own enjoyment, so that in deciding how much to bid they had to consult only their own private preferences. In fact, even in art auctions, many buyers care not only about their own enjoyment of an object but also about how much the object may fetch on the market in the future. This is not a subjective matter but an objective (though still unknown) fact. In auctions of spectrum licenses, the differences that exist between companies are small compared to the uncertainty they all face about how profitable the markets for third-generation mobile telephony will turn out to be. In these circumstances there is a real danger that the auction may allocate the objects in question not to those who really value them most but simply to those who are the most wildly optimistic.

"It's bad news: you've won the auction." The discovery that you were the greatest optimist of the bunch should often lead you to wonder what it is that other people know and you don't. It is a question Didius Julianus might well have asked himself. The economist Paul Klemperer has described Julianus's victory in the auction for the Roman Empire as "an early and sad case of the winner's curse," since he reigned for only two months before being overthrown and executed by Septimius Severus.[4] Less violently, the telecom companies that won licenses in the European spectrums auction have seen their credit ratings downgraded, their share prices fall, and some of their executives depart to a comfortable but nevertheless unwilling retirement. Not many readers will shed tears for Julianus, and many will likewise feel that the directors of large companies are paid very large sums of money not to be wildly optimistic and do not deserve great sympathy for suffering the winner's curse. But these examples suggest a question about the merits of a system that awards the spoils systematically to the optimists: is this compatible with a role for prices as summarizing and transmitting reliable information about the future?

Actually, this is a misleading way to put the question. Auctions, like ordinary markets, tend (when they work smoothly) to allocate goods to those people who most want to own them, without asking questions about whether this strength of desire is intrinsic or springs from foolish optimism. Prices for any transaction will settle, as we saw above, at a level that compromises between the valuations of the more optimistic traders and the valuations of the more pessimistic. The fact that traders will end up owning the goods about which they have been most optimistic (relative to others) is what gives both optimists and pessimists the best incentive to avoid casual misjudgments. You pay the price of your optimism by being obliged to own the goods about which you were so optimistic. Even the most enlightened committee of inquiry lacks so keen an incentive to reach a reasonable collective judgment. As we shall see in chapter 12, there are strong grounds for saying that markets can sometimes reflect, and even magnify, collective bouts of overoptimism or overpessimism in modern society. What is remarkable about market prices is their capacity for reflecting individuals' valuations at all; if these valuations are foolish, nothing can prevent the resulting market prices from being foolish too.

Still, auctions would not continue to attract participants if only the foolish ever won. Most of those who take part in auctions know about the winner's curse and adjust their bidding behavior to take it into account. This makes them cautious, and the greater the uncertainty about what they are buying, the more cautious they will be (a tendency that has been well documented in studies of auctions where significant amounts of money are at stake, notably auctions of oil-drilling rights).[5] Cautious buyers mean less revenue for sellers, who therefore have good reason to reveal as much information as they can about what they are selling and to find ways to make that information as trustworthy as they can. It's not always easy to convince skeptical buyers that your information is trustworthy, but the ingenious feedback system used by eBay has been an important reason for the remarkable success of this web-based auction firm. Buyers and sellers leave ratings about each other, as well as comments, and other buyers and sellers use them to decide whether they can trust someone they have never met. As a cruise around the eBay site will quickly reveal, a high proportion of sellers receive ratings from buyers that are over 99 percent positive. All well-designed auctions not only rest upon trust but propagate it: eBay has found a remarkable institutional mechanism for spreading trust across a vast and widely dispersed community of internet users.

IS EVERYTHING FOR SALE?

Modern economic life has resulted in the use of explicit prices for a far greater proportion of exchanges between individuals than was true for our ancestors. This follows from the uncontroversial fact that the division of labor has become more extensive and sophisticated, involving more transactions between strangers. When you're exchanging with strangers you need to be particularly careful about keeping accounts — indeed, accounting systems are central to the systematic symbolic reasoning human beings have evolved to handle a complex division of labor, as we saw in chapters 2 and 3. Some people also believe (though this is much more speculative) that more exchanges than in the past are made on explicitly reciprocal terms even between people who know each other, as part of a deal and involving a clear understanding about the quality and quantity of both sides of the exchange. In contrast to actions taken unilaterally, with the actions of some other party in the future remaining opaque or uncertain, these explicit deals can be said to bring prices into the realm of familiar relationships. Some people have seen this latter tendency as an unfortunate consequence of the more widespread use of explicit prices, as a regrettable commercialization of modern life. If we are all becoming, in Oscar Wilde's famous description of a cynic, people who know "the price of everything and the value of nothing," then modern markets are institutions of vulgar calculation that have been sweeping away a subtle heritage of gift exchange based on trust and mutual esteem.

However we feel about modern markets, it is important not to exaggerate the degree of spontaneity in the interactions of our ancestors. The anthropologist Marcel Mauss argued in his book *The Gift* that in what he called "archaic societies" gifts are "in theory voluntary, in reality given and returned obligatorily," and that gift exchange constituted the major mechanism of circulation of goods in such societies.[6] If so, one might imagine that in such societies prices could be established for transactions just as they are in market societies even if they were not prices expressed in terms of money ("six sheep for one cow"). Exchanges might easily be every bit as explicit, just as much the product of wheeling and dealing, even if they come described as gifts. Vulgar calculation in period costume, you might say. The impression that prices have become more central to familiar relationships in the modern world might be due simply to our failure nowadays to be realistic about the nature of relationships in traditional societies.

In fact, though, Mauss argued that gifts were different from monetary transactions in an important way. In particular, the nature of obligation incurred on receipt of a gift was not determined wholly or even primarily by the nature of the goods received but owed a great deal to relative status, and to other social and emotional links between donor and recipient. At times he seemed to believe that the complexity of these links was under threat from market transactions and that modern societies would reach a phase "of purely individual contract, of the market where money circulates, of sale proper, and above all of the notion of price reckoned in coinage weighed and stamped with its value." At other times he rejoiced in the fact that "a considerable part of our morality and our lives themselves are still permeated with this same atmosphere of the gift, where obligation and liberty intermingle. Fortunately, everything is still not wholly categorized in terms of buying and selling. Things still have sentimental as well as venal value."

Given that gifts entailed reciprocal obligations, it is not obvious how they escaped being considered venal. But it seems to have been part of the strategy of reciprocity in the societies described by Mauss that its venality should be hidden, or at least made more opaque. Natalie Zemon Davis has shown in *The Gift in Sixteenth Century France*[7] that multiple conceptions of gift-giving have coexisted for centuries; complex rules of reciprocity have been cloaked by more high-minded ideals of "gratuitous and non-calculating values" and of a liberality whose only reward was the gratitude of the recipient. Individuals might be no less (and no more) self-interested than their modern descendants, but in the language of their transactions interests were more tacit than obligations and ties. Seen in this light, what makes transactions with explicit prices different from others is not their motivation, not their venality per se, but the lack of subtlety with which that venality is communicated. Selling a good is like giving it to someone and simultaneously reminding them of their debt to you, a debt that (it is implied) sensitive and intelligent individuals ought to have been aware of without a reminder and might resent being brought so vulgarly to their attention.

Gifts may indeed have been a more delicate and refined way than commercial trade to undertake economic exchange. Like many delicate and refined arts, therefore, they gave an advantage to those who had the aristocratic privileges that made their mastery easier to acquire. As Davis's study makes clear, the rich and privileged could sometimes give away a great deal, but they rarely gave away real control over important resources. She writes: "gifts opened channels of communication across boundaries of status and literacy. They gave expression to the highly strained but genuine reciprocity between unequals in the social and economic order." She hardly needs to add that they did nothing to change that order. The terms on which gifts were exchanged were less transparent than monetary prices, because those who benefited from the social order had no interest in allowing others to see just how its benefits were distributed.

Suppose it were true that transactions even between people who know each other well have become more transparent, more governed by explicit prices, in the modern world than they were for our ancestors. Why might this have happened? One reason could be that the very habits of systematic reasoning and account-keeping we need in order to handle dealings with strangers have also been applied to our dealings with those we know well. Once a set of mental habits has been developed for an area of life where it is urgently needed, it can be applied with much less trouble and effort to other areas where the need has previously been less urgent.

Another reason could be that property rights have become more clearly defined than they once were. We saw in chapter 3 that any successful large-scale division of labor requires a degree of social consensus about who owns what, and particularly about who is entitled to offer goods and services in an exchange. This consensus may be embodied in a formal system of law, such as a registry of land title, an appropriate set of statutes governing the exercise of this title, and a system of enforcement that allows people to exercise their rights. Or the consensus may be more informal, provided it is considered no less reliable by those who have to use it. For the more uncertain your right to the goods you offer to give me tomorrow, the less I shall be able to rely upon your promise to repay the favor you are demanding of me today.

Some kinds of property right have become clearer and more formal than they were in ancient and medieval times, though this is particularly true of the industrialized Western societies. In ancient Rome there was no system of title to urban land. People built their houses anywhere they could get away with it. Something similar is true of the slum areas of many cities in poor countries today, though in practice the ability of people to get away with building even in slum areas is heavily influenced by both legal and illegal constraints. Much of the agricultural land of Western Europe in the Middle Ages was also operated in ways that gave less clear rights to individuals than they were subsequently to obtain from the "enclosure" movement. That's not to say that individuals had no private property; on the contrary, the English open-field system consisted, in the words of Deirdre McCloskey, of "scattered strips communally regulated but privately owned."[8] True common land consisted of pasture land that was useless for arable cultivation and could only be used for grazing. But the communal regulation, as well as the frequency of disputes brought about by the fragmented and dispersed plots, meant that individuals had limited control over the uses to which their own land could be put. Importantly for our purposes, they bore fewer of the costs and gained fewer of the benefits of using land in the most fruitful way.

Creating clear property rights is most important where the resources over which the rights to be held are valuable (which is another way of saying that they are scarce). For otherwise decisions will be made, and activities undertaken, which affect these resources — deplete or degrade them — without taking their value properly into account. We saw in chapter 8 that it was in the water-scarce regions of the western United States that the most comprehensive systems of property rights to water were developed in the last century. Throughout the world, title to land has become more systematic in areas where land is in shortest supply relative to the demands of people for food and housing. That's the most important reason why land titles in much of Africa remain collective, because in much of Africa it isn't land that is scarce but people able to work the land. Wherever it matters that some resource should be treated as valuable, instead of being considered in limitless supply, it will be important that someone should have clear rights to the resource; otherwise care for the resource will be overlooked by the tunnel vision of all concerned. But when the world's ecology is changing, systems of property rights can take a long time to adapt to the new realities. Some of the earth's environmental resources — its atmosphere, for example — have no individual owners to speak for them and must rely on the collective conscience of us all.

Buying and selling anything, whether land or grain or financial contracts, requires that the individual selling has a clear set of rights to the object concerned, *including the right to transfer those rights to someone else*. It's probably true that now more of the objects in our world have had such rights defined over them than was true in the Middle Ages, but it would be quite misleading to suggest that this has been a continuous progression. There are many things that I value but I have no right to transfer to someone else, beginning with the right to my own freedom, the transferability of which has been illegal since the abolition of slavery. And it follows from this, that there are many things I value that have no price, for a price implies a transfer with an explicit return. Sometimes this restraint on the right of transfer rests on a social consensus, as with slavery (a consensus that nevertheless did not exist in the United States until after a savage civil war). Sometimes it rests on what can only be described as a catastrophic social failure. The economist Hernando De Soto has written of the startling paradox that many of the poor in the developing world actually "own" highly valuable assets, beginning with houses that have been constructed in urban slums.[9] But their ownership is purely informal, unrecognized by any legal system, a fact that makes it impossible for them to use these assets as collateral against loans, and thereby to raise capital that might be put to productive ends and help lift the theoretical owners from their socially enforced poverty. Without the right of transfer, in other words, ownership may leave the owners powerless, unable to benefit from the rights of exchange that lie at the heart of the modern division of labor.

The boundaries between the things that have prices and those that do not are often tested. Here is a striking case, described by Jennifer Gann:

In September 1999 an individual offered his right kidney for sale on eBay, an internet based auction site. In America, where there are over 47,000 patients awaiting kidney transplants, and where the average wait for a kidney transplant nearly doubled between 1988 and 1996, this excited considerable interest. The bidding had reached $5.8 million before being shut down by the administrators of eBay because the sale would violate the US National Organ Transplant Act, passed in 1984, which prohibits the sale of human body parts. The Act itself is silent regarding the reason for the prohibition, but the language used during the congressional hearings debating it leaves no doubt as to the motivation of its sponsors: *"if . . . organs of living people should be offered for buying and selling, then I think this would represent a major degradation for humankind. . . . this "free-market" sale of an individual's organs is morally offensive and ethically indefensible."* Indeed, the moral repugnance which we feel at the thought of selling part of our bodies appears to be near-universal. The UN and the European Union have, respectively, encouraged and instructed their member countries to prohibit the sale of human body parts. The World Health Organization has interpreted the Universal Treaty on Human Rights as prohibiting the sale of human organs.[10]

It's important to note that what many people find offensive about selling body parts is not the fact that one person's organs will be transferred to someone else. A significant proportion of transplanted kidneys come from live donors, almost all from close relatives of the recipient. We usually applaud the generosity of such donors. What offends some people is the thought of donating body parts as an element in an explicit transaction, for a price. (Similar reactions are often expressed toward surrogate childbearing, commercial sex, and—in some countries—toward donating blood for money.)[11] As a consequence of this repugnance, we deny people full property rights in their own bodies. By doing so we preserve a sense of the integrity of the human body—and lengthen the queues for organ transplants.

Whether or not we are right to draw the boundaries between market transactions and implicit or gift exchanges where we do, the fact is that there are such boundaries and always have been. Even if we keep careful account of our dealings with strangers, there are many other arenas of social life where our interactions are less explicitly reciprocal, less overtly part of a deal. Sometimes this is because we are tied by the impulses and obligations of kinship, as within families. Sometimes it is because we act out of a wish to participate in some voluntary and collective activity, as in clubs or within relationships of friendship and community. Sometimes it is because habit or spontaneity are more agreeable to us than calculation, and are a luxury whose indulgence does us no real harm.

But sometimes it is because, for all the remarkable achievements of markets in coordinating the many component activities of modern life, there are other institutions that can perform feats of coordination that rival those of markets. Perhaps the most remarkable of such institutions is the modern firm. Many individuals join firms as part of an explicit deal, usually involving the promise of a salary against the promise of work. But once they are in firms, the day-to-day decisions they take are governed by a logic quite different from the explicit logic of markets. It is a logic of administrative hierarchies, in which people exercise discretion and issue and obey instructions, few of which bear any resemblance to explicit deals that can be characterized by prices. In chapter 10 we shall explore what firms can do, why they have grown in size and importance in modern life, and where the boundaries lie between them and markets. The fact that firms have such a central role in the modern division of labor alerts us to some of the many things that markets cannot do.

CHAPTER 10

Families and Firms

THE BOUNDARIES OF THE FIRM

The side streets of any major city in the developing world are full of small workshops in which manufacturing, repair work, and assorted services are carried out by groups of people of all ages, often related to each other. Tailors, garage mechanics, assemblers of radios or plastic toys, jewelers, and pawnbrokers carry on their business for long hours each day, usually cooking, sleeping, and doing their laundry in the same building, fitting their domestic lives and their work complicatedly and — to a bureaucratic eye — messily around each other. These people depend on markets for their livelihood, but their relationships with each other have little of the market about them: they are regulated by a system of instructions passing between those who exercise authority and those who are subject to it, with no explicit reciprocity and certainly no price system to coordinate their actions. Someone is always in charge, even if the outsider might not always be able to guess who it is. In the sea of decentralized market relationships, with no one in overall charge, there are countless such islands of centralization, planning, and hierarchy. These islands are as necessary to the organization of modern society as is the sea of markets. One of the great challenges of modern life is to understand where the shoreline should be: where the islands need to end and the sea to begin.[1]

The answer matters for many reasons, not least because the modern firm has been responsible for a spectacular increase in our ability to produce goods and services. The qualitative psychological leap from hunter-gatherers to modern humans was made many thousands of years ago, and citizens of ancient Greece or medieval Paris were already used to dealing with strangers in a way that brings them mentally much closer to us than to our common Paleolithic ancestors. But in terms of the sheer quantity of resources we control and consume, the most dramatic changes have taken place in the last two or three hundred years and especially in the last century. The human species now produces around fifty times as much output, consuming over seventy-five times as much energy and over sixty times as much freshwater, as we did two hundred years ago.[2] This is not the result of market exchange on its own but of the ability of firms to fit market exchange and internal organization together in an unprecedentedly busy and productive partnership. To see how this has happened, we need to know how firms respond to the opportunities market exchange makes possible.

Sometimes small family organizations like the ones in the back streets of Jakarta or Marrakech carry out operations that in richer countries are more likely to take place in large factories. Assembling simple electronic equipment is one example: radios, alarm clocks, amplifiers, keyboards. On the whole, though, the organizations that perform the ordinary work of society have evolved in size and structure over time, often in similar ways in very different parts of the world. Some sizes and structures come through experience to seem better equipped to manage particular tasks. Except when using slave labor on large estates, farming is an activity that throughout much of history has relied mainly on families;[3] the large industrial farms that dotted the Soviet landscape were a historical anomaly imposed by the central planners' liking for size at any price. Car manufacture, on the other hand, started out as a small workshop activity but quickly evolved, under Henry Ford's pioneering example, into one dominated by large firms.[4] Already in 1913 Ford produced nearly half the output of the American car industry, while 299 other firms produced the other half (employing five times as many workers in total as Ford did). Within a few years most of those other firms had disappeared. So what makes the difference between these two kinds of activity — one suitable for the small workshop, the other requiring the large factory?

The answer is not as simple as "technology" or "standardization." Some hi-tech activities, like building aircraft, do indeed take place in large firms: the Boeing Aircraft Corporation employs over 150,000 workers. But others, like the manufacture of precision instruments, are carried out overwhelmingly in small firms of thirty, fifty, at most a hundred employees. Silicon Valley is full of such firms, as are the areas around Cambridge in England and Munich in Germany. And standardization works both ways: just as it enabled Henry Ford to concentrate production in large factories, today it enables Nissan and General Motors to demand very exact specifications from suppliers of components, who may be small firms located hundreds or thousands of miles away from the main assembly plant.

To understand the answer we need to go back to families, who at the dawn of history were the only form of centrally organized institution known to mankind. Families are a form of cooperative organization that evolved originally around the care of children, who are helpless for longer in the human species than in any other, the only mammalian young to require parental feeding long after they have been weaned.

Feeding and mutual protection were tasks that hunter-gatherers could undertake in relatively small bands, but once settled agriculture began, both feeding and protection could benefit from organized cooperation on a larger scale. The ordinary tasks of agriculture — plowing, sowing, reaping — were and have remained within the grasp of individual families operating on their own, sometimes calling on friends and neighbors for help at critical periods such as harvest time. But as we saw in chapter 8, irrigation has sometimes needed much more complex organization, especially when diverting entire rivers along canal systems to thirsty land some distance away. Protection, too, required both individual initiative and collective solidarity. Each family needed an element of prudence, some skill in combat, and — in particular — the judgment to know when to fight in defense of its home and possessions and when to flee. Some families relied on individual prudence alone, finding protection through invisibility — like the woodcutter in the forest, a figure famous from countless children's stories, who hoped that marauding armies would not think his poor hovel worthy of pillage and that he could run and hide in the unlikely event that they did.

But solidarity was often a wiser strategy. Just as fish find safety in the school even if the school becomes more conspicuous as a result (and as merchant ships in wartime sail in convoy even when this makes them more visible to submarines), so many of the first farmers found that banding together in units larger than families gave them an important advantage in defense. Farmers are conspicuous anyway, both because their carving of the fields leaves unmistakable scars on the landscape and because they need somewhere to store their harvests and tether their livestock. So the formation of villages and towns provided a means for them to band together in their own defense, and subsequently to build fortifications more solid than anything a family could manage on its own. The first village settlement at Jericho has been dated to before 9000 B.C., and within a thousand years it had grown to a substantial settlement of several hectares of mud-brick houses with thick walls. The first evidence of the famous city walls comes from the early eighth century B.C., and the presence of great water tanks, probably for irrigation, is attested from the seventh century. And a massive ditch, thirty feet deep and ten feet wide, was dug into the rock without metal tools. A single family could never have managed protection on this scale.

The growth of villages, towns, and cities took time. Fortifications were a great investment of time and energy for people who had a more pressing need to grow or find food. And the very conspicuousness of fortifications could attract as well as deter attack, for they signaled the presence of something worth stealing. The walls of Jericho were destroyed and rebuilt many times. Settlements on the scale of Jericho were extremely rare before about 3000 B.C. (Çatal Hüyük in Turkey was another, flourishing in the seventh and sixth millennia B.C.). But slowly the advantages of scale came to seem decisive to those builders of cities who could mobilize the necessary manpower, a discovery that crystallized onto the map of the world the urban civilizations of Mesopotamia, Egypt, the Ganges Valley, Minoan Crete, and China, all before the end of the second millennium B.C. With defense came a vast increase in each family's exposure to strangers, who came to trade, to admire, and to beg, as well as sometimes to conquer, and who brought with them their animals, their exotic foods, and their diseases, as well as their strange and sometimes beautiful ideas. With defense also came subjection to the law and the whim of rulers.

Although much of the interdependence of human beings since the birth of agriculture has been driven by bilateral trade (by what Adam Smith called the human propensity to "truck, barter and exchange"), the foundation of villages, towns, and cities is a sign that there are many important things that bilateral trade between individual families cannot achieve. These are tasks that need collective action on a larger scale, and for most of recorded history these tasks have comprised what has come to be known as "governance," namely, the building, the management, and the defense of the collective assets of the community. Families have joined together to hunt, to build, to defend themselves, to hold festivals, and to debate and police the rules that govern their communities, including the rules by which bilateral trade is conducted and its agreements enforced. These tasks — building the physical and social infrastructure of modern life — are the subject of chapter 13.

In contrast to the great collective tasks of governance, those of ordinary business — planting, weaving, milking, smelting, cooking, trading, hairdressing, creating the goods and services that furnish the lives of individuals and families — have remained for most of history well within the capacity of an ordinary family. Large armies may have a history as old as that of cities, but large firms are, with rare exceptions, an invention of the last three or four hundred years and did not become common until around two centuries ago.[5] Why did these activities remain exclusively family activities for so long, and why did they cease to be? The answer in a word is industrialization, though it is an answer that raises a host of new questions. At all events, it is industrialization that explains how some organizations founded simply to carry on business have become, in scale and sophistication, formidable enough to challenge the power of governments.

In fact, large firms have found a place in modern life partly by applying some of the lessons of the successful armies of the past, notably the discovery that certain tasks can be simplified and standardized so as to be easily learned and effectively implemented by a large team of people.[6] As one study of the U.S. Navy records: "In boot camp [the] inductee's credo is: "If it moves, salute it. If it doesn't move, pick it up. If you can't pick it up, paint it white."[7] Some of the earliest of the large firms founded in the early modern period even had a semimilitary mandate, like the East India Company, founded in 1600 with a charter from Queen Elizabeth I to carry out trade, but also entitled to make and enforce laws in the territories it entered. (Similar dual-purpose mandates characterized the Hudson's Bay Company of 1670 and the Royal African Company.) But most large firms, though they have no literal military function, have much in common with fighting forces. What firms shared with armies was a commitment to control over their members, an insistence on supervising their activities, behavior, even their personal habits. To cite the U.S. Navy study again: "The [naval] base is a place of close-cropped haircuts and close-cropped lawns. Here nature and the human form are controlled, arranged, disciplined, ready to make a good impression."[8] The same ambition fired some of the early firms of Europe's industrial revolution.

STANDARDIZATION AND SURVEILLANCE

The royal manufactory at Villeneuvette, in southwestern France, provides an early example of this development at work. Today it is a quiet village invaded by grass and wildflowers and full of crumbling buildings, some of which have been restored to house the artists and craft workers selling to tourists who come to enjoy its bucolic charm. But it was once a center of intense manufacturing activity. Established in the early seventeenth century by King Louis XIV's finance minister, Colbert, it not only provided a site on which the work of cloth-making—weaving and dyeing—could take place but also housed, fed, and supervised the workers, both on the job and in their few hours of leisure. It was a forerunner of the mill towns of the nineteenth century, like Bournville near Birmingham and Pullman outside Chicago,[9] whose purpose was avowedly paternalistic: to see to the welfare of workers, because they would be more productive if well fed, healthy, and closely watched. Supervisors were to check on the state of workers' families, enforce churchgoing, and above all watch for signs of excessive drinking. Productivity, it was thought, required an investment of the whole person, not just their presence and effort during the hours of work.

Nevertheless, Villeneuvette and one or two other places like it (the silk factories of Northern Italy, for example) were exceptional in the Europe of the time.[10] As the medieval guild system began to break down, its immediate successor was not industrial production but a flexible and decentralized system (known in England as "putting out"), in which spinning, weaving, dyeing, and tailoring were carried out in people's homes. Various intermediaries—merchants, financiers, general organizers—would organize for the delivery of raw material and collect finished work. This system, with some local differences, made up the bulk of textile manufacture in many countries in Europe and was dominant in Japan until the late 1920s. It first began to give way to the factory system in England in the eighteenth century, under the influence both of technical inventions (such as the water frame, a machine for spinning with rollers) and of innovations in factory organization. The two went together: Richard Arkwright, who patented the water frame (although he had stolen the idea from someone else, as emerged in a famous trial in 1785), was attracted to the invention in large part because it enabled the centralization of production and the location of the workforce under a single large roof. This made it possible to engage in rigorous surveillance of the workers. One near-contemporary observed that "the difficulties which Arkwright encountered in organising his factory system were much greater than is commonly imagined. In the first place, he had to train his work-people to a precision and assiduity altogether unknown before, against which their listless and restless habits rose in continual rebellion; in the second place, he had to form a body of accurate mechanics, very different from the rude hands which then satisfied the manufacturer." As the historian Sidney Pollard has put it, "what was needed was regularity and steady intensity in the place of individual design; and care of equipment and material instead of pride in one's tools. . . . None of this came easily to the new workforce." In the more sinister words of another historian, "throughout the manufacturing districts, mill owners were faced with the problem of keeping at regular work men who loved their independence and their ale."[11]

Controversy raged then and has continued to this day over whether the habits of mind and body necessary for industrialization were compatible with human dignity. Karl Marx famously thought industrialization "alienated" mankind from its true nature, though he admired enormously the huge increases in productivity that capitalism had made possible. Lenin was a great admirer of the scientific-industrial principles of Frederick Taylor (and notoriously re-defined socialism as "Soviet power plus electrification"), though again it seems to have been the sheer productivity that impressed him; Lenin's spirit was nothing if not competitive. One of the more thoughtful defenses of the factory system's effect upon its workers came from Henry Ford: "I have heard it said, in fact I believe it is quite a current thought, that we have taken the skill out of work. We have not. We have put in skill. We have put a higher skill into planning, management, and tool building, and the results of that skill are enjoyed by the man who is not skilled."[12]

Of course, the factory system was not just about standardizing the working habits of individual people. It was about standardization in many other dimensions too: Henry Ford's innovations radically changed the nature of parts manufacture. "The parts were so precisely manufactured that several cars could be disassembled, their parts mixed, and reassembled; this was said to be impossible with any other low-priced car before 1913."[13] It was not the idea in itself that was new; precision-engineered, interchangeable parts had been introduced into gun manufacture in New England a century before,[14] and the so-called "American system" was a source of much wonder at the Great Exhibition of 1851 in London.[15] What was new was its application at a scale and with a thoroughness that had never been achieved, or even attempted, before.

Standardization certainly had its costs, notably a reduction in the variety of goods produced. Henry Ford again: "in 1909 I announced one morning, without any previous warning, that in the future we were going to build only one model, that the model was going to be the 'Model T,' and that the chassis would be exactly the same for all cars, and I remarked: 'Any customer can have a car painted any color that he wants so long as it is black.' I cannot say that any one agreed with me."[16]

Ford had understood that by drastically reducing variety in the things he produced and in the processes by which they were made, he could make so much more with his workers and his machinery that ownership of a motorcar could be brought within the reach of the ordinary working family. Unlike some industrialists since, Ford was not blind to the virtues of variety. Far from it: he had once worked as a farmhand and expressed the hope that his Model T car might liberate the American farmer from what Ford saw as the stultifying monotony of rural life.[17] His gamble worked, and worked spectacularly, because the monotony to which he consigned his workers did not outweigh for them the very much better wages he offered than other employers, while the monotony in the design of his cars did not outweigh for them the very much lower prices he offered than other carmakers.

And the gamble perhaps worked better in America than it could ever have worked in Europe. One reason was that Europe was more divided by legal and regulatory barriers erected by its patchwork of (often fiercely nationalistic) states, so the emergence of a genuine mass market across the content was much less likely than in America. More subtly, the historian David Landes has suggested that one of the main reasons why the American economy caught up with the British economy during the nineteenth century, and had overtaken it (in terms of income per person) by the eve of the First World War, was that America was socially and culturally ready for a mass market.[18] Millions of Americans were prepared to tolerate cheap, standardized cars, clothes, and furniture — enough potential customers to permit production on a continental scale. But Europe remained a continent divided by language and class differences, where those who could afford to buy cars, clothes, and furniture preferred to pay high prices for craft production whose subtle gradations of quality advertised the buyer's social aspirations and achievements. In a world where the leading manufacturers compete to serve an elite, the ordinary citizen may never get a chance to express a preference for cheap and plentiful monotony.

What exactly was the connection, though, between standardization and production on a large scale? Standardization both permitted and required large scale. It *permitted* large scale because it allowed procedures to be automated, often through separating out the many component parts of a complex activity, allowing them to be performed repetitively at high speed, by people or machines or both. Adam Smith has a famous discussion in *The Wealth of Nations* of the way in which even something so apparently simple as pin-making can be divided into many component activities (today we would call them subroutines). This not only makes them faster to perform but also much easier to learn, particularly by people who lack a craft training. Indeed, the factory system played an important role in the transmission of certain kinds of knowledge from one person to another, a role that is even more important in the modern world than it was in Smith's time, and one that we shall look at more closely in chapter 11.

Standardization also *required* large scale because of the need for close surveillance of the quality of work at each stage of the manufacturing process. A putting-out system, where people worked in their own homes, was all very well if anyone could tell at a glance whether their work was of good enough quality for the purpose in hand. But as soon as the finer details of quality came to matter, ones that might not be instantly visible to the naked eye, it became important to oversee the process of production as it was going on, so that flaws and errors could be corrected before they caused too much damage to the overall product. This lesson, learned by the early industrialists, was never quite appreciated by their heirs in the Soviet factory system a century and a half later: uniting factory workers under one roof was regarded as important by the Soviets for surveillance of workers' general discipline and effort but not for detailed oversight of quality. Not until the car or tank left the production line (and sometimes not until it reached the eventual user) would anybody discover whether the parts inside were faulty — by which time the damage they could do was far greater than if they had been properly tested when they were first made.

Sometimes, of course, large scale has other advantages because it enables particularly big or expensive machines or buildings to be more effectively utilized. More and more, too, large firms in the modern world are in fact networks of factories that may individually be of quite modest size. The size of the firm (as opposed to the factories) is necessary to take advantage of some more intangible and indivisible asset, such as a brand name, a set of relationships with banks and other investors, a particular capacity in research and development, or even simply the attention span of an unusually gifted management team. But scale is often needed when standardization places a premium on effective oversight of quality, and where monitoring that quality is hard to do at a distance. As economists studying the characteristics of different organizations tend to put it, we should expect to see large firms when there are fewer "transactions costs" associated with bringing different activities inside the firm than with conducting them at arm's length, through the market.

For activities where scale is less important, by contrast, families may have a big advantage over large firms. Typically, scale matters less when the work cannot really be standardized: perhaps it's a service that doesn't require much technological support and for which personal contact with the client is everything, or the manufacture of a product that must be customized to the needs of individual buyers. Scale also matters less when it's easy to specify the requirements for doing well, so the job can be done at arm's length from the person who wants it done. Alternatively, perhaps the work consists of tasks that individual people just have to go out and do, like plowing a field or painting a wall. You can't bring the field or the wall to your production line, and though it may help to have a machine to assist you, many people will not necessarily work proportionately more effectively than one person. (Such customized, field-bound activities can even involve quite advanced technology, such as tailoring a software package to an unusual business or devising a series of flow meters for an underground mine.) Then, when scale matters less, it's more important that the different members of a team should work together with a general trust in each other's effort and goodwill. Unlike networks of strangers, families have been tackling the cooperation problem at a small scale since human prehistory. Notoriously, they have often failed at this, but their collective experience is matched by no other human institution.

OUTGROWING THE FAMILY

Firms usually begin as family concerns, in fact: even in the United States today some 90 percent of all registered businesses are family businesses, though the remaining 10 percent account for a large proportion of total economic activity. The interesting question is what makes some firms outgrow their family origins and reach a scale out of the scope of any single family to manage.[19] Firms that employ one hundred or more people, to take one simple statistical measure, represent a tiny fraction — less than 0.5 percent — of all registered firms in the United States, but their importance is immense: they employ over 60 percent of all employees and account for nearly 70 percent of total sales revenues.[20]

Outgrowing the family scale is one of the most significant challenges a family business can face. The historian Alfred Chandler has argued that the failure of many British businesses to outgrow the dominance of single families is an important reason for the disappointing performance of British industry in the twentieth century in comparison with both Germany and the United States, where professional managers took the reins of many important firms at a comparatively earlier stage in their development.[21] Why then do countries differ in their ability to face this challenge? Francis Fukuyama has argued that national culture exerts a subtle but very important influence on the size of firms.[22] Any family firm that needs to undertake activities requiring large scale will be faced with the need to bring outsiders into positions of discretion and responsibility; eventually there will not be enough family members to do the job. But bringing in outsiders is risky: How do you know whom to trust? How much responsibility should you grant them? And what can you do if you begin to doubt their loyalty? In fact, argues Fukuyama, all cultures have traditions of dealing with outsiders, and it is to these traditions that people look for models when they are considering how to structure their relations with outsiders in a business setting. Most obviously, families bring in outsiders through marriage. Some cultures, as in Japan, treat it as normal for those who marry into a family to be given a full say in family decisions, to share ownership of family assets, and to be trusted in positions of family responsibility. Other cultures, as in much of China, are more protective of blood ties, and less commonly give outsiders who marry into the family a real say in decisions or real control over assets. The difference may seem subtle (and is extremely hard to document in more than an impressionistic way); it certainly appears to have escaped those who think there is such a thing as a single set of "Asian values." But the result is an important difference in the average size of firms between Japan and comparably capitalistic Chinese societies like Taiwan, Hong Kong, and Singapore. Large firms are proportionately much more common in Japan, claims Fukuyama, because when family businesses are thinking of expanding, they have cultural models for the inclusion of outsiders that are not available to family businesses in China.

Naturally, cultural models are not all that a family has to hold on to when thinking about the right size for its business. There is also the law. The law plays a particularly important role in protecting the interests of minority shareholders — which is what family members almost inevitably become once their firm grows large enough. An expanding business requires not only manpower but also capital — the resources to finance current activities and investment in the future. A family firm that lacks these resources will need to find other investors willing to pledge their own funds. They in turn will do so only if assured of mechanisms that make it more likely that they will be repaid. Broadly speaking, two kinds of mechanism exist. One, which is much the more common for small firms, is debt. Debt is a legally enforceable promise that if the firm does not repay, the lender can request either seizure of assets or a full bankruptcy (namely, the administration of the firm by a court-appointed official who operates in the interest of repaying the firm's creditors). The second mechanism is equity, which means a share in the control over the firm's operations, not just in the event of non-repayment but on a regular basis, through the power to appoint the board of directors at a shareholders' meeting.[23]

Families seeking to expand their businesses usually face a difficult choice. Debt leaves them in control but forces them to make repayments at a fixed level — one that takes no account of the varying fortunes of the firm (though it may perhaps vary with overall conditions in the economy). The inflexibility of these repayment promises leaves the family vulnerable to losing control altogether. Equity, on the other hand, involves much more flexibility; a firm can simply declare no dividend if business conditions have been bad that year. But this greater flexibility comes at a real cost: handing over a share in control today, now.

Shared control is a delicate concept. Anybody who controls more than half of a firm's voting shares can theoretically take all of the decisions without consulting those who own the rest. This is where the law comes in. The law typically protects (to different degrees in different legal systems) the rights of minority shareholders. The most obvious way in which it does so is by requiring the same dividend per share to be paid to all shareholders; the majority may not vote itself a large dividend while voting a small one to the minority. The law often protects minorities in other ways as well, for example, by ensuring that takeover bidders must extend share offers to minorities on the same terms as to others. And minorities in terms of a firm's capital may nevertheless entrench themselves by remaining majorities in terms of votes; many families have retained voting control over their firms by raising outside capital on a nonvoting basis. In these circumstances the law protects the outsiders against the insiders, not vice versa.

There is much controversy over whether the law is right to intervene in detail in the conditions under which a firm's current owners may raise capital from outsiders. Some argue that restrictions on what majority shareholders may do merely diminish the flexibility of available financial arrangements without really making investors better off. After all, investors might reasonably choose to forgo explicit legal protection in exchange for higher returns, just as they may invest in riskier debt ("junk bonds") in return for higher interest rates. Others reply that if the range of possible levels of protection is too great, investors may simply become confused, so it is important to assure a certain basic level of protection for everyone. This debate has had important repercussions in Europe, where in July 2001 a controversial Takeover Directive that would have made it easier for outsiders to dislodge controlling insiders was defeated in the European Parliament by the narrowest possible margin: the vote was tied, 273 on each side.[24] Whatever the merits of one or another form of legal protection, it is important to see what the debate is fundamentally about. It is about whether those who have started up a business (who are often, though not always, families) and who now need the help of strangers in order to finance its expansion need the protection or the restriction of the law, or both, in order to establish the necessary mutual trust.

As we have seen in previous chapters, markets provide a way for strangers to exchange with one another. The complex institutions that underpin modern markets can be understood as ways to establish the trust that such exchange requires. In just the same way, modern firms provide a way for strangers to collaborate on those productive tasks that require more than exchange and would be impossible without centralization, planning, and hierarchy on a significant scale. The formal and informal institutions underpinning modern firms (everything from company law and accounting systems to dress codes, safety procedures, and management-speak) can be understood as ways of making trust achievable between strangers. They allow people who share no blood ties and who know rather little about each other to place their resources, their welfare, and sometimes even their lives in each other's hands. Nevertheless, the advantages of large-scale production remain delicate. No one doubts them when it comes to building aircraft or managing the transmission of electricity, but in many other spheres of life even sophisticated networks of artificial trust are no match for the spontaneous, face-to-face variety. Restaurants remain small businesses for the most part. Those that don't (like McDonald's) sell standardization to customers in lieu of refinement or creativity.[25]

TECHNOLOGY AND FIRM SIZE

How is modern technology changing all of this? Before we look at information technology and other such wonders of the modern firm, it's worth looking backward at the way in which earlier technological revolutions affected the scale of business operations. Eighteenth- and nineteenth-century technology favored large-scale activity, and in two main ways: by enabling standardization through precision engineering and by harnessing the greater energy efficiency of single large machines, whether these were steamships or railroads or factory equipment. The later developments of electricity and telecommunications in the early twentieth century had a more ambiguous effect: production no longer had to take place near the customer and thus could be concentrated in a few small centers, but at the same time, small workshop activity no longer had to cluster around sources of power and information and thus could compete effectively with larger hubs of production. Alfred Chandler has emphasized, though, that there was nothing automatic about the benefits from scale. First, producing at large scale makes sense only if you face large markets (American firms in the nineteenth and twentieth centuries were obviously in a better position than those in other countries). Even if you do, investing in large-scale production facilities is worthwhile only if you have the management skills necessary to keep your factories running at high capacity and the marketing skills necessary to reach the many customers that are theoretically out there.[26] What made Du Pont, General Motors, Standard Oil, Sears Roebuck, and U.S. Steel different from other less successful firms was not that they had different technological opportunities but rather that they had the organizational and managerial capacity to exploit those opportunities to the full. They supplemented the invisible hand of the market with the visible hand of management. (*The Visible Hand* is the title of Chandler's best-known book).[27] One consequence of this was that many firms became large not simply because they had large production plants but because the best way to ensure high capacity for these plants was to integrate backward into raw material production and forward into distribution and marketing.*

The Visible Hand was published in 1977, ironically around the very

---

* This trend was copied, usually disastrously, by central planners under communism, who thought that vertical integration, including health services, holiday *dachas*, and the farms producing food for the workers' canteen, was a sufficient condition for efficient production. A Polish minister for industry in the early 1990s told me that the Nowa Huta steelworks outside Cracow would need only to strengthen its perimeter fence to be able to declare itself a separate state.

time that changing economic conditions were starting to reveal the limitations in Chandler's vision of American business.[28] In the two and a half decades since then, more and more large firms, particularly in the traditional production industries, have found themselves outperformed by smaller, nimbler competitors. These competitors are more focused on certain core activities and tend to coordinate with their suppliers in other ways than through complete vertical integration. The reasons for this are not simply technological. For instance, growing international trade and increased competition at home have forced many firms to be more hard-headed about which activities they undertake for themselves and which they buy outside. In-house suppliers that can't match the competition are a luxury firms can increasingly ill afford.

But technology matters too: the information revolution of the late twentieth and early twenty-first centuries is having a powerful impact on the structure of firms. To begin with, information technology makes it possible to produce items to order, with highly individualized specifications, without losing economies of scale. It also makes it possible to supply a customer from any distance away, provided the customer and the supplier can reach agreement at that distance as to what constitutes acceptable quality. It works for software: much of the software for the American banking industry is produced in India. It works for precision-engineered components whose tolerance limits can be written down and objectively tested ("objectively" means that the test can be performed in Milan or Manila and still reach the same result). It works — up to a point — for financial services. It doesn't work, though, for paintings, or for fresh fish. Smoked salmon can be bought over the internet, but to buy the fresh kind, you need to see it directly. Similarly, the internet works for most books, but not for most clothes. It works — also up to a point — for cut diamonds and diamond jewelery but hardly at all for rough diamonds, which still need physical inspection to determine their natural characteristics. On a day in April 2003 when I made the comparison, the most expensive of over 68,000 polished diamonds or pieces of diamond jewelry for sale on eBay had a price of $4 million, while the most expensive of a mere 101 rough diamonds had a price of only $299, a tiny fraction of the levels at which some rough diamonds change hands at the De Beers sales (known as "sights") in London.

What exactly is revolutionary about the information revolution? Part of what information technology brings to firms is the standardization of procedures, enabling knowledge of their operation to be transmitted from one individual to another without the painstaking apprenticeship of the craft system at each stage in the chain. As I pointed out above, this is certainly not a new phenomenon; it's a good description of what made the Roman army so much more powerful than its predecessors and rivals. And the growth of the corporation in the late nineteenth century was about exploiting exactly such standardization. But two features of this process as we experience it today are new. First, we have learned to standardize procedures that are more complex, more flexible and of a higher order — not just those required to fasten the nut to the bolt, Chaplin-style, but those required to stop the entire production line and retool it for a different model of car, an operation that can now be carried out very much faster than before. As a result, we can decentralize much more sophisticated operations within a single firm than the pin-making tasks described by Adam Smith, benefiting in the process from advantages of motivation and adaptability without sacrificing advantages of scale.[29] Secondly, this standardization of procedures is much more likely to be recorded in reproducible, often digital form. This means that the knowledge can be easily transmitted across firms and not just within them, leading to more unstable and uncontrolled forms of competition. To learn the Roman army's procedures you had to be a Roman soldier, whereas to copy a rival firm's accounting system you just have to buy (or pirate) its software. (Blueprints and chemical formulas have, of course, performed a similar function for decades and even centuries, as systems of patents and licenses have sought to recognize.)

Increasing digitization is making the boundaries of the corporation more porous to valuable information. We should not exaggerate how new this is. The invention of printing had exactly such an effect on the medieval church. The alphabet is itself a form of digitally encoding ideas, but for as long as reproduction of books meant copying by hand in a monastic scriptorium, the dissemination of these ideas had made little progress outside the church that controlled the copying process and a handful of wealthy laypeople who were in a position to own the product. But printing allowed ideas to seep through the church's walls to those outside who owed the institution no particular loyalty. And since the dawn of history, technical inventions have often spread through imitation far beyond the contexts in which they first appeared. The domestication of the horse and the development of wheeled chariots transformed warfare across Europe and Asia during the third millennium B.C. More prosaically, most of the benefits from the invention of air conditioning accrued not to the inventors or even to the manufacturers of air-conditioning equipment but instead to the owners of real estate in places such as Florida.[30] Land proved ultimately much scarcer than the know-how needed to replicate this valuable but relatively low-tech process.

Nor should we exaggerate how much of our stock of useful knowledge can be transmitted across the globe at the click of a mouse. As was pointed out in chapter 1, many procedures central to modern life will not be mastered by information technology any time soon — cleaning a hotel room and weeding a flowerbed, to name but two. Information technology still cannot tell you how to value a rough diamond, or whether that fish smells really fresh, or whether you're going to look good in that dress. And many corporate cultures involve intangible qualities that prove extremely resistant to imitation (though hope springs eternal, as shelf after dreary shelf of business books in airports attest). Recent research has shown that distance still matters to a large extent in the spread of knowledge even in fields characterized by high scientific precision: the use of licenses for inventions patented in American universities tends to cluster closely around the sites where the inventions originated.[31] The explanation seems to be that there is no substitute for face-to-face contact in transmitting some of the intangible components of knowledge and skill — and without these intangible components even the tangible ones will not work very well. Face-to-face contact, sometimes mediated through a complex chain of responsibility and command, is what distinguishes the island of the firm from the sea of market transactions around it.

Still, even if it sometimes seems as though nothing is truly new under the sun, the cumulative effect of many subtle changes can make a large impact on the corporate landscape. If firms in many traditional production industries have been slimming down and focusing on their core activities, firms in some service industries and those where branding is important have been growing very large. One force for size is the fact that digital information can be almost costlessly reproduced. A firm such as Microsoft can devote billions of dollars to developing the first copy of a software product, and then make millions more copies for no more than the cost of producing a CD-Rom. This is useful if there are many millions of potential users of the product, but useless if it is a highly specialized product with only a tiny niche of users. Another force for size is the importance of networks: a credit card company relies on users being able to find outlets that will take their cards and on outlets being able to find users — and the value of such linked networks is increasing as people travel further and more often across the world. A third force is the power of branding: a visitor to a Sheraton hotel or a buyer of Coca-Cola needs to feel confident that the service they receive or the liquid they drink is recognizably similar to what they might have received from the same brand on the other side of the world. And that in turn is credible only if the firms that own these brands are large, coherent, and organized in a reliably uniform way. Staff in the Hong Kong Sheraton may have trained in New York; the Coke sold in Africa may have been bottled in France. As communications and broadcasting give a bigger share of the world's population access to a common pool of information, more firms are finding that it pays to be large.

Nevertheless, at the same time that these forces are favoring size, modern technology is also playing a part in promoting diversity. The internet may make more people aware of Sheraton Hotels but it also enables the intelligent surfer to see that all hotels are not alike and that some reflect a local spirit far better than any large chain could. When I travel to a different country on vacation, I want some things to be like what I have at home: drinkable water, a reasonable level of hygiene, peace and quiet. But there are other things I probably want to change: food, scenery, décor, the ingredients of that elusive element called charm. A brand name is often a crude signal: it promises reliability without diversity. So I may use the internet to search for smaller local hotels. Not that branding becomes irrelevant; on the contrary, some sites, like some series of travel guides, specialize in what might be called "local branding," in which they offer users an assurance that hotels will share a certain quality and charm even though they express those attributes in different ways. The point about such branding is that if hotels wish to share the qualities of a hotel chain, they need to belong to the same firm, or at least to a highly organized franchise. If instead they wish merely to share a more elusive character such as "charm," it is enough for them to belong to the same information network. Information technology, then, can help to make some firms very large, but can bring to others the advantages of size even when they stay small.

FIRMS AND THE CONSTRAINTS OF THEIR ENVIRONMENT

Let's return, then, to the question with which this chapter began. What makes some activities suitable for large firms and others suitable for small ones? And can we really explain the growth of large corporations as a phenomenon rooted in the underlying soil of economic life? Is it not just an accident based on fashion, convention, or a quest for power by those who run them? Few people who have ever set foot inside a modern corporation would deny that the quest for power is a palpable motive shaping people's everyday lives. Executives thirst to command others and burn with resentment at the slights that come from submitting to the command of others; junior employees sometimes live out a kind of prolonged adolescence in continued deference to their supervisors. And there is ample evidence from more systematic studies, as well as from journalistic reports, that takeovers and merger deals struck in company boardrooms can be driven by greed, vanity, and wish for power, the desire to run a large firm (regardless of whether it is an effective one), the urge to be Number One, the need to belong to what investment bankers call the "Bulge Bracket." None of this should be surprising to anyone familiar with the raw material of human nature. But though none of it is surprising, none of it — surprisingly — may matter very much. The theatrical emotions may be speaking the lines, but larger economic forces are writing the script.

Why? Greed, vanity, and the wish for power have always driven human beings' conquest of their natural environment, but that conquest has often failed. Those who have succeeded have not necessarily been greedier or vainer nor wished more ardently for power than those who failed. They have simply adapted those motives more successfully to the possibilities of the environment, including the environment created by the motives of others. It's the same in the business world. It's not the desire to run a large firm that makes you capable of doing so. It's not the thirst to take over a competitor, or to diversify your business into new markets, that makes these strategies viable. Just as in nature, the strategies need to match the opportunities afforded by the environment. The big animals that wander the Serengeti may impress competitors, or zoologists, or tourists, but they also consume huge quantities of energy, and no large animal can survive unless its environment obligingly feeds it. That's why so few of the world's successfully adapted animals are very large; and why the largest, like the dinosaurs, have proved so vulnerable to environmental disruption; and why the most favorable environments for large animals are to be found in the relatively stable surroundings of the oceans. Big firms, likewise, consume enormous quantities of resources just to keep running, and no large firm can survive for long unless its environment — its owners, its customers, its government — obligingly feeds it. Firms that have tried to grow too large — Enron, Vivendi, WorldCom — have often been checked when the food supply dried up.

Sometimes, in spite of failing dismally to adapt to their environment, firms survive through finding powerful individual backers. In the mid-1990s, a few years after the collapse of communism, I visited a factory close to the Ukrainian capital, Kiev. I was used to visiting firms that made a wide array of products, but even so this firm astonished me. It made docking equipment for space stations. It made pine kitchen furniture. It made plastic medical syringes. It made video arcade games. It made aircraft. It made mining equipment. It made keyboards for personal computers. It made precision instruments. None of this was based on any coherent vision, any idea of whether there were intrinsic complementarities between the skills needed to make precision instruments and those needed to make furniture. The firm made anything its team of twelve hundred ingenious inventors felt like making, regardless of whether anyone wanted to buy it. It had survived because the firm's director had excellent contacts in the Ministry for Industry, which for several decades had been prepared to pour bad money after worse.

In the company of the director and several of his colleagues, I enjoyed a lengthy discussion of the theories of economist John Sutton, who has done more than any other modern researcher to document the different forces that make some firms grow while others stay small.[32] "Surely it makes sense for us to keep our aircraft division together with our precision instruments division," said the director. "It's all high-technology, after all." Sutton would have pointed out that this makes no more sense than for a Bond Street tailor making made-to-measure suits to set up shop in the entrance to Marks & Spencer, on the grounds that "it's all cloth." For a Bond Street tailor has to deal with individual measurements and requirements that vary subtly (or not so subtly) from one client to another. Marks & Spencer can go for large-scale production, invest in advertising, cut its prices, and put lots of identical items on the rails in the knowledge that subtle differences need not matter, and that the large amounts of money it has spent on the strategy will be justified by the large number of extra customers the strategy will bring in. Both strategies may make sense, but they are quite different from each other, and customers need to know which one they are getting. If I buy a suit from Marks & Spencer, I may be able to ask for the trousers to be slightly altered, but if I ask for too many alterations, I shall be politely directed to go to a tailor. It's the same with aerospace, which tends to make aircraft in large numbers by throwing money at a design problem (like how to transport several hundred people for several hundred miles at minimum fuel cost). This is quite different from precision instruments, which are bespoke items designed for the precise needs of small numbers of individual clients. Aircraft manufacturers are the big hunting mammals of the industrial world, while precision instrument makers are the small rodents, the opportunists. Neither could survive on the same diet as the other.

Similar contrasts can be seen across the world. Aid workers and government officials in many poor countries have often expressed bafflement and despair at the inability of government-subsidized banks and credit schemes to displace the traditional moneylender from his place in village life. But the moneylender is a rodent too, benefiting from information about his borrowers more detailed than any bank could ever acquire, adapting his strategy, his terms, and the availability of his funds to the needs, circumstances, and weaknesses of his borrowers. The modern bank, with its air-conditioned offices, and computerized loan records, has powerful skills, but it is a large mammal that occupies a quite different ecological niche. Neither looks remotely ready to displace the other.

My conversations in Ukraine also revealed a striking parallel between the worlds of politics and business. Under communism, Ukrainian firms were run along autocratic lines, as befitted their tsarist political origins. An individual director might be good or bad, plodding or inspired, but what he said (and it was almost always "he") was the law for his firm. Firms in America or Western Europe, by contrast, are coalitions, products of the eighteenth-century political theory of checks and balances that underlies the American Constitution. Standing behind the inspired inventor is an accountant asking what it will cost, or a marketing director asking how anyone will ever be persuaded to buy it, or a personnel director asking what will be the impact on the workforce. These are frustrating voices for the creative thinker or inventor to hear, and it's sometimes tempting to think that modern society would be better off without them. Inventors and entrepreneurs can often be seen on television or in the letters columns of newspapers bemoaning the pettifogging constraints of bankers, accountants, and bureaucrats that stop them from taking their creativity to truly inspiring heights. They deserve just as much skepticism as politicians who bemoan the constraints placed on them by advisors, bureaucrats, and voters. A look at the mess made in that factory in Kiev is enough to dispel this fantasy.

Many of the most spectacular corporate failures in modern times have been produced by great creative individuals who overreached themselves, in part because the normal restraining mechanisms of the modern firm failed to work. Just as the sensory capacities of a large mammal enable it to see, or hear, or scent danger before the danger arrives, and thereby check the urge to act on the impulses of hunger or libido, so the checks and balances of a modern corporation are means to sense disaster before it arrives, and thereby restrain the urge to act on an impulse, even a great and creative impulse. When a corporation's internal checks begin to fail, its days are as surely numbered as those of a large hunting mammal whose scent or hearing fades. And the larger it is, the faster it will run out of fuel for its daily metabolic needs.

So the answer to the question at the beginning of this chapter is clear. Groups of strangers can sometimes collaborate to perform the ordinary productive tasks of modern life, but large groups will predominate over small groups only when they have a strategy better adapted to their environment. Brute force and ambition are never enough. Only when the environment demands large-scale coordination, using skills that can be transmitted within an organization through personal contact more effectively (with lower "transactions costs") than through the anonymity of markets and information networks, will large groups enjoy a systematic advantage over small ones. Otherwise they will fall victim to the suspicion that is endemic between strangers, and that dates back to the very origin of our species.

Modern corporations are not the only organizations to coordinate the division of labor outside markets. Charities, mafia organizations, government departments, churches, ethnic networks, and armies all do something recognizably similar. As we saw at the start of the chapter, the large firm is a relatively modern invention, and it has enjoyed its remarkable success only because it has proved extremely effective at creating, absorbing, and transmitting knowledge and skill from one person to another. For much of human history since the dawn of agriculture — for perhaps nine and a half of the last ten millennia — control of knowledge remained the prerogative of generals, priests, and (more recently) master craftsmen. As we shall see in chapter 11, the escape of knowledge from the exclusive control of these groups is what has enabled the division of labor to take such an elaborate, prosperous, and dangerous form in the modern world.

CHAPTER 11

Knowledge and Symbolism

Late one Sunday afternoon in 1994, a week before Christmas, three friends were coming to the end of an afternoon's potholing in the Ardèche in southern France. In a small cavity in the rock, a site well known to cavers and walkers, they stumbled across an opening that led to a passage widening out into a large, empty space. They would need further equipment to continue, which would mean adjourning to their car, but it was already night and they were tired. Once back at the car, they nearly decided not to return, but when they did, they discovered a series of passages linking vast chambers, the whole site extending over several hundred meters. One of the trio, Eliette Brunel, spotted a small painting of a mammoth in red ochre on a piece of hanging rock. Alerted by this discovery, they searched the walls and discovered hundreds of paintings and rock carvings, some of them of extraordinary energy and sophistication. Although they did not realize it at the time, the oldest of these paintings date back a little over thirty thousand years, making them twice the age of the famous cave paintings in Lascaux. In one evening they had extended our understanding of the origins of human culture back in time by many millennia.

The Chauvet cave (named after the expedition's leader, Jean-Marie Chauvet) has now attained worldwide fame and is a central point of reference for those wishing to understand human evolution.[1] The really surprising thing about the Chauvet paintings, though, is not that such remarkable works of art should have been created so long ago, but rather that we have not found more of them. Those who made these paintings and carvings were clearly beings with both imagination and skill; they had a capacity for symbolic representation and a curiosity about their world for which there is absolutely no evidence among any earlier European peoples. Evidence of tool-making has been found in archaeological sites well over a million years old, but if stone tools were useful, they were very far from being creative. For most of that million-year span, stone tools showed a tedious lack of variety, of adaptability to local materials, or of evolution over time.[2] The earliest human beings went on flaking and chipping in exactly the same way that their ancestors did, with no learning apart from the acquisition of the same ancient skill, no accumulation of collective knowledge or experience. Nor did humans show any signs of gradual experimentation with culture — with pictures, artworks, or personal decoration — or evidence of natural or metaphysical curiosity. When these interests arrived, they seem to have done so very suddenly.

The likely explanation of their sudden arrival in Europe is not, in fact, that they suddenly evolved. Instead, they almost certainly evolved elsewhere, namely, in Africa; like many of the creative members of any society, the master artists of the Chauvet cave were probably recent immigrants, at least as measured in evolutionary time.[3] Over forty thousand years ago, people living in the cave of Enkapune Ya Muto, or "Twilight Cave," in East Africa's Rift Valley, carved ostrich egg shells into delicate beads, which they may have used to exchange with others as symbols of reciprocity in the same way that !Kung San tribesmen in the Kalahari Desert of Botswana do today.[4] Stones engraved with patterns, found in a cave called Blombos in South Africa, have been dated even earlier, to seventy thousand years ago or more, leading some archaeologists to claim that a capacity for modern cultural behavior may have evolved gradually over many tens, and possibly some hundreds, of millennia. The suddenness of the break in the archaeological record may owe more to the accidents of preservation and discovery than to any suddenness in the developments it records.

This interpretation of the evidence is highly controversial, not least because no one can do more than speculate whether such a revolutionary development in human behavioral capacities could possibly have been the result of a relatively slight adjustment in the anatomical microstructure of the human brain. Brains leave no fossils; only skulls do, and the skulls of the first culturally modern humans were no different from those of their cultureless immediate predecessors. There is also much argument among specialists about how precisely to describe the mental capacities that were necessary for human beings to develop culture in this way. Susan Blackmore, for example, argues in her book *The Meme Machine* that all that was needed was an ability to imitate others, an ability that makes us very different from other animals and that, once acquired, set off an unstoppable flood of copying that has led our ideas and institutions to take on lives of their own. Michael Tomasello argues in *The Cultural Origins of Human Cognition* that the capacity to imitate to the extent that we do itself requires *other* skills — notably an ability to project ourselves into the point of view of other people.

What is not controversial, though, is how revolutionary this development was; it made possible the whole future of human culture. To see why, think of it as combining two preexisting elements in human behavior: symbolic representation and the creation of physical artifacts.[5] Each of these elements was remarkable enough in its own right, but they had a truly startling potential in combination. Symbolic representation means the use of signs for communication, signs whose reference to the external world is potentially arbitrary but whose meaning depends on and is reinforced by social convention. The signs used by modern man could and did draw upon pictorial representation, but their potential for recombination in new and unexpected ways gave them a fluidity and expressiveness far surpassing any mechanical copying of nature: one of the paintings in the Chauvet cave is of a creature with the head and torso of a bison and the legs of a human being. Symbolic reasoning radically transformed the ability of human beings to communicate information about their world, allowing them to represent past and future events as well as present ones, imaginary events as well as real ones, general ideas as well as brute instances, hopes and fears and dreams as well as cries and demands.

Symbolism as such almost certainly long predates modern man: language, after all, uses arbitrary sounds to refer to objects,[6] and anatomical evidence suggests that our probable ancestors (such as *Homo ergaster*) and cousins (such as *Homo neanderthalis*) must have spoken languages that served complex social purposes.[7] These languages would have involved arbitrary systems of signs: when Neanderthal man told Neanderthal woman that he had seen two mammoths, he must have uttered sounds that were neither binary nor mammothlike. But the symbolism of Neanderthal man vanished into the air as soon as it was uttered; it left no physical traces and gave subsequent generations only the shifting sands of memory on which to build. What made symbolism revolutionary was its embodiment in physical artifacts, manufactured objects that could outlast the behavior that created them and even the lifespan of their creator. Of course, artifacts as such were not new either. Stone tools are artifacts — very complex ones, which even today require long training and a high degree of skill to reproduce. But the stone tools of premodern man had absolutely no symbolic content. What made the cognitive revolution we see in the Twilight cave and the Chauvet cave so remarkable was that it combined these two features. For the first time in the story of humanity, artifacts that were also symbols appeared. For the first, time man could leave his descendants objects with a meaning, one that would make his own ideas live after him.

The ability to learn from those who have preceded us is at the heart of the story of humanity. Anthropologists sometimes use the term "culture" to mean any kind of behavior that is learned and that differs from one community to another for no other reason than historical accident. In this sense some nonhuman animals have culture too: for instance, zoologists working with chimpanzees have identified some kinds of foraging behavior that varies between troops in exactly this way.[8] Nevertheless, culture in the sense of a collective store of ideas that can be used to meet various challenges in our lives, without all having to be learned and absorbed in advance, is a uniquely human phenomenon. One of the features that distinguished anatomically modern man from his forerunners was a significantly longer life-span, and it seems likely that the female menopause evolved around the same time.[9] Both developments greatly increased the probability that grandchildren would have access to grandparents and other senior adults who were not directly preoccupied with raising children of their own. In this way the memories of these adults could serve as a repository of knowledge to help the tribe meet the challenges of an unpredictable environment. But, on its own, such an oral encyclopaedia was perishable and short-lived. It took symbolic artifacts to put culture on a more lasting footing.

Symbolic artifacts offer several major advantages over a purely oral culture. They are typically more durable than brain tissue. They can be shared: many people may look at a picture or read an inscription (these have some of the features of what economists call "public goods"). As a result any single individual has access to a vastly greater library of ideas than she could ever store in her own brain. And finally, the fact that symbols can be recombined in new and unexpected ways allows their users to experiment, to invent as well as to record their inventions for future users. This "cognitive fluidity," as archaeologist Steven Mithen has called it, may have been responsible for the invention of agriculture, through allowing human beings to fashion a new relationship with the animals and plants they had previously gone out to hunt. At any rate, it is remarkable that after some millions of years of human evolution, agriculture should have been invented independently in at least seven different places in the world only a few thousand years after the first symbolic artifacts were created. Although it has been plausibly argued that other factors, such as climate change, were involved, there had been radical climate changes before that had not produced so radical a shift in human behavior. It could be coincidence, but it is far more likely that one invention (symbolic artifacts) facilitated the other (agriculture) once the ecological conditions were suitable.

For the first time in human evolution, then, symbolic artifacts allowed knowledge to become both collective and cumulative. The greatest inventions are those that make it easier for others to become inventive in turn. The invention of writing is almost certainly another example of multiple independent invention, one that occurred a little over five thousand years ago in as many as five widely separated parts of the world: Egypt, Mesopotamia, China, Pakistan, and Central America. It made possible a vast range of subsequent inventions that depended on writing for their expression, their dissemination, and possibly even their conception. The invention of printing by Johannes Gutenberg around 1450 looks more like a single formative event, though even this took place at a time of parallel developments (both in Europe and in China) that suggest printing would soon have been invented even if Gutenberg had never lived. Its impact was extraordinary, and not just for the immediate benefits it brought to those newly able to afford books. As historian Elizabeth Eisenstein has written: "In 1483, the Ripoli Press charged three florins per quinterno for setting up and printing Ficino's translation of Plato's Dialogues. A scribe might have charged one florin per quinterno for duplicating the same work. The Ripoli Press produced 1,025 copies; the scribe would have turned out one." The cost of making books had fallen to around one three-hundredth of what it had been a few years before.[10]

Some of the many new readers who would have access to books as a result would just read for their own pleasure and instruction. Others would be inspired by their reading to further invention. For instance, to cite Eisenstein again, the astronomers Copernicus, Tycho Brahe, and Johannes Kepler "had an opportunity to survey a wider range of records and to use more reference guides than any astronomer before." Others again would use the invention as a means of founding businesses, like William Caxton, who in 1476 set up England's first printing press (on which he printed not only the Bible but also the first popular edition of Chaucer's *Canterbury Tales*). Even if the original motive was business rather than further invention, Caxton's subsequent contributions to spelling and editing played a large part in the growing standardization of the English language.

In our own time, the fact that symbolic artifacts can multiply a thousand- or a millionfold the power of a single idea has had striking implications for the rewards that accrue to those who have ideas that others find useful or attractive. Some people, like Bill Gates, can become billionaires because their ideas can be copied: genius is less than 1 percent inspiration, more than 99 percent replication. Similarly, although musicians worry about the effect of copying on the rewards for their work, it is only since copying of musical performances became possible that some musicians have become seriously rich. Prior to the twentieth century, musicians relied for their rewards on the audiences for their performances, which limited the number of paying admirers to those who could be fitted into a single concert hall. One or two became prosperous through royal patronage, like Jean-Baptiste Lully, who worked for King Louis XIV of France. Others of great creativity could barely scrape a living: Mozart died a pauper. Now musicians of microscopic talent compared to Mozart are multimillionaires, and complain when copies of their songs are downloaded free on the internet. In fact, the evidence is strong that ideas feed the demand for more ideas—as any website manager knows, you will never get people to subscribe for content if you don't give some pretty interesting content away for free. The invention of video recorders did not impoverish, but rather has massively enriched, the studios of Hollywood, which now earn more from video rentals than from ticket sales. It is similarly unlikely that improved copying technology will impoverish the music industry any time soon.

What it will certainly do, though, is to increase spectacularly the gap between the rewards enjoyed by the people whose talents appeal (for whatever reason) to many people and the rewards enjoyed by those whose talents appeal to relatively few.[11] As the economist Robert Frank describes the process:

> Winner-take-all markets have proliferated in part because technology has greatly extended the power and reach of the planet's most gifted performers. At the turn of the century, when the state of Iowa alone had more than 1,300 opera houses, thousands of tenors earned adequate, if modest livings performing before live audiences. Now that most music we listen to is pre-recorded, however, the world's best tenor can be literally everywhere at once. And since it costs no more to stamp out compact discs from Luciano Pavarotti's master recording than from a less renowned tenor's most of us now listen to Pavarotti. Millions of us are each willing to pay a little extra to hear him rather than other singers who are only marginally less able or well known; and this explains why Pavarotti earns several millions of dollars a year even as most other tenors, many of them nearly as talented, struggle to get by.[12]

Not all the rewards of creativity are financial. Some people become less rich than opera stars but nevertheless attract the esteem and admiration of others (esteem being a way in which we reward those who have done things for us that we value more than the market does). As printing increased the audience for books (and reproducible artworks such as engravings) in the seventeenth, eighteenth, and nineteenth centuries, more attention came to be focused on the notion of the individual literary or artistic genius. The quality of the symbolic artifact came to count for more than the sum total of the actions of the person that produced it. This was understandable, given that the former was much more long-lived and had much more direct influence on other people than the latter. Indeed, by a kind of reverse logic, the idea that individual artists might have messy, unfocused, unaesthetic lives came to be seen almost as the touchstone of their artistic authenticity, as though it were a proof of the perfection of the artifact that it could only come to birth at a supreme culminating moment in an individual life. It is a curious flowering of the notion of spiritual attainment that had its roots in the ancient and medieval injunction to people to fashion their whole lives to the glory of God.

Trust between Generations

Thanks to the collective and cumulative knowledge made possible by symbolic artifacts, individual human beings can undertake challenges unimaginable to our hunter-gatherer ancestors. As we have seen in earlier chapters, the possibilities open to humanity have vastly expanded because of the division of labor. But even a single modern, educated individual trying to survive unaided on a desert island would in some respects fare much better than one of our hunter-gatherer ancestors. He would lack the knowledge a hunter-gatherer would have learned from his living elders — and on occasion such knowledge might prove critical for his survival. He might also find that the habits of depending on others for the supply of the goods needed for his daily existence were too difficult to unlearn. But he would have the accumulated knowledge of many generations of those no longer living, transmitted through the symbolic artifacts of cultural exchange. If he survived the initial challenges he would be able to avoid many of the false starts, painful experiences, and deadly traps that lay in wait for our ancestors. Conversely, what hunter-gatherers parachuted into modern life would require in order to cope with its challenges would be not just a capacity to share tasks as elaborately as we do but also the cultural and intellectual inheritance of the generations that have preceded us and which frees us from the need to make every invention anew. To put the matter another way, symbolic artifacts enable an elaborate division of labor *across* generations and not just within them.

In a similar way to the division of labor within generations, therefore, the use of symbolic artifacts also requires an element of trust — trust in the strangers who will interpret our communications in the future. We saw in earlier chapters how trust in modern societies is no longer just a matter of personal psychology, of how you feel about a particular individual. More fundamentally, it is about the set of social institutions that make it reasonable to trust someone enough to exchange with them, regardless of how you feel about them personally. These institutions comprise the law, the mechanisms for enforcing the law, and a whole range of conventions — informal habits and incentives that, taken together, give us a reason to predict the trustworthy behavior of others with an acceptable level of confidence. To the extent that these affect the degree of confidence that a person can have in the contractual promises made by others, such factors make up what we can call the system of property rights in a society. In a similar way, the exercise of symbolic communication is subject to property rights. To use this terminology sounds less strange once we reflect that the purpose of such rights is to enhance our trust in those who will interpret our communications. For trust is of importance to us in a variety of ways, and it will affect the kinds of symbolic communication we are willing to make. And when we look more closely, we see that property rights in symbolic communication have a number of features that make them even more complex than property rights in ordinary physical things.

Take a simple example. Build a better mousetrap, said Emerson, and the world will beat a path to your door, though you build your house in the woods. Suppose I do just that, but my mousetrap is not a piece of elaborate machinery that I must make for you but rather a simple idea that you could implement yourself at a cost much lower than the total benefit to you. I may reasonably think that since my idea benefits you I should obtain some share of that benefit. Indeed, the days I may have spent dreaming up the better mousetrap may have been motivated precisely by the vision of the world's beating a path to my door — my own problems with mice may be rather minor by comparison. What can I do to ensure that you give me some of the benefit you receive from my invention?

In theory, perhaps, I could just sell the idea to you. But that suggestion is more complicated than it sounds, for how can I describe the idea to you with sufficient precision for you to know whether it is worth buying, without revealing the idea to you for free? This problem has been recognized in the public system of intellectual property rights, embodied in the laws on patents, copyright, and trademarks. The basic philosophy is simple. I may be wary of describing the idea of my mousetrap to you, for you may then announce that it is not worth buying, while secretly using it all the same. But suppose I could describe it to a trusted third party, who would ensure that my idea is not trivial, and is genuinely mine, and will exercise some sanctions against you if you use it without paying me. I may be willing to trust such a third party even if I have my doubts about trusting you. The patent office is just such a third party. It acts as an intermediary between those who have ideas and those who wish to use the ideas of others.

Suppose I succeed in patenting my idea, so that others cannot copy it; they must buy the mousetrap that I make and that embodies my idea. The world beats a path to my door and I now become very rich. But I may choose to set a high price that makes me a monopoly profit but denies the product to many potential buyers who could afford the cost of making more mousetraps. Alternatively, although my idea may have been a stroke of genius, I may just not be very good at turning it into a functioning product. My mousetraps may break down more often than if I had sold the rights of manufacture to someone else. A third possibility is that my mousetrap works just fine, but not nearly as well as it might work if someone else were to improve the idea by adding a truly revolutionary improvement of their own. In each of these cases, the property right has rewarded me comfortably for my invention, but at the cost of restricting the transmission of my idea to others. Does this matter, or is it the necessary price a society must pay for the establishment of the institution of trust in the development of ideas?

Until recently most economists and lawyers would have given a fairly simple answer to this question. Monopoly rights over ideas are indeed a cost, but a necessary cost, of giving incentives to people to produce ideas in the first place. After all, most inventions require a large investment of time and resources; the majority don't come serendipitously to the mind of the inventor, as (perhaps) the idea for my mousetrap did. Without the prospect of monopoly rights, people would stop trying to invent and would do something less useful instead. But precisely because they are a cost, the system of patent rights is restricted in time: patents are typically granted for twenty years, no longer. Furthermore, the costs of my monopoly power consist just in the number of mousetraps I refuse to manufacture in order to keep the price high by restricting supply. There's no reason to fear that I shall hold on to my idea when it would be better to sell the idea to someone else who could either manufacture it or improve it better than I could. I can license my patent to another user. And if the other user has a better use for it than I have, I will license the patent, since that other user will be able to pay me more than I would have earned by holding on to it myself. I have every interest, so the argument goes, in the development of better ideas, better versions, than my own. Such better ideas don't compete with mine, but rather enhance them, make them more valuable. If I know what is good for me, I shall encourage their development.

So indeed the argument goes. But the evidence from history is, to say the least, ambiguous on this point, for many innovators have sought to restrict the further development of their ideas. It took the end of Richard Arkwright's patent on the water frame for other inventors to set to work to improve it and incorporate it into related inventions; the most important improvements to James Watt's steam engine had to wait for his patents to expire.[13] Neither of these two great inventors showed much interest in letting others improve on their work, even when these others were willing to pay to do so. Earlier, the Roman Catholic Church had made great efforts to restrict the circulation of printed books, notably through the Index of prohibited publications. These efforts were ultimately unsuccessful, because they caused a flight of intellectuals and their ideas to Protestant countries. In Elizabeth Eisenstein's words, "the influx of religious refugees into Calvin's Geneva in the 1550s radically altered the professional structure of the city. The number of printers and booksellers jumped from somewhere between three and six to some three hundred or more . . . Geneva gained at the French expense." In more recent times, the United States Government alleged, and the American courts upheld, that Microsoft Corporation had sought to block development of the web browser software Netscape Navigator, in spite of the fact that this software would in principle only enhance the value of the Windows operating system to which it was added as an application. Indeed, the vigorous development of the software industry in recent years is evidence (as economists James Bessen and Eric Maskin have argued)[14] that property rights can sometimes block rather than encourage innovation. Patents and copyrights play only a minor role in the software industry; as soon as an important innovation appears, other innovators set to work to try to improve it, rather than waiting twenty years for patents to expire. Similar things happen in other industries, like financial services, where innovation is vigorous and continuous although intellectual property rights play virtually no role.

Although at first sight it might seem strange that those who have new ideas should seek to block the ideas of others that apparently enhance their own, the Catholic Church (like James Watt, Richard Arkwright, and perhaps Microsoft, if the U.S. government's suspicions were correct) may have had a better grasp of its own long-term interests than the conventional argument gives it credit for. Ideas that build on mine and enhance them today may return to challenge them tomorrow — that is not just an unfortunate accident but inherent to the nature of symbolic communication, with its flexibility and its potential for recombining symbols in new and unexpected ways. The Catholic Church understood only too well that a widespread readership even for orthodox works would create a pool of educated outsiders from which heresy might one day return strengthened to challenge the ideas by which it had first been nourished. Microsoft may have feared that even if Netscape's web browser enhanced the value of Windows today, it might develop into a substitute for Windows in the future. Indeed, a number of scholars have recently proposed explanations for the otherwise puzzling wish of some firms to block complementary developments of their existing products in terms of a fear that these developments will provide a springboard for future inventors to challenge those products themselves.[15] The key to this fear is symbolic recombination.

Suppose I have a monopoly over the manufacture of a product with a low level of symbolic complexity: anvils, say, or railway lines. Then anything that improves the quality of other goods that are complementary to my monopoly product — horseshoes and railway services, respectively — will be good news for me, because it will increase the willingness of people to buy my anvils (or railway lines). I may even have an interest in encouraging inventors of new types of horseshoe (or developers of innovative kinds of railway service). Perhaps I give them free access to my monopoly product while they are working on their inventions. Similarly, if I have a monopoly on the production of electricity, I shall be delighted to see inventors develop refrigerators and washing machines, and may even give them cheap electricity to help them to do so; every new power-thirsty invention will give an upward nudge to the demand for my electricity. In each case, the low level of symbolic complexity of my own product makes it extremely unlikely that such generosity will rebound upon me, by giving rise to substitute anvils, alternatives to railways lines, or refrigerators that generate their own electricity. But whenever the symbolic content of my product is high, that is exactly what I shall fear; the possibilities for symbolic recombination are so rich. My ideas may spawn others that turn on their own progenitors.

The human brain's capacity for symbolic tinkering is capable of reinterpreting ideas in a startling and sometimes frightening range of ways. Engineers see in airplanes a triumph of technological coordination and a soaring of the human spirit; psychoanalysts see them as fantasized penises. Some poets and isolated preindustrial peoples have seen them as giant birds, while Japanese wartime strategists and present-day Islamic fundamentalists have looked at the same masses of metal and seen them as bombs. The human mind's capacity for creating poetry is also what has made it so clever at plotting ambush.

By definition, innovators are those who have not been deterred from expressing their ideas in the form of symbolic artifacts. When the first cave painters daubed shapes by firelight onto the walls of the caves of Chauvet, Altamira, or Lascaux, did they fear that one day enemies might use them as evidence of habitation, with which to track down and kill the artists or their descendants? When warriors first used wheels to make chariots, were they deterred by the thought that their enemies would soon copy their ingenuity and come thundering against them in chariots of their own? When the U.S. Department of Defense first developed electronic mail, did it foresee that one day terrorists plotting to attack the United States would use this technology to coordinate their plans? The evidence of successful creativity is all around us, and it may seem on this evidence that the problem of trust between generations has, in this respect at least, been solved, for innovation has been rapid, and accelerating, in recent centuries. But if we focus exclusively on this fact, we may overlook the more subtle fact that innovators have often sought to restrict the subsequent dissemination of their own ideas. How fast innovation takes place will be critical to mankind's ability in the coming century to solve problems that are not standing still, problems such as poverty, disease, and terrorism. So it becomes critical to ask: How well do our systems of intellectual property cope with the problem of intergenerational trust? Do they do enough to make the knowledge of each generation of humanity available to its successors?

PROTECTING THINGS, PROTECTING IDEAS

One way of reacting to the evidence that innovators often block the dissemination of their own ideas is to challenge the very idea that intellectual property should be protected. Economists Michele Boldrin and David Levine have made the radical proposal that society should recognize no property rights at all in ideas as such.[16] Property rights, they suggest, should belong to the world of exchangeable things — many of which, of course, embody ideas. The more powerful the idea embodied in an object, the more valuable it will be to copy, but that is to the advantage, not the disadvantage, of the person who owns the object. For instance, the more people who will eventually want to listen to copies of my new CD, the greater the price I can extract from the first purchaser, who will then enjoy the right to make (and sell) as many copies as he or she desires.

In fact, it is not hard to show that even in a world in which there were no intellectual property rights at all, and the law protected only the ownership of physical objects, creators might be able to receive the full rewards of their creativity. For this to happen, though, requires some quite special circumstances. Imagine I have discovered a new drug that has some remarkable properties. It reverses aging, turns frogs into princes, and cures cancer, all three.[17] Not everyone will value these properties equally, but the drug is nevertheless very valuable indeed. Now imagine that all the possible users of the drug are lined up in an order that reflects how much they value the drug. To the left are the elderly frogs with cancer, to the far right are the healthy young princes. The person at the very far right is someone who values the drug only just fractionally above the cost of producing it and would therefore pay no more than this cost. To his left stands someone who values it a little more. How much would he pay? He would pay as much as it is worth to him, plus what he can get for reselling it to the last person in the line. The person next to *him* would likewise pay what it is worth to him, plus what he might get for reselling it to the person on his right. Adding up along the line, we can see that the first buyer should be willing to pay a sum up to the total of all the values that the buyers in the line attach to taking the drug. In other words, simply by respecting property rights in the physical object *without separately protecting property rights in the idea*, it should be possible to reward the innovators with the full value of what they have created.

Like the Coase theorem that we met in chapter 8,[18] this argument is of course a fantasy rather than a realistic proposal (in fact, the argument is really just an instance of the Coase theorem in another guise). But it is an instructive fantasy, for it helps to draw attention to the particular obstacles that real life places in the way of innovators. One reason why this kind of sequential bargain could not work in reality is that when I invent my drug, I may have difficulty knowing who are the people who value it most (people do not come neatly sorted into lines according to their need for the drug).[19] Another is that even if I could organize an auction to find out who valued it most, it would require a separate auction to transfer each unit of the drug to the next buyer in the fictional line, and by the time these had all been conducted, even the healthy young princes might have died of cancer, old age, or mad frog disease. A third problem is that buyers in each auction might not know how much to bid until they had learned enough about the drug's characteristics to be in a good position to make a pirate copy of it themselves. A fourth problem is that some buyers in the auction might be dissuaded from bidding their true value for the drug by the hope of waiting until its price had come down in a later auction. In short, it's unlikely that without at least some protection for ideas, innovators can ever realistically hope to receive the full value of their innovations to all their users. That is the understanding on which the admittedly imperfect institution of intellectual property is based.

Nevertheless, even with these obstacles the fact remains that the easier it is to copy my drug (and therefore the more patients can potentially benefit from taking it), the greater, in principle, are the rewards I should be able to reap for having invented it. This is a lesson that should be borne in mind when firms complain that they are unable to enforce patent rights in some developing countries. The very possibility of exporting to developing countries at all increases the rewards to be made from selling their products, so increased trade benefits innovators, even if not always by as much as they think they deserve. Indeed, the greater ease of communications across the world has done much to raise the rewards of innovation. Just as satellite dishes make it easier for internationally recognized brands to extend their global reach, so telephones, faxes, email, and the internet have all increased the ease with which products, processes, and business methods can diffuse across national frontiers. Not all of the effects of this are positive, but overall the returns to both innovation and the adoption of the innovations of others are likely to rise.

Intellectual property is best understood, therefore, as an institution — combining a set of formal laws, such as patent and copyright laws, with a set of social conventions, such as those governing scientific citations — that tries to increase our trust in the willingness of others to reward us for our valuable ideas. Assuring us of the complete and unconditional ownership of our ideas would be too extreme a way to do this, since we might do too little to spread the ideas to others. Denying us any ownership of our ideas would also be too extreme: it would encourage the spreading of such ideas as we chose to develop but would make us reluctant to develop them in the first place. (Imagine if the contents of your personal diary and your digital camera were instantly posted on an open-access website as soon as they were created — would you not be more cautious about what you wrote and photographed?) The balance we strike between these two will always be imperfect, will work better in some circumstances than in others, and will in any case need to evolve over time. But when thinking about the right way to strike that balance, we need to remember not just the trust that is its purpose but also how many of our other social institutions have that trust among their intended or unintended consequences. And many of the other institutions of our modern social life need also to be understood as vehicles for the propagation of ideas.

IDEAS AND THE SHAPING OF MODERN INSTITUTIONS

In fact, what Boldrin and Levine have proposed — protect things, not ideas — is no more than many innovators have been doing informally for centuries, and in this idea lies the key to understanding the growth of the modern firm. Much more important to the growth of ideas than the formal protection of the patent system has been a combination of two kinds of informal protection. The first is to embody ideas in things — or, even better, in organizations and institutions. As we saw in chapter 10, what makes firms a distinct alternative to markets as a way of organizing the complex task-sharing of modern society is that firms are able to transmit certain kinds of knowledge between users more effectively than markets can. Partly this is because many important innovations are simply organizational ones: many kinds of international technology transfer, even in the twenty first century, take place not in the high-science contexts of pharmaceuticals and aeronautics but in such diverse and comparatively unglamorous fields as accounting and international hotel management. Partly, though, it is because even technologies which are embodied in physical things — machines or products — need some skill or know-how to be used to their full effect, or to be debugged and maintained, or to be operated with a full awareness of their associated dangers (like the side effects of drug treatments). Many innovators have therefore realized that an organization (a hospital or a firm, for instance) can deliver the innovation in a more effective and trustworthy fashion than through any mere transfer of the physical object via a market transaction. And what a market transaction cannot accomplish, mere theft will never be able to achieve. So no innovator who can provide the organizational support for her innovation need fear that theft will deprive her of all rewards.

Far from making organizations redundant, the information revolution of the late twentieth and early twenty-first centuries has made organizations more important than ever. As anyone who has ever found a million responses to an internet search will realize, more information does not imply more understanding. More and more we need to know what information to screen out in order to help us to understand our world. *Homo sapiens sapiens* has come a long way from the caves of Blombos, Enkapune Ya Muto, and Chauvet. The colorful symbols illuminated by firelight were like beacons in a night that was empty of human meaning (and that prompted man, in his hunger for symbols, to people the forests and the skies with gods). The contrast with the visual cacophony of symbols in the modern urban environment could not be more striking. The psychoanalyst and art critic Adrian Stokes even saw in the jagged sights and sounds of the modern city a version of the disorder suffered by many of the mentally ill.[20] This is not an eccentric hypothesis: one influential recent theory of the causes of schizophrenia, for example, suggests that sufferers lack the ability to screen out irrelevant sensory information that the rest of us unconsciously ignore, and for them the world is an unending howl.[21] Modern man could easily suffer from a collectively generated paranoid schizophrenia in the absence of guidance on how to evaluate the results of each other's endlessly restless creativity.[22] To sort out the emails offering purported remedies for everything from poverty to sexual impotence, or the torrent of solutions for the problems of the world offered by aspiring political leaders, or the bewildering variety of technical specifications for products and processes available from suppliers across the world, all of us will continue to need the advice and good judgment of people we can trust. Symbolic communication has not abolished the problem of trust but has merely shifted it: from wanting to know whether we can trust an individual to wanting to know whether we can trust some collective source of information. As a result, the internet, like the other manifestations of the information revolution, may radically change the nature of firms and other such organizations, but it will never make them disappear.

There is a second way in which creativity has been historically protected without formal systems of intellectual property rights, and that is through the support of political organizations of various kinds. The historian David Landes has written, following earlier work by Eric Jones, that one of the main reasons why the industrial revolution took place in Europe before China (in spite of China's awesome technological advances during the Middle Ages and a period of impressive growth under the Sung Dynasty over seven centuries before Europe's industrialization) was the continual competition for supremacy between Europe's shifting and decentralized political powers.[23] This meant that innovators whose ideas were insufficiently appreciated in one place might seek out the support and protection of another (we saw above how this worked to the benefit of Protestant Geneva). In China an innovation that failed to capture the favor of the emperor might not merely languish but even be suppressed. Landes recounts how the magnificent Chinese naval expeditions of the early fifteenth century, whose "flotillas far surpassed in grandeur the small Portuguese fleets that came later," were deliberately halted by imperial decree: "By 1500, anyone who built a ship of more than two masts was liable to the death penalty, and in 1525 coastal authorities were enjoined to destroy all oceangoing ships and arrest their owners. Finally, in 1551, it became a crime to go to sea on a multi-masted ship, even for trade."[24] The Chinese emperor feared no one, certainly no foreigner. Europe's potentates, in contrast, lived in a continual climate of beneficial and creative fear.

Political organizations have intervened in many ways in the workings of modern societies, often to very good effect. But just as with the merchants about whom Adam Smith was so cynical, their motivations have often been far less elevated than their rhetoric. Creativity has received much support from emperors and princes throughout the ages, often in the hope that it could be turned to aggressive as well as defensive ends. We shall explore some of the consequences of this public support for innovation in chapter 13. First, however, we shall look at one more of the great unintended consequences of the division of labor in modern society: the exclusion of the unfortunate.

CHAPTER 12

Exclusion: Unemployment, Poverty, and Illness

The Unemployed

I visited Kiev, the capital of Ukraine, for the first time in 1995. The country was in a deep economic recession, so I was surprised to see evidence of a great deal of construction activity. For several kilometers along the road from the airport to the center of town, half-finished tower blocks could be seen, clad in scaffolding and dominated by soaring cranes. There were trucks, cement-mixers, piles of builders' sand. After we had driven for some minutes past this astonishing expanse of building site, I was struck by an oddity, and asked my host, "Is today a public holiday?" He shook his head. "I know what you're thinking," he said. "There's no one working there. There hasn't been anyone for at least a couple of years." Suddenly this great panorama of buildings, vehicles, and equipment, which had seemed to bear witness to a frenzy of activity, became a bleak symbol of exactly the opposite — of so catastrophic a slump in construction work that no one had bothered to remove those items of equipment that could be salvaged. There was no point in salvaging them if there was no work elsewhere for them to do.

In this scene the unemployed workers, in contrast to the unemployed equipment, were invisible. They were probably at home, either fired from their jobs or on what is euphemistically termed "short-time working," which consoles them with the theoretical possibility of being recalled in the unlikely event that demand picks up sometime soon. In modern Western societies, many of the casualties of economic recession, like the casualties of poverty or illness, are similarly inconspicuous, but this does not mean they are nonexistent, or few in number. Sometimes they become visible in ways that can seem startling to those used to the apparently orderly activity of busy people. The historian Piers Brendon has described what he calls "one of the most shocking instances of state coercion in American history." It took place during the Great Depression, when in 1932 "20,000 unemployed Great War veterans converged on Washington DC":

> Arriving in the capital from all over the country, their numbers swollen by the attendant publicity . . . the veterans put up huts in open spaces or squatted in empty buildings near the seat of government. Most camped on the mosquito-

ridden Anacostia mud-flats, nicknamed "Hard-Luck-on-the-River" . . . They kept it as clean and sanitary as possible, digging latrines . . . and even cultivating small gardens. Some brought their families. The men were dignified and disciplined . . . [but nevertheless] frustration led to confrontation.[1]

When veterans occupied several buildings near the Capitol that were due for demolition, General Douglas MacArthur, the army chief of staff later to achieve fame and notoriety in the Pacific and Korea, decided to "break the back" of the demonstration. "So, late in the afternoon of 28 July, four troops of cavalry, six whippet tanks and four companies of steel-helmeted infantry with fixed bayonets and machine guns advanced down Pennsylvania Avenue . . . beating terrified people with the flats of their sabers. . . . Scores of people were injured." The buildings were emptied and the shantytown was torched. The government defended the actions of MacArthur although the latter had exceeded his orders, as he was later to do more dramatically and dangerously during the Korean War. (He had already provoked widespread derision when he claimed to the press that the veterans were "animated by the essence of revolution"). Though there is evidence that many members of the administration, even Hoover himself, were genuinely disturbed by the massive numbers of unemployed in depression America, the episode made clear that the unemployed were expected by the authorities to remain inconspicuous. The more visible they were, the greater the panic their presence induced. It was the sense of breaking a prohibition that gave a hard political edge to the work of a photographer like Walker Evans, who sought to make the victims of the depression visible to the rest of America. In fact Evans came into conflict with his employer the Farm Security Administration, whose photographic project was intended to show the possibility of a "better future" for America's rural poor, a possibility Evans's bleak documentary realism seemed to deny.[2]

The Great Depression popularized the notion that unemployment and periodic economic collapse were particular characteristics of industrial capitalism, the dark side of capitalism's undoubted vigor and productivity in its sunnier spells. Coming so soon after the boom years of the 1920s, the depression also provoked the belief that capitalism was, of all economic systems, the one most peculiarly prone to cycles of boom and bust, with the good times buoyed up by nothing more solid than optimism and the bad times locked in by collective gloom. Wall Street, the center of the financial markets, was nothing more than the casino in which these paroxysms of optimism and pessimism were played out in gambles made by financiers with other people's money and other people's lives.

Boom, Bust and the Division of Labor

In fact, though boom and bust in the modern world are alarmingly dependent on an evanescent state of confidence, this is neither new nor peculiar to modern industrial capitalism. It is deeply embedded in the division of labor itself and is a danger in purely agricultural societies as well as industrial ones. To see why, think of a simple society, without the use of money, in which farmers face a choice between growing grain and doing one of two other activities: baking bread or raising cattle for meat and milk. Both of these activities have characteristics that make them dependent on trust. In a society where the division of labor is well established, some farmers will grow grain and exchange it with others who bake bread or raise cattle, since there are advantages in specialization. Not everyone wants to own or can effectively operate a baking oven; not everyone has the skills or the equipment appropriate to cattle-farming. We may suppose that both bakers and cattle-farmers will need grain to use in their own production, for feeding the ovens or the bovines, as well as to eat while they are waiting for their own production to take place. The difference between them is that cattle-farmers need more grain, and they need it for longer. Bakers can take grain and return it to the donor in a day or so in the form of bread; cattle-farmers take grain and return it in the form of meat or milk many months later. This implies that while both baking and cattle-farming need trust, they need it to different degrees.

For much of the time, we can imagine, the need for trust in this society is fairly latent. Bakers give bread directly in return for grain; cattle-farmers offer meat and milk directly for the grain they need — each one acquires the inputs necessary for future production by offering the output of production in the past. For established citizens, there is no problem; it's a straight swap. Young bakers and cattle-farmers starting up in business, on the other hand, have to persuade grain-growers to lend them grain until they have produced enough bread, milk, or meat to repay the loan. Becoming a cattle-farmer needs more trustworthiness than becoming a baker, but normally speaking there should be a ready supply of young recruits to both activities.

Now imagine a crisis of trust in this simple society. Perhaps the word goes round that the harvest may fail, grain may become scarce, and the bakers and livestock farmers will no longer repay the grain they owe, preferring to hoard it instead. Or perhaps echoes of a distant ethnic conflict make arable farmers (from tribe A) suddenly doubtful about the trustworthiness of bakers (from tribe B) and openly hostile to cattle-farmers (from tribe C). In this new atmosphere of suspicion, arable farmers may no longer be willing to lend their grain to either bakers or cattle-farmers.

If the crisis is comparatively mild, it may be bakers who suffer worst, since cattle-farmers can live for some time off their own stocks of meat and milk, while the bakers have only a few days' stock to live on. In a more severe crisis, the cattle-farmers may suffer more, since their cattle will die or be taken from them by force, to repay the past loans of grain on which they have defaulted purely because no one would lend them any grain for the future. The bakers will have no grain either, but they will have fewer debts hanging over them and may be able to pick themselves up more easily if the crisis passes. Both bakers and cattle-farmers may think wistfully how much easier everything would have been if they had only stuck to growing grain (siren voices may even call for a return to permanent self-sufficiency in the future). Eventually, the scarcity of bread, meat, and milk will make some more adventurous spirits think about setting up as bakers or cattle-farmers again, and some adventurous fellow-citizens willing to lend them grain in order to get going. But there will have been a cycle of boom and bust driven by nothing more than the waxing and waning of trust. And not a factory or a stock-market in sight.

This parable naturally simplifies many of the processes at work in modern industrial societies. We are supposing that cattle-farmers may become bankrupt and unemployed because other people stop trusting cattle-farmers. In modern societies, though, it is just as likely that machine operators will become unemployed because other people stop trusting finance directors. Or a crisis of confidence in the housing market may lead to a fall in house prices, which means that banks will earn less on mortgage loans and thus have less capital to lend to businesses. So a firm making shirts can go bankrupt purely because some people have changed their minds about the reliability of houses as investments for the future. Because of the multiplicity of trust relations in the modern world, the failure of some particular trust relation can hurt individuals who were never part of that trust relation in the first place. In spite of its simplification, though, what the parable shows very clearly is that losses of confidence are a risk that is inherent in any society dependent on the division of labor, whenever that division of labor requires (as it almost always does) that some individuals depend on the trust of others in order to be able to specialize. And the more elaborate the division of labor the greater the possibilities for the web of trust that sustains it to unravel.

Sometimes trust is too easily gained, and charlatans abuse it. Would-be cattle-ranchers may find it easy to borrow enormous quantities of grain on the strength of a swagger and a Stetson. Or shares in dot.com start-ups may trade for vast prices without any profits in prospect (the strength of the share price is an indicator of the ease with which the firm's owners are borrowing money). Sometimes, on the other hand, trust is too hard to acquire, and honest, competent people cannot make a living or may even lose the living they had previously been making. In the early twenty-first century, as in the 1930s, we may think that stock markets are primarily to blame, since in the late 1990s, as in the late 1920s, stock markets inflated the boom in a way that postponed and magnified the subsequent bust. Stock markets increase the dangers, by their very efficiency at bringing together borrowers and lenders, entrepreneurs and investors, people with ideas and families with savings. No way has yet been devised, nor will any ever be, to give us more opportunities to invest for our future without giving us more chances to be cheated through others' exploiting our overwhelming desire to become rich. But as this parable should teach us, stock market booms and crashes are just one particular modern manifestation of trust cycles, and trust cycles are a problem that has much older roots.

The economist Robert Shiller has argued that modern stock markets are vulnerable to cycles of collective optimism and pessimism for reasons that are due to our evolutionary history:

> Evolutionary changes within the human brain have optimized the channels of communication and created an emotional drive to communicate effectively. It is because of this emotional drive that most people's favorite activity is conversation. Look around you. Everywhere you go, when two or more people are not working or playing or sleeping (and in some cases, even when they are doing these things), they are talking. . . . The information that tends to flow most rapidly is the kind that would have helped society in centuries past in its everyday living: information about such things as food sources, dangers, or other members of society. For this reason, in modern society there is likely to be rapidly spreading conversation about a buying opportunity for a hot stock, or about immediate threats to personal wealth, or about the story of people who run a company.[3]

The research of Shiller and his colleagues has shown that many share-buying decisions are made as a result of word-of-mouth communication, especially around crucial events such as stock market crashes. This makes sense if the information being communicated is information that is fundamentally about trust. The false intimacy of television can also reinforce the impression that we are being given reliable information, directed to us as individuals by trustworthy people. Such communication creates the possibility of "information cascades," whereby small pieces of news, or rumor, or even changes in gut sentiment, can be magnified into large movements in share prices that have momentous consequences for whole societies. Such movements can often correct themselves, and it is unlikely that information cascades would be so powerful if they were always or even usually misleading. As Shiller emphasizes, there is nothing irrational about relying on word-of-mouth information; over our evolutionary history as a whole, it has proved a spectacularly successful way of coping with threats to our survival and prosperity. But in a world of crowds it can sometimes have consequences evolution could not possibly have foreseen. Trust as the social glue of mass societies was an unintended by-product of the word-of-mouth communication developed in hunter-gatherer bands. And unintended by-products cannot possibly be guaranteed free of flaws.

The 1930s, with their terrible economic conditions and the terrible political events to which they gave rise popularized the idea that modern industrial capitalism was peculiarly unstable. The experience of the Great Depression also popularized the idea that the job of modern governments was to step in to control this instability. This is an attractive and reasonable idea, but also a dangerous one. Modern industrial capitalism is indeed unstable, though not uniquely so in our history and not for historically unprecedented reasons. Markets are indeed full of charming optimists (not to mention downright charlatans) seeking to capitalize on our trust, but so are governments and political parties. Our political opinions are no less dependent on word-of-mouth communication and no less vulnerable to information cascades than our investment opinions — sometimes more so, since we are less often required to back our opinions with our own money. Experts too are vulnerable: while it's true that normally shrewd investors can become strangely gullible under the influence of market enthusiasm, so can normally shrewd regulators. After all, it was the famously cautious Alan Greenspan, chairman of the United States Federal Reserve Board and the most powerful economic official in the world, who in 1996 warned about the "irrational exuberance" of stock markets and within a year, having overlooked his own warning, was suggesting that the extraordinary levels of share prices were warranted by a radical change in the nature of the American economy — rather as the economist Irving Fisher had crowed in 1929 that "stock prices have reached what looks like a permanently high plateau." In effect, Greenspan was so conscious of the need to avoid undermining public confidence in the level of stock prices, and thus creating a crash, that he did nothing but talk stock prices up, with damaging effects on confidence that were the more serious for being delayed.[4] The moral, therefore, is that the division of economic labor certainly leaves us open to cycles of boom and bust. But so does the division of labor between citizens, the politicians they elect, and the regulators whom those politicians appoint. Only if we are alive to the way in which trust is taken and given in the various arenas that make up modern society will we be able to use the institutions in which trust remains healthy to cure the deficiency of the institutions in which trust has decayed.

In a year when the world economy is functioning comparatively well, there are perhaps 30 million people in the industrialized countries alone who are registered as unemployed — roughly equal to the populations of Canada or Morocco. In a bad year, there may be over twice that number, and if they all stood in a single line for their dole payments, the line might stretch from New York to Las Vegas or from London to Moscow. In fact, they are dispersed and comparatively inconspicuous. Many of them — and proportionately more in the bad years — are like the bakers and cattle-farmers in our parable. They are people whose role in the division of labor was established on the basis of a trust that has now evaporated, and who will now have to pick themselves up and start again, perhaps in the same role once the blizzard has passed, perhaps in a new one. In the meantime, though, the stresses upon them are severe, since unemployment means the loss not just of income but also of self-confidence and the sense of belonging. Some of the unemployed, less disturbingly, are between jobs. (In just the same way, some of the passengers on a railway will be waiting at the station, between trains.) Some, however, are unemployed for a different reason: the only work they can do is so unproductive and so exhausting that it is better to opt out altogether. This last kind of unemployment certainly occurs in the industrialized world and can be unintentionally provoked by tax-and-benefit systems that penalize people by withdrawing benefits as soon as they begin to earn even a small wage. But it is in the developing world, and especially in its rural areas, that this kind of unemployment is chronic, desperate — and visible everywhere.

POVERTY AND INFORMATION ISLANDS

Kovilur is a small hamlet in the arid plain at the center of the state of Tamil Nadu in south India. After the rains, the inhabitants plant fields of sorghum and millet in the newly softened earth, but in the dry season the ground is a dusty brick-red. The village is made up of around thirty houses, some of mud, some of concrete, grouped in straggling fashion around a temple whose high, trapezoid tower, decorated with statues of Hindu gods, stands in magnificent silhouette against the evening sky. The temple, though run-down and rarely visited, is unusually fine even by the standards of southern India, but in many other respects this village and its neighboring hamlets are little different from millions of others across the developing world. There is significant malnutrition among their inhabitants; preventable illnesses like polio still claim victims; few children go to school. And many people spend long hours motionless, inactive, in whatever shade they can find. They are unemployed.

That's not to say they have nothing to do. Most women still rise at 4 A.M., to sweep the house and prepare breakfast for their men and profit from the cool hours around dawn to fetch water and firewood, often walking several kilometers with a cluster of branches on their head or a swaying pot on their hip. They may not get to sleep before 11 P.M. or midnight, and most complain that exhaustion is the permanent color of their lives. The younger and fitter men rise at six and leave their village by seven in quest of work. Those who have bicycles are lucky. Those who don't, like the women whom social regulation prevents from riding alone, are confined to searching for work within walking distance.

Such work exists. The village of Manipuram, some twelve kilometers away, is a crowded, bustling place in the green zone irrigated by the waters of the great river Cauvery.[5] Fields of rice paddy, banana, and sugarcane crowd the available space, and in the waterlogged areas, reeds are harvested, to be woven into mats. Preparing and drying the reeds provides work for many, especially for women and children, though men will work at this too during lean times. The merchants who manage the preparations, delivering bundles of harvested reeds to the workers and collecting the dried results, complain that it is hard to get as many workers as they would like. So why are the workers only twelve kilometers away still unemployed?

It makes no sense for the merchants to take the reeds to the workers. Newly harvested reeds are heavy, full of moisture, and expensive to transport. Processed reeds are dry and light, so it makes sense for the processing to happen near to where the reeds are grown and for the transport to happen afterward. So why don't the workers come to the reeds? Twelve kilometers may seem like nothing to a visiting foreigner with a car, but it is a whole pilgrimage to an undernourished worker who must walk in the hot sun with no assurance of being able to find work at the end (those who do make the journey find work only three-quarters of the time, and they are the optimistic, well-connected ones). When you have little enough to eat in the first place, you must conserve your limited energy rather than gamble it on speculative ventures.

To put it another way, a hungry man can be a formidable competitor, but a hungry man who has to walk a long way first is no competitor at

all. The result is that the comparatively flourishing job market in Manipuram has little impact on the lives of those who live in Kovilur.
These two villages may be no more than a few kilometers apart, but
economically they are in different worlds.

How can we understand why the world excludes some of its potentially productive citizens in this way? The answer lies in the kinds of
connection that individual citizens have with others in their society.
Much of the history of the last ten thousand years, as we have seen in
earlier chapters, has been about individuals being brought closer to
strangers—either physically closer, as the barriers to movement have
fallen, or closer in the space of knowledge (two people on opposite sides
of the world can know enough about each other to engage in multi-
million dollar transactions with as much confidence as they have in
crossing the street). Yet the more sophisticated the modern division of
labor becomes, the more we risk being brought up sharply against its
limits. Someone may feel comfortable lending money to a foreign banker
she has never met, but hesitant to lend money to the man in the next-
door apartment. Who is he, and what is his track record with other
people's money? The man next door is not physically remote from her,
but as far as her ability to trust him is concerned, he is living on an
information island.

Every village in a poor country is an information island. This does
much to explain why decades of foreign aid, not to mention large flows
of private capital from rich to poor countries, have made so much less
impact on poverty in the developing world than optimists about global
integration have hoped. Investors remain reluctant to invest in societies
about which they know very little, and for good reason, since when
they do invest, they often make foolish choices. And the ignorance of
investors may begin as close as the end of the street. So villagers in
Kovilur cannot raise funds for businesses or schools—some cannot even
raise money to buy bicycles. They remain confined to farm labor which
leaves them hungry and weak. Their hunger and weakness leave them
less able to impress outsiders with their potential for making good use
of investment resources, or even with their reliability for a simple but
demanding task like working the land.

Not only does modern society often fail to build bridges to those on
information islands; it can even, in subtle but sometimes devastating
ways, weaken those bridges that already exist. The way it does so is
through a process known as "assortative matching," whose importance
in explaining the persistence of poverty and exclusion is only gradually
coming to be given proper recognition.[6] We saw in chapter 11 that some
of society's most important institutions, such as firms, are those that
channel information more effectively among their members than is pos-

sible through the comparatively anonymous institutions of the market. Something similar is true of villages in the developing world; their inhabitants, rich and poor, have far fewer secrets from each other than is possible in cities or in the dormitory villages common in parts of the rich world. Certainly, information flows far more freely within villages than between them. A bank official might know exactly who could be trusted to repay a loan among the inhabitants of his own village but might be completely baffled when required to make the same judgment in a village a few kilometers away, and might not even know whom he could reliably ask for advice.

If institutions such as firms and villages are effective information channels, it matters who belongs to the same institutions as you do. People who can make effective use of the information they have are also people who can transmit such information effectively to their fellow members. This is a simple point but one with profound consequences. For as modern society has improved the ease with which people can travel, search for jobs, choose where to live, or find suitable marriage partners or business associates, the membership of society's most important institutions has begun to sort itself into a hierarchy of skill that increasingly replaces the old hierarchy of birth. Talented individuals move out of their villages to mingle with other talented individuals in the towns. High earners marry other high earners. Gifted workers frustrated by the constraints of a large organization leave to form start-ups with similarly gifted colleagues. Parents dissatisfied with the education their children are receiving sell their house to move to a better-funded (because more prosperous) school district. This restless ambition of the talented is often the source of much creativity, but it has consequences for those they leave behind. In recent years, for instance, it has been cited as the source of important changes in the structure of businesses in rich countries. Whereas (to caricature the facts a little) the typical American firm of the 1950s might have been General Motors, a firm employing both high-skill and low-skill individuals, the typical firms of the twentieth century are Microsoft (employing mainly high-skill people) and McDonald's (employing mainly low-skill people). The fact that the high-skilled and the low-skilled are now less likely even to work in the same firms matters, precisely because of the way that information flows more effectively within firms than between them.

ASSORTATIVE MATCHING

How is this happening? Recent theories of assortative matching have been casting important light on the process, in contexts as diverse as labor markets, education, sexual behavior, and financial markets. A fundamental insight of such theories is that each person's productivity — the value to herself or to others of what she produces — depends not just on her own talent and effort but on the talent and effort of those she works with. This is an insight with which most people who work in large organizations and dream of how productive they might be if they were not held back by their mediocre colleagues would wholeheartedly agree (their colleagues probably feel the same way about them). It implies that individuals impose externalities on each other in firms, just as they do in cities, as we saw in chapter 7 (cities, after all, are information channels, just as firms are). The presence of such externalities alerts us to the possibility of some pathological effects at the level of society as a whole.

A powerful implication of such theories is that if individuals can choose their working colleagues, the result is likely to be much more damaging to those with low ability than it would be if individuals were obliged to work with those whom chance (or birth, tradition, or family history) had happened to give them as neighbors. In effect, free choice leads to sorting, in which the talented pair off with the talented and the rest with the rest. As a result, people of low ability are twice cursed: first by their own low ability and then again by the low ability of those with whom they are obliged to work.[7] Another consequence is that people of high ability have a greater incentive to invest in making themselves even more productive, because the value of that investment will not be diminished by the low productivity of the people they have to work with.

It's worth looking a little more carefully at how this happens. Consider an extreme version of the theory that says a person's productivity depends on her colleagues. Call it the "weakest-link" theory of production: the productivity of a whole team depends on the talent and effort of the weakest member of the team. (The economist Michael Kremer has dubbed this the "O-ring" theory of production, after the ring of rubber sealant whose failure caused the explosion of the space shuttle *challenger* on takeoff in 1986, thereby illustrating the dependence of a vast and expensive piece of equipment on the functioning of one simple component).[8] Suppose teams are initially made up of random mixes of talented and untalented people, and that with a bit of investment any person's talents can be improved by the appropriate training. In each team it makes sense to concentrate the investment on the least talented person, because that person is the weakest link whose lack of talent weakens the whole team. So, through society as a whole, looking after the disadvantaged turns out to be a good bet for the others.

Now suppose people can choose their colleagues. Everyone would like to have talented colleagues, of course, so somehow there has to be a mechanism for rationing such people out. Suppose the mechanism is like an auction. It doesn't have to be a literal auction: it could work through the job market or the housing market, in which people (or the firms they represent) pay for the privilege of having talented colleagues or successful neighbors. It's easy to see that those who are talented and successful themselves will be willing to bid more in this auction, because those whom they recruit will be more productive than if they worked with less talented bidders. Consequently the talented will match with the talented.

Let's now consider the effect of this on incentives to invest in making people more productive, through education or on-the-job training. It will still be true that, within any one working group, it makes sense to concentrate investment on the least talented (because of the "weakest link" effect). But more talented groups will face a higher return on their investment than less talented groups, because each newly educated person will be working with more talented colleagues. The result is likely to be ghettoes of low talent, with low rates of investment and growth, and neighborhoods of high talent with high rates of investment and growth.

A useful analogy is with investment in the bandwidth of internet connections. Many people who have installed broadband connections advertising download speeds of ten megabytes per second have been disappointed to discover that their actual download speeds are a tiny fraction of this rate. The speed of anyone's download is determined by the slowest connection in the link between the source and destination computers. Consequently, in any one network it makes sense to concentrate investment on the slowest connection. But a network with faster connections on average will still see a bigger improvement in download times for any given investment. This accounts for the snowball effect of broadband connections: when nobody else has them, they are not worth the expense, but the more other people own them the more valuable they become. Such effects — sometimes called "network externalities" — arise whenever technologies connect people, whether by broadband, by telephone, or even by horse and cart along a dirt track.[9] Put simply, it takes two to connect, and it's not worth connecting if there's no one to connect to. The loneliness of the underconnected global citizen accounts, in one way or another, for much of the economic stagnation that persists in the midst of global plenty, blighting the lives of billions of people across the world.

This is not to say that technology alone is the answer to the problems of the isolated poor like the villagers of Kovilur. Kovilur is not cut off physically from the world. Its inhabitants make the journey out; development workers, government officials, traveling merchants (balancing pots and pans precariously in beehive formation on the back of their bicycles) all make the journey in. Travelers with a religious mission occasionally arrive to do puja at the temple, which was a famous pilgrimage destination in former years. Bankers visit to make loans to those farmers who can credibly promise to repay. But in spite of these contacts, the village moneylenders still do regular business at interest rates far above those charged by banks in the towns. Too many children leave school after a year or two of fruitless study, barely able to sign their names. Those who do continue their studies, in a school whose single teacher often does not show up for class, may be unable afterward to find any work more rewarding than hard labor in the fields. Toddlers can be seen sitting in front of their huts with the sticky look of the malnourished; polio victims move around angularly on skeletal legs. The village has much potential, but it is not developed. Those who might help it to develop cannot trust its inhabitants enough to make the effort seem worthwhile, and its inhabitants lack the experience and self-confidence to project themselves as credible participants in the demanding rituals of the outside world. In the center of a world that is interconnected as never before in history, Kovilur, like hundreds of thousands of villages across India and millions across the world, remains an information island.

Illness and Exclusion

Some prosperous citizens of rich countries can also feel like islands in an uncomprehending sea, cut off from the compact of trust that sustains the majority of their fellow citizens. In any year it is estimated that some 17.5 million Americans suffer from clinical depression, though fewer than half of these receive treatment. In 1999 just under 30,000 Americans committed suicide (according to official figures), making it the third most common cause of death among young people, only a little less common than homicide; it's likely that quite a number of deaths classified as accidents (especially car accidents) were suicide as well. In the world as a whole, around a million people a year commit suicide, and the rate has been climbing steadily in the half century that internationally comparable records have been kept. The cause of suicide is mysterious. At an individual level, it's often linked to economic distress: suicide rates go up in recessions and down in booms (the rates in America declined every year from 1994 to 1999, for instance). Yet poor countries are not necessarily more vulnerable than rich ones. Countries in Latin America have much lower rates than the United States or Canada, and the Latin countries in southern Europe (Italy, Spain, and Portugal) have much lower rates than Austria, Germany, and Switzerland. There are some other startling discrepancies in the incidence of suicide. Men kill themselves four times as often as women, though women make more suicide attempts. The Netherlands has a male suicide rate only 40 percent that of neighboring Belgium. Norway, Sweden, and Denmark have only middling rates by world standards (contrary to folk wisdom and the impression cultivated assiduously by Ibsen, Strindberg, and Bergman), but Finland has a male suicide rate nearly twice as high as theirs. Contrary to folk wisdom too, the suicide rate among blacks and Native Americans in the United States is lower than it is among whites. It is in Eastern Europe and the former Soviet Union that suicide has reached epidemic proportions, with more than one in two thousand Russian, Ukrainian, Kazakh, Latvian, Hungarian, and Lithuanian men killing themselves every year.[10]

No economic theory is ever likely to explain convincingly why one person rather than another succumbs to depression or suicide: depression is an illness, with organic as well as cognitive causes. But the treatment of depression is an economic phenomenon, consuming enormous economic resources. Both the reported incidence and the nature of depression, like that of other mental and nonmental illnesses, respond to economic incentives and are shaped by economic constraints. Most of the difficult choices in medicine, involving how much to spend on a person's treatment and what exactly to spend it on, are made by healthy people on behalf of people who are sick. That means they respond to the healthy person's sense of priorities. This, though it sounds alarming, is both inevitable and, on balance, desirable. But the result is to increase the isolation felt by the sick themselves.

The healthy decide on behalf of the sick in two main ways. First, healthy people decide how much to spend on care of the sick, instead of on other things. Often those decisions are made by the patients themselves, before they become sick. I may choose between different levels of health insurance, some of which cost more today but give me more generous benefits if I fall ill. When illness strikes, I may regret that I was not more generous in my choice of insurance program, but that doesn't imply that my choice was foolish. We should all make provision for a rainy day, but we should also live while the sun shines without expecting to know just when or how often rain will fall. Our choices of health insurance will depend on how great we think the risks are, as well as how much we need to put aside to pay for them. Yet however wisely we make these choices, when we fall ill we come to know something we did not know before, something which estranges us a little from the healthy person we were then.

Often, though, decisions are made by some healthy members of society about the resources to be devoted to other people who are sick. This may be because there is a national health service in the country concerned, as there is in the United Kingdom; we can think of this as a choice to have collective health insurance, with premiums paid compulsorily through the tax system. Or it may be because some individuals have not insured themselves (whether through ignorance, poverty, or deliberate choice) and lack the resources to fund their own treatment. Most modern societies are unwilling to live with the consequences of letting uninsured people fend entirely for themselves. There exist public hospitals, albeit crowded and underfunded ones, in many countries that have no national health service as such. Alternatively, healthy people may direct resources to the sick because they have a direct individual interest in their fate. Particularly through infectious disease, the sick create important externalities for others that, as we saw in chapter 7, no modern society can afford to ignore.

The second way the healthy decide on behalf of the sick is by advising how given health budgets should be spent. This can be a matter of advising a sick person how to make choices among the various treatments available, given the resources she has. Or it can be a matter of advising a funder — an insurance company, a hospital, a public authority — as to who is sick and how sick they are. Usually, in fact, it is both at the same time. In either case, the decision must be made not just by someone who is well but by someone with the appropriate medical skills. The patient herself may need advice not just because she is inexpert but also because her illness interferes with her judgment. But even a patient with unimpaired judgment will need the advice of someone with experience and scientific knowledge. And in the face of serious illness, in which a patient is brought into the anteroom of her own mortality, she needs to feel she can trust the humanity and not just the expertise of her medical advisers.

So the patient has someone making decisions on her behalf, decisions that have important consequences for her state of health but also for the resources available to treat others (every time a doctor recommends a patient for urgent surgery, other patients on the surgeon's list have to wait a little longer). The patient trusts the doctor to act on her behalf, and the doctor's Hippocratic oath is a solemn commitment to do just that. And yet (though the Hippocratic oath does not state this explicitly, and many doctors feel acutely uncomfortable even discussing this awkward fact about their professional orientation) almost all medical consultations are conducted on behalf of some funder, some economic institution, as well as on behalf of the patient herself. The doctor must not exaggerate the patient's condition purely in order to win her more rapid treatment, although common sense and simple humanity often lead doctors to give the patient the benefit of the doubt. Doctors may prescribe a drug or an operation but they do so knowing the rules of the institution they represent, rules that determine priorities for allocating resources. When is an operation to remove secondary tumors a waste of resources that could save a patient whose cancer is less far advanced? When is cosmetic surgery a vital aid for recovery after a disfiguring accident rather than just a way of pretending to avoid the aging process? When is Viagra appropriate? Medical decisions are not simply diagnostic; they are economic through and through.

The Inevitable Distortions of Delegated Decision-Making

The economic consequences of having someone else make decisions on your behalf have been studied in a vast array of contexts in recent years, from the relations between bosses and workers to those between politicians and the electorate, from the way farmers made decisions to the way governments allocate foreign aid. What has come to be known as the "principal-agent problem" describes the many ways in which a person who needs something done (known as the principal) can motivate her agent (her doctor, say) to act as closely in accordance with her interests as possible.[11] The motivations that matter most in medicine are rarely simply financial; doctors may care about money, but they rarely care just about money. They also care about their patients, about their role as objective scientists, and about the esteem of their professional colleagues — being struck off for medical negligence is a blow that costs a doctor far more than loss of earnings. But economic incentives can work through manipulating esteem as well. A system in which doctors can be sued for failing to operate but cannot be sued for performing an operation that was unnecessary will ineluctably lead to an increase in unnecessary operations. And fear of being held responsible can work through even more indirect channels. As one medical case study puts it, "one reason doctors put patients in the hospital is simply to have them rest and be taken care of . . . [but] in the hospital it is easy for physicians (unless they stop and think about it) to perform unnecessary procedures simply because the means for doing so are readily available."[12] Sometimes the pressure is in the other direction: it can be difficult to get admission to the hospital at all for some conditions, particularly where diagnosis is as difficult as it is in mental health. The outcome is paradoxical: too much treatment for some conditions, too little for others, and inadequate time in the hospital combined with too much high-technology intervention while there.

Many case studies of medical practice have emphasized how economic pressures shape the way doctors think about their patients, and how these pressures can affect trust. Two features of medicine make this tension particularly acute. One is that doctors are forced to be servants of two masters: their patients and those who are paying their patients' bills. In many industrialized countries the costs of health care have been rising dramatically, as technology has advanced, as expectations have risen, and as the comparatively cheap diseases of poverty have given way to the expensive, chronic diseases of affluence. The response, both by public authorities and by private insurers, has been to squeeze budgets, demand more explicit justification for each intervention, and demand that doctors play the role of resource managers in much more explicit ways than they have been used to. In the United States this has come about largely through what is known as "managed care," in which insurance companies, instead of simply reimbursing medical expenses after treatment, require hospitals to negotiate explicit treatment regimes with them even before such treatment takes place. Though such pressures are in some respects inevitable, many doctors find them not only difficult but counterproductive. They can undermine the very relationship of trust that is central to the therapeutic relationship between doctor and patient in the first place.

The second feature of medicine that adds to the tension is that only some treatments for illness have an immediate, verifiable impact. Those that don't may be no less important, but their appropriateness for the particular case is much harder to demonstrate to the satisfaction of an insurer or a hospital manager. The economists Bengt Holmstrom and Paul Milgrom have shown that when agents working for a principal are forced to choose between tasks whose results are easy to verify and tasks that are important but hard to verify, they not only cut back on the tasks that are hard to verify but may even put too much effort into the easy ones![13] In medical terms that means too many drugs, too little of almost everything else. Anthropologist Tanya Luhrmann has described this process at work in American psychiatry. It's harder to do research on the effectiveness of psychotherapy than on the effectiveness of drug treatments. And it's harder to do research on the long-term impact of drug treatments than on their ability to provide immediate symptomatic relief. It's harder to show the value of in-patient treatment beyond its effect on stabilizing the condition of individuals in crisis. So the budgetary pressures on American medical care have had a more dramatic impact on psychiatry than on other branches of medicine, and within psychiatry there has been a sharp move away from therapy-based "talking cures" toward purely drug-based interventions.[14]

Undeniably, some kinds of talking cure are ineffective, and others may go on for longer than their therapeutic effectiveness warrants. Nevertheless, there is growing evidence that drug-based treatments are more effective when combined with psychotherapy than they are on their own. Even in the narrow terms of reducing the length of hospital stays, the pressures of managed care have often been counterproductive, by encouraging hospitals to offload their problem cases onto each other in a way that is collectively self-defeating for everyone. Psychotic or depressed patients discharged too quickly from one hospital may stop taking their medication and quickly find themselves in the emergency admissions room of another hospital in the same city; they bounce from one institution to another, often being treated by doctors unfamiliar with their case, and in the end require much more extensive hospitalization than they would have if they had simply stayed longer in the original facility. Worse, as Luhrmann describes the situation, whole states and regions compete to play pass-the-parcel: "One of the startling consequences of psychiatric illness is the way state administrators sometimes offload patients onto other states. In southern California, patients would show up in the psychiatric emergency room and explain that they had been in Minnesota or Illinois and had gone to the bus station and a nice man from the county mental health had bought them a bus ticket to San Diego, which they thought they'd like to visit."[15]

Economic pressures can even affect the very character of illness itself. In Luhrmann's words:

> Our psychiatric professionals, as well as the rest of us, have expectations of the psychiatrically ill, and we institutionalize those expectations in subtle and unsubtle ways that can lead people to mimic the symptoms we think they should have. If a homeless veteran wants a warm bed for the night, he can learn what words and gestures will persuade the psychiatrist on call to admit him to the hospital. If a woman receives a disability check each month for her psychiatric diagnosis, she will learn how to avoid having the support curtailed. . . . the psychiatrically ill learn to play roles our society has designed for them.[16]

As the rest of Luhrmann's study makes distressingly plain, the fact that the mentally ill learn to play the roles we assign them does not make them any less ill.

Exclusion and Collective Action

The unemployed, the poor, the seriously ill, all in their different ways can find themselves excluded from the compact of trust that, by and large, succeeds in sustaining the baroque edifice that is modern human society. No one planned it that way, but that's no less reason to find the result unacceptable. True, the process should not be caricatured: in most cases it's less awful to be unemployed, poor, or sick today than it was two hundred or two thousand years ago.[17] Romanticized accounts of bucolic poverty in the Middle Ages, or claims that the mentally ill are creative souls who would have been revered as saints in the days before psychiatric drugs and hospitalization, are mostly fantasies that gloss over the sheer grim misery of most poverty and mental illness, not to mention the cruelty with which earlier ages often treated their own unfortunates (burning mentally ill women as witches, for example).[18] Nevertheless, the fact remains that for many citizens of modern society the compact of trust works, if not perfectly, far better than our ancestors could ever have imagined, while for the excluded it works haphazardly, if at all. And to the extent that the condition of the excluded has improved in comparison with previous ages, that is largely due to a conscious effort of collective action. Modern societies have sought, through coercion or persuasion, to act in groups so as to modify the results of the uncoordinated division of labor—and fortunately, that division of labor has, by increasing overall prosperity, made it easier to afford the costs of doing so. This collective action is what we can call politics, in a very broad sense of the term.

If a society with no one in charge, characterized by tunnel vision and dependent on a fragile web of trust, cannot protect its environment or look after its excluded, what can be expected from collective action? How well can collective action make up for the deficiencies of the division of labor? This is the subject of part 4.

Epilogue to Part III

The theme of part 3 has been the way in which the character of human societies in the mass is shaped by the pervasive presence of externalities. This character may be attractive or repellent, but it has been endlessly fascinating to economists.[1] Entire branches of economics have sprung up to deal with various themes that have been touched on in these chapters: the geography of cities and of economic development more generally,[2] the way in which environmental resources are depleted in the absence of incentives to take care of them,[3] the way in which different types of markets allocate resources and summarize the information that traders unwittingly reveal about their motivations and beliefs.[4] This last example shows that some of the most subtle but important externalities are those created by information: what one person does can reveal to others, often for free, information the person herself may have had to spend a lot of time, money, or effort to acquire. Jealous of these revelations, people can be driven to hoard information, often with only partial success. Whether successful or not, their efforts to hoard information shape the institutions of which human society is made up.[5] Firms, for example, can channel some kinds of information more effectively than markets can, and this advantage gives firms an edge over markets in coordinating some kinds of activity. When this advantage is strong, firms can even become quite large, standing out as great islands of hierarchy and planning in a sea of decentralized market activity.

Just as fishermen deplete the stock of cod left in the open sea without wishing to do so, subject only to the iron law that today's catch leaves fewer fish for the trawlermen of tomorrow, so human beings in their manipulation of symbols are shaping the stock of knowledge available for the knowledge users of tomorrow. The use of knowledge, though, adds to the stock rather than depleting it, so the efforts of today's researchers mean that, whether they intend this or not, our descendants will know many things that we did not know today. As we shall see, this is not always a good thing.

Part 4 explores one of the most deadly externalities of all: the way that cooperation within a group (often motivated by a wish to overcome some of the failings of uncoordinated individual action) can make the group more lethally aggressive in its dealings with outsiders. Of all the legacies of our hunter-gatherer past, this poses by far the most troubling threat to the great experiment launched by humanity ten thousand years ago.

Prologue to Part IV

One of the great puzzles of prehistory is why agriculture caught on so fast. You might think that, once the idea appeared and the climate made it possible, the answer was obvious: why go out to hunt and gather when you can sit home and watch the grass grow? The reality, though, is more complex. Sitting and watching the grass grow is not the idyll it seems, for those who are sedentary are also vulnerable. When enemies attack, hunter-gatherers can simply melt into the forest, but farmers have much more to lose: houses, chattels, stores of food. So farmers not only face high risks but also need to spend time, energy, and resources defending themselves — building walls, manning watchtowers, guarding herds, patrolling fields. This means less time and energy, fewer resources, devoted to making food. It could even happen that the greater productivity of the hours they spend growing and raising food is outweighed by the greater number of hours they must spend defending themselves and the food they have grown — meaning that, all in all, they produce less food. Indeed, studies of the bones and teeth of some of the earliest agricultural communities of the Near East show that farmers had *worse* health (due to poorer nutrition) than the hunter-gatherers who preceded them. Increases in agricultural productivity in later millennia more than made up for this eventually, but even so, the puzzle remains: what prompted agriculture to be adopted so quickly and often within a comparatively short space of time? Agriculture seems to have been independently adopted in at least seven places: Anatolia, Mexico, the Andes of South America, northern China, southern China, the eastern United States, and sub-Saharan Africa (at least once and possibly up to four times). Almost certainly the end of the last ice age dramatically improved the productivity of agriculture compared with the hostile conditions beforehand. But what would that have mattered if all of the additional benefits of the new farming technology ended up being spent on defense? Why adopt such a technology at all?[1]

We shall never know for sure. The need for communities to defend themselves sometimes leaves clear traces, in the form of walls and weapons, but most of the time and energy absorbed by defense leave no archaeological record, so we cannot be certain that this is what explains the poorer nutrition of the first farmers. Still, here's a reasonable guess.

Agriculture dramatically raised the advantages to mankind of banding together for self-defense. Once constrained by a sedentary lifestyle and unable any longer to play hide-and-seek with its enemies, a large group is much more secure than its members could be in multiple smaller groups. But the result of devoting time, effort, and resources to defending yourself is not just to make you feel more secure. It usually also makes your neighbor feel *less* secure. And in that simple but grim externality lies one of the driving forces of modern society, of its stunning technological achievements as well as its capacity for brutality on an industrial scale.

Once the very first farming communities began to invest systematically in defense, the fact that they could do so began to make them a threat to their neighbors, including communities who were on the margins of adopting agriculture themselves. For there is no such thing as a purely defensive technology. Even walls around a town can make it easier for attacking parties to travel out to raid nearby communities in the knowledge they have a secure retreat. The club that prehistoric man used to ward off attackers was the same club he used to attack others. Once a community has invested in even a modest army, whether of mercenaries or of its own citizens, the temptation to encourage that army to earn its keep by preying on weaker neighbors can become overwhelming. So, even if the first farming communities were not necessarily any better off than they would have been without agriculture, once the process had started, many communities had an interest in joining in. Like the externalities of congestion and disease we saw earlier among city-dwellers, these interactions could lead each to act ineluctably against the collective interests of all.

Part 4 sketches the implications of this simple logic of attack and defense for the structure of modern societies. The double-edged sword of defense has posed three main threats. The first is the threat posed by communities to their neighbors, a threat that encouraged a spiral of competitive investment between rivals. The second threat is internal: as communities became more prosperous and could hand over the task of defense to others (either to mercenaries or to professional armies of their own citizens), they could find themselves threatened by the very people upon whose protection they had come to rely. This threat seriously preoccupied some of the great political thinkers of the past, from the great Tunisian philosopher Ibn Khaldun in the fourteenth century to the Scottish political economist Adam Ferguson in the eighteenth. As Ferguson put it in his *Essay on the History of Civil Society*:

> By having separated the arts of the clothier and the tanner, we are the better
> supplied with shoes and with cloth. But to separate the arts which form the

citizen and the statesman, the arts of policy and war, is an attempt to dismember the human character, and to destroy those very arts which we mean to improve. By this separation, we in effect deprive a free people of what is necessary for their safety; or we prepare a defense against invasion from abroad, which gives a prospect of usurpation, and threatens the establishment of military government at home.[2]

The third main threat comes from the turbulent and unregulated character of the very economic prosperity that is the foundation for military strength. States that have grown prosperous on commerce have realized, sometimes too late, that the same traders and entrepreneurs who supply their defense needs are also arming their enemies. The democratic liberality of the division of labor, which arms friends and enemies alike, was a feature of the warfare of antiquity and continues unabated to this day.

Chapter 13 looks at the way in which the modern state has grown since its foundation as a simple means of defense among members of sedentary agricultural communities. Historically, although the common force of gravity holding all communities together has been the need to band together for defense, in dealing with their neighbors societies have faced a continual choice between two kinds of strategy: strength through prosperity and prosperity through strength. Though these represent points along a continuum rather than a difference in kind, the first has, broadly speaking, been the strategy of city- and nation-states, the second of empires. Paradoxically, the more successful states have been in pursuit of strength through prosperity, the more they have been tempted to abandon it in pursuit of prosperity through strength. In this cycle of economic growth, military adventurism, political overreach and subsequent economic decline lies much of the turbulent dynamic of world history.

The temptation to abandon the strategy of peaceful trade with their neighbors in favor of impatient confiscation is not the only danger faced by prosperous states. As the tasks undertaken by the state have multiplied and grown more complex, the ambition of the state to cure the ills of the modern division of labor has grown in turn. The state now taxes and subsidizes, redistributes income, regulates markets, intervenes in response to unemployment. In short, modern states constrain the operation of citizens, firms, and markets in historically unprecedented ways. These activities have the potential to compensate for the failings of a society where everyone has tunnel vision and no one is in charge. At the same time they have increased the need for constraints on what the state itself can do. For as the task of managing modern society becomes more complex, the state itself has (necessarily and inevitably) reproduced within its own internal structure the very division of labor whose failings it seeks to address. There is no longer a king; instead there are finance ministries, regulatory agencies, legislatures, committees, embassies, consultative bodies, cabinets, courts, lobby groups, each with their own agenda and given to rivalries outsiders can only guess at. A president or prime minister still holds life-or-death power, notably to send citizens to war, but the forces shaping such decisions are the result of many conflicting political pressures and subject to tunnel vision in ways eerily similar to those of market society itself. This does not make the state impotent in regulating the market economy, nor is it exactly a case of the blind leading the blind. But the narrow-sighted lead the narrow-sighted, in a world in which the long reach and destructiveness of modern technology require panoramic vision as never before.

Chapter 14 asks where the long experiment begun ten thousand years ago has brought us at the beginning of the twenty-first century. Globalization is not a new phenomenon, though it continually reinvents the disguises it wears. *Homo sapiens sapiens* has built institutions of startling complexity that have enabled a hunter-gatherer psychology to dominate its environment in a way quite unprecedented in nature. Those institutions nevertheless have the potential to do great damage to us and to our world. Any lasting solutions to these dangers need to be adapted both to the dangers themselves and to our own hunter-gatherer psychology, which constrains our ability to respond to them.

Collective Action: From Belligerent States to a Marketplace of Nations

CHAPTER 13

States and Empires

DEFENSE AND ATTACK

Effective defense requires teamwork. Each member of a team of fighters almost always has a much better chance of survival in a battle than its individual members would on their own. The only important exception is when fighters are mobile and can survive by running away (as guerrilla fighters have always known). Then and only then can it be an advantage to be fighting alone.

When our ancestors began farming and herding, they gave up the advantages of mobility. It's true that domesticating sheep, cattle, or pigs does not bind you as tightly to one place as planting grain does. But it certainly becomes more costly to flee an enemy, who can then help himself to your accumulated stores of food, even if these have to be rounded up rather than just plundered from the storehouse. So the beginning of agriculture implied almost inevitably that our ancestors would band together in larger groups than they had previously been used to, even if these were probably just larger family groups at first. Hunter-gatherer families could easily split up once food got scarce or rivalries and tensions grew difficult to manage, but early farmers knew that splitting up had become a much more dangerous thing to do. It became more than ever essential to learn to live with others and to manage conflict rather than to escape it.

Banding together was not just a matter of living in larger groups. It also implied living physically closer together. If you're going to stay in one place, it makes sense for that place to be defended; even a simple wall or fence can gain you valuable seconds in a fight, as well as keeping out casual scavengers. And it follows from the laws of simple geometry that the larger the settlement you are trying to defend, the greater the area protected per meter of wall (the circumference of a circle increases with its diameter, but its area increases with the *square* of the diameter). So agricultural settlements naturally tended to contain more people than hunter-gatherer bands. Yet living together also brings its challenges—how to share space, how to dispose of waste (as we saw in chapter 7). Solutions to these problems, like strategies for self-defense, have the character of *public goods*, as economists call them. This means that they apply indiscriminately, more or less, to everyone in the community, regardless of who has contributed to them. A defensive wall defends everyone, even the shirkers who tried to avoid being part of the building crew. A system for disposing of human waste is to everyone's benefit, including those who try to avoid the costs of managing it. So unless there were some arrangement for sharing tasks, backed by the threat of coercion, everyone would try to free-ride on the efforts of others. And such an arrangement implies the concentration and exercise of power. We can therefore understand how a system of collective order was the natural consequence of the first agricultural revolution.

If the system works, the community prospers. Prosperous communities soon acquire neighbors, either those envious of their prosperity (or simply curious about it) or the inhabitants of regions into which the community expands as its prosperity leads to population growth and pressure on the limited land. And there are only two main ways you can behave toward your neighbors: you can fight them, or you can try to live with them. Historically, communities that successfully fought their neighbors have slaughtered them, driven them off their land, or enslaved them; sometimes a combination of all three. Communities that have sought to live with their neighbors have either exchanged goods and favors actively with them (sometimes resulting in an eventual merger) or tolerated them while attempting to minimize active contact.

We have no written records to tell us which of these ways of dealing with neighbors was most common during the several thousands of years immediately after the invention of agriculture. But we have records of a different kind that can rule out at least some possibilities. The work of human geneticist Luigi Cavalli-Sforza and his colleagues has shown a remarkable fit between the diffusion of agricultural technology (chiefly wheat) from the Middle East to various parts of Europe from 7,500 B.C. to around 3000 B.C. and the pattern of human genetic variation across Europe.[1] The most reasonable interpretation of this evidence is that farmers gradually expanded across the continent (at no more than an average of one kilometer per year for over four thousand years). They interbred with local hunter-gatherer communities, who had different frequencies of certain particular genes that have left traces in their descendants alive today. For instance, we know that inhabitants of the Basque region of southwestern France and northern Spain have significantly different gene frequencies from those of other Europeans, indicating that they resisted longer and more successfully against interbreeding with migrant agricultural groups from further east (though significant interbreeding certainly took place). They also speak a radically different language.

What does this show us? First of all, it rules out the possibility that

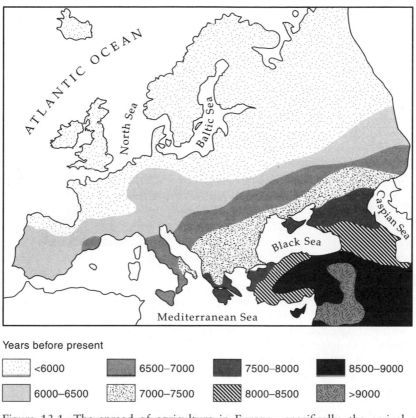

Years before present

<6000		6500–7000		7500–8000		8500–9000	
6000–6500		7000–7500		8000–8500		>9000	

Figure 13.1. The spread of agriculture in Europe—specifically, the arrival of wheat from the Middle East to the various parts of Europe, from 9,500 years to 5,000 years ago. Reprinted by permission from Luigi Luca Cavalli-Sforza, *Genes, Peoples, and Languages*, trans. Mark Seielstad (New York: North Point Press, a division of Farrar, Straus and Giroux, 2000), p.109, fig. 5. Originally published in A. J. Ammerman and L. L. Cavalli-Sforza, *The Neolithic Transition and the Genetics of Populations in Europe* (Princeton: Princeton University Press, 1984).

the agricultural way of life spread mainly by cultural emulation, as hunter-gatherers simply copied the practices of their visibly prosperous neighbors. On the contrary, these practices were spread by migration: people and techniques moved together. This was not just a European phenomenon: it was true also of the other instances of agricultural diffusion that have so far been studied, such as the expansion from Mexico southward to the Andes or the Bantu expansion south- and eastward through Africa beginning about three thousand years ago.

Secondly, it rules out the possibility that migrant agriculturalists sim-

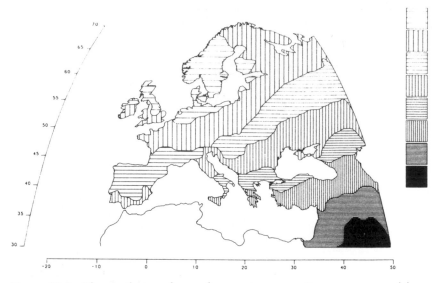

Figure 13.2. The similarity of gene frequencies across Europe, measured by a statistical technique known as principal components analysis. Its remarkable similarity to figure 13.1 makes it likely that there was an expansion of farmers from the Middle East into Europe, mixing with local hunter-gatherers (who had different gene frequencies). Reprinted by permission from Luigi Luca Cavalli-Sforza, Paolo Menozzi, and Alberto Piazza, *The History and Geography of Human Genes* (Princeton: Princeton University Press, 1994), p. 292, fig. 5.11.1.

ply massacred all those hunter-gatherer communities they found along the way, or even just drove them permanently off the land. We don't know, of course, how many of the men they massacred even as they sought diligently to impregnate the women. Evidence from later societies strongly suggests that, where agriculture was yielded more than a mere subsistence, many of the captured males would have been put to work as slaves. Indeed, economic historians have now established that almost no societies did not enslave others at some time in their history, with slavery becoming more likely the wealthier the society concerned, at least until they became wealthy enough to afford to take a stand against slavery on principle.[2]

At the same time, though, relations between different agricultural communities in the same region must have oscillated between periodic hostilities and cautious exchange. Both would have been the product of opportunism and the random demands of subsistence, the rhythm driven by reactions to events as much as by deliberate policy. But once societies reached a significant size, the choice between fighting their neighbors and trading with them assumed a major strategic importance.

It became a policy, and one that different societies shaped in different ways.

STRENGTH AND PROSPERITY

For around half of the last ten thousand years, settlements of any size were extremely rare (towns like Jericho remained quite exceptional till around 3,000 B.C.). But a series of inventions — writing, the wheel, the domestication of the horse, the combination of the wheel and the horse to make the chariot, ironworking, brick-making, improved techniques of building in stone, the sail and the oar, as well as the improved agricultural productivity that allowed farmers to support more nonfarmers — made it possible to organize societies in larger cities, and to coordinate the activity of larger and more deadly armies, than had ever been seen before. Larger cities were themselves a means of raising larger armies, and larger armies had proportionately much better prospects of success in battle. This made them a source of fear to their neighbors and enemies and enabled them to extort enough resources from those neighbors to compensate comfortably for the cost of the armies themselves. The competitive spiral thereby became more intense, as neighbors drew the conclusion that the only escape from permanent payment of tribute lay in having large armies too.

Nevertheless, from as early as the eleventh century B.C. and the rise of the Phoenician city states, some societies have pursued a different strategy, of seeking strength through prosperity rather than prosperity through strength. In these, production and trade paid for defense, and diplomacy (usually fostered by trade) allowed states to call on more defensive resources than they could afford to employ on a full-time basis. These societies needed a comparatively high degree of internal coordination, which limited their size to the territory within which information and instructions could be transmitted rapidly — in effect, for more than two millennia, to the city and its hinterland. Such societies usually needed to offer their citizens a stake in the collective wealth, even if (as in the Greek city-states) that wealth was in part made possible by the work of slaves. They also developed, for the first time in history, a substantial merchant class, which represented the city to the outside world.

It's important not to misunderstand this distinction: all city-states were concerned about defense and invested heavily in physical means of protection. Indeed, defense was the main reason these predominantly agricultural communities concentrated in urban settlements at all, as the work of the political scientist Azar Gat has shown.[3] What distinguished the strategy of strength through prosperity was that it required treating some of one's neighbors as resources rather than simply as threats. City-states articulated, then, an importantly different strategy toward their neighbors from any that had yet been seen on the part of large organized societies. Some neighbors, at least, were best considered allies and trading partners rather than enemies, even if their trustworthiness could never be taken for granted. Such a strategy was risky, but its payoff was potentially vast, not just in economic but even in purely military terms, as the work of military historian Victor Davis Hanson has recently shown.[4] Economic strength allowed states to buy the most reliably lethal weaponry, regardless of where it was produced (including technologically advanced items such as ships, siege engines, and artillery). It allowed them to pay for mercenary armies when they were needed. And, at least as importantly, it provided *motivation*. Hanson argues that the Greek city-states were "the first consensual governments in the history of civilization that fielded soldiers who were independent and free property owners — militiamen, family farmers, and voters all in one." This encouraged a preference for decisive pitched battle instead of the skirmishes and extended campaigns often favored by their enemies; Greek citizens "had no wish to be absent from their farms on long campaigns." The Greeks elaborated pitched battle into a strategy of murderous effectiveness, as the initial victory of the army in which Xenophon fought at Cunaxa was to demonstrate, when an entire wing of the Persian army was destroyed at the price of a single Greek soldier wounded by an arrow.

The Athenians were themselves fully aware how much their military strength depended on their trading economy. In the first book of Thucydides' history of the Peloponnesian War, Pericles tells his fellow Athenians that their rivals lack the necessary long purse:

> Personally engaged in the cultivation of their lands, without funds either private or public, the Peloponnesians are also without experience in long wars across the sea, from the strict limit which poverty imposes on their attacks upon each other. Powers of this description are quite incapable of often manning a fleet or often sending out an army: they cannot afford the absence from their homes, the expenditure from their own funds. . . . Capital, it must be remembered, maintains a war more than forced contributions.[5]

The paradox was that societies that had sought to build prosperity on strength became not only less prosperous but even less strong than societies that conceived the relation the other way round. And yet, once the strength was there, the temptation to exercise it against weaker neighbors could become overwhelming. Both Athens and Rome outgrew their city-statehood, and for a long time were able to put their merchant skills to work in the interests of a more expansionist and imperial project. Hanson contrasts the economic approach to warfare of Greece and Rome with the more coercive approach of the armies they faced in battle:

> The looting of the Achaemenid treasuries by Alexander the Great spurred a military renaissance in the eastern Mediterranean for more than two centuries as relatively small cadres of Greek-speaking dynasts ruled vast Asiatic populations in Seleucid Asia and Ptolemaic Egypt. . . . Rome was the capitalist war machine par excellence of the ancient world [with an] intricate system of logistical supply contracted out to private businessmen. . . . The alternative to capitalist-finance warfare was either simple coercion — the forced impressments of warriors without pay — or tribal musters fueled by promises of booty. Both systems could result in enormous and spirited armies: Vercingetorix's quarter-million-man Gallic army that nearly defeated Caesar at Alesia (52 BC) and the nomadic invasions of Genghis Khan (1206–27) and Tamerlane (1381–1405), who overran much of Asia, are the most notable examples. . . . But even the most murderous hordes could not sustain — feed, clothe and pay — a military force with sophisticated weaponry for a lengthy period of time. At some point farmers, traders and merchants do not work if they are not paid.[6]

Put this way, as a matter of simple incentives, the point may seem obvious. What was not obvious to many of the world's early political leaders was that societies unwilling to treat at least some of their neighbors as partners rather than as enemies would never be able to build up the capital to underwrite a successful long-term military project in the first place.

THREE FLAWS IN THE COMMERCIAL STRATEGY

During the last five thousand years, the competition between states and empires (the former founded substantially on commerce, the latter substantially on coercion) has undergone many fluctuations of fortune, not unlike the competition between firms that was discussed in chapter 10. Successful city-states sometimes metamorphosed into empires, and unsuccessful empires fell apart into squabbling states. Some scholars, such as Paul Kennedy, writing about the period since 1500, have seen an inherent dynamic in which imperial success led intrinsically to overreach, because the kinds of investment required to maintain an empire were incompatible with the kinds of investment needed to maintain the commercial foundations of their military success.[7] Be that as it may (and Hanson's description of the Greek empire in the eastern Mediterranean suggests that imperial overreach might sometimes take a long time to set in), the process was also highly dependent on chance. Whether states could survive against the depredations of empires, for instance, has depended not just on the skill of their diplomacy but also on changes in offensive and defensive technology. The training of horses to carry armored fighters, the development of the trireme in Athens, and the organizational innovations of the Roman state (including those famous roads) all tilted the balance in favor of scale, and therefore of empires; improved building in stone and the invention of the crossbow and longbow tilted it back in favor of small defensive formations, and therefore of states.

Many apparently small developments could have large and distant consequences: the historian Lynn White suggested that the humble stirrup (an invention imported from Asia) made possible large-scale combat between mounted knights in Europe and thereby laid the foundations of feudalism.[8] White's theory is no longer taken seriously in its original form, but it is not disputed that the stirrup had consequences out of all proportion to its size. Changes in the cost of transport and communication over large distances could make a crucial difference to the viability of empires (the collapse of the Roman empire fed upon itself as the impoverished regions were no longer able to afford the upkeep of the infrastructure that had kept the empire together). Organizational innovations counted as much as physical ones; for example, the census, which was instituted by both the Chinese and the Roman empires and was systematically implemented by the nation-states of Europe in the early modern period in their attempts to consolidate their political, geographical, and above all fiscal hold over their territories. Along with the census came the innovation of personal surnames, first imposed on the population in China in around the fourth century B.C. and attempted many times elsewhere in the world in subsequent centuries, not always successfully.[9] Indeed, whether a state was capable of standardizing surnames was as much a test of organizational capacity as a means of achieving it.

Many innovations had highly ambivalent consequences for the contest between states and empires: an innovation might favor states initially but empires in the course of time. Before 1000 B.C. the Phoenicians' remarkable mastery of shipbuilding had laid the foundations of their trading economy, but these same skills were later to be refined for military as well as trading purposes by their Greek and Roman rivals. This shows that although the strategy of building a commercial foundation for military strength has proved, over the millennia, spectacularly more successful than the rival strategy of building a purely military foundation for economic strength, it is a strategy with a major flaw.

THE DANGER OF DISPARITY IN STRENGTH

In fact it has three major flaws, each of them due to the fact that even defensive technologies always have some potential for being used in attack. The first flaw is that wealthy states can become a source of fear to their neighbors, since the strategy of trading with those neighbors rather than fighting them may not outlast the emergence of a major disparity in military strength. And insecure neighbors are not necessarily good news. They divert resources from peaceful investments that might help both parties toward expensive and dangerous military technology, and they can be tempted by opportunities to strike preemptively in order to forestall the risk of facing a preemptive strike themselves. It was the insecurity of Sparta in the face of Athens' growing prosperity that led to the Peloponnesian War. The popular modern view that trade between neighbors makes warfare less likely (a view central to the establishment of the European Economic Community in Western Europe after the Second World War) is one that has no reliable basis in history.[10] We can be sure that the only reasonable alternative to warfare between neighbors is indeed trade, but that does not mean that trade by itself is a significant assurance of stability.

Even when immediate neighbors establish a reasonable, if temporary, equilibrium between themselves, there are always more distant neighbors who can be threatened. The imperial ambitions of the Western European nations over the last five hundred years have been particularly intense at periods of delicately balanced rivalry between those imperial powers, whether we look at the sixteenth century, the late eighteenth, or the later nineteenth. Nor have attempts to "civilize" the process on the part of the rivals themselves necessarily helped the neighbors. The European powers abolished the transatlantic slave trade in the early nineteenth century, but the systematic slaughter of indigenous inhabitants of their colonies continued. These included the aboriginal inhabitants of Australia and Tasmania (the latter of whom were entirely wiped out), the Hereros of German South-West Africa (now Namibia) in 1904,[11] and what may possibly be the largest single genocide in history, the killing of up to ten million Congolese by Belgian colonists between 1880 and 1920 — a startling average of one murder every two minutes, day and night, for forty years.[12] Such slaughter may even have been encouraged by the fact that, with the end of slavery, these inhabitants no longer represented an economic resource for their murderers; they were simply in the way.

Military strategists have long known that a disparity in strength between rivals — and especially a *growing* disparity in strength — is the most important single reason to expect an outbreak of hostilities. Intriguingly, a similar explanation has been advanced for one of the puzzles of animal behavior, namely, the much greater frequency of violence among adults of some species than among others. Chimpanzees (like lions, wolves, and spotted hyenas) regularly kill other adults of their own species; gorillas, like most other animals, very rarely do. Yet their propensity for violence as such is about equal. Gorillas—again, like many other species—engage in high rates of infanticide (for instance, one in seven of the infants recorded at Dian Fossey's site in Rwanda were judged to have been killed by adult gorillas). Infanticide is common in nature, but killing of adults is rare, and for a simple reason: infants are overwhelmingly weaker than adults. So it is not surprising that the species where killing of adults regularly occurs are those in which the accidents of foraging behavior regularly lead to meetings between groups of unequal size and strength.[13] Chimpanzees, operating within an environment where the most effective group size varies according to the particular task, and where groups will wander in pursuit of food in exploratory and unpredictable ways over a wide area, are one such species. Human beings, unfortunately, are another. Although a move toward a sedentary agricultural existence at any time in the last ten thousand years might temporarily have slowed the wanderings of any one particular group, the resulting migrations as population growth took off, as well as the strikingly different size and strength of cities and states, dramatically multiplied both the opportunities and the incentives for warfare. In our own century, globalization may be doing something similar—a point that will be taken up again in chapter 14. And the enormous disparity in military strength between the United States and all other countries that has emerged since the end of the Cold War may be bad news even for the United States itself, a point to which I shall return.

SOLDIERS AND CIVILIANS

The second flaw in the strategy of building strength through prosperity is that a successful commercial strategy of defense requires, like a successful commercial strategy for anything else, a division of labor between specialists and the rest. As Ibn Khaldun pointed out so clearly six centuries ago (and Adam Ferguson again nearly four centuries after him), when a society hands over military decisions to professional soldiers in order to get on with building prosperity, those soldiers wield immense power over those whom they have been asked to protect. Over and over again, that power has been used, not always to kill or enslave, but at the least to tax or extort (these last two terms meaning often the same thing). The philosopher Thomas Hobbes famously argued that the absolute power of a single monarch was better than the contested power of rivalrous local gangsters. Hobbes lived in a period of intense and bloody rivalry between the European powers (he claimed that his mother had given birth to him in fright at the coming of the Spanish Armada in 1588). The English version of his great work *Leviathan* was published shortly after the end of the Thirty Years War, one of the bloodiest episodes of fighting to which the European continent had ever been subjected. This suggests that Hobbes was so alive to the human costs of rivalry *between* political powers that he underplayed the costs of inequality in power *within* states, costs that were to preoccupy political thought in subsequent centuries. Indeed, it is no exaggeration to say that the problem of how to constrain the exercise of power within the state has come to be seen as the central problem of political philosophy in the modern era (the accidents of intellectual terminology mean that the problem of constraining the exercise of power *between* states is no longer considered philosophical at all but falls under the disciplinary heading of international relations).

THE ARMS BAZAAR

Both of these flaws in the strategy of commercial states have been horribly exposed by the political and military evolution of the world's nation-states in recent centuries. But there is a third flaw, no less deadly, of which the Greeks themselves were well aware, and which threatens us in the modern world as much as either of the first two. A successful commercial strategy for defense requires, as part of the division of labor, that those who invent, design, and build weapons should be given considerable freedom. It needs commercial rivalry, room for the maverick, the ingenious but unexpected solution. And free designers will sell to whoever will pay them. Victor Hanson writes that in Athens "the impetus was largely capitalistic and democratic: designers were free to profit by building better weapons than their competitors, while rulers sought to arm as many of their subjects as possible as cheaply and lethally as possible."[14] Another historian, Edward Cohen, points out that maritime commerce in Athens was "characterized by extreme market fragmentation: there existed at Athens no single owner of a multi-ship fleet, no dominant trading companies, no enterprise controlling the harbor."[15] Even during the Dark and Middle Ages in Europe, writes Hanson, "Europeans were adept at fabricating a variety of superior military goods in great numbers, from plate armor to matchless double-edged swords, crossbows and Greek fire, prompting many states to publish decrees forbidding their merchants from exporting such arms to potential enemies." One example of such a decree was that published in 1198 by Pope Innocent III excommunicating "those who presume to give arms, iron, or wood to the Saracens for their galleys."

These export controls did not work. They have never worked when strong enough economic interests are at stake. Indeed, Pope Innocent himself was lobbied by Venetian trading interests to relax his decree. He replied in a spirit of compromise in this letter to the city of Venice:

> Our beloved sons Andreas Donatus and Benedict Grilion, your messengers, recently came to the apostolic see and were at pains to explain to us that by this decree your city was suffering no small loss, for she is not devoted to agriculture but rather to shipping and to commerce. We, therefore, induced by the paternal affection we have for you, and commanding you under pain of anathema not to aid the Saracens by selling or giving to them or exchanging with them iron, flax, pitch, pointed stakes, ropes, arms, helmets, ships, and boards, or unfinished wood, do permit for the present, until we issue further orders, the taking of goods, other than those mentioned, to Egypt and Babylon, whenever necessary. We hope that in consideration of this kindness you will bear in mind the aiding of Jerusalem, taking care not to abuse the apostolic decree, for there is no doubt that whosoever violates his conscience in evading this order will incur the anger of God.[16]

The failure of export controls was not just an incidental blemish on Europe's statecraft. Far from it: the continual rivalry between producers and exporters of technology (notably, though not exclusively, military technology) was one of the main motors of Europe's remarkable economic development in the medieval and early modern periods. David Landes contrasts the different approaches of Europe and Ming dynasty China. In spite of having invented gunpowder, "the Chinese never learned to make modern guns. Worse yet, having known and used cannon as early as the thirteenth century, they had let knowledge and skill slip away. Their city walls and gates had emplacements for cannon, but no cannon. Who needed them? No enemy of China had them. . . . [However] no European nation would have been deterred from armament by enemy weakness; when it came to death, Europeans maximized."[17]

The underlying logic of military exports is that developing military technology takes a lot of investment and creates a strong incentive to sell as much of the resulting equipment as possible to recoup that fixed investment. This is as true now, in the early twenty-first century, as it has ever been. Like their medieval predecessors, the most ingenious engineers in the world's most powerful nations compete to sell the products of their defense industries to other countries, many of whom will eventually use the weapons against their one-time benefactors.

The major conventional arms-producing countries between them exported over $16 billion of conventional armaments in 2001, according to official figures reported by the Stockholm International Peace Research Institute.[18] Naturally, this is dwarfed by total military spending across the world, estimated at over $800 billion dollars in the same year: much military expenditure consists of paying wages rather than buying hardware. However, it is almost certainly an underestimate, as it does not include military equipment smuggled or stolen or simply underreported, of which there is certainly a great deal. The most dangerous weaponry is not always the most obviously destructive, because there is a trade-off between size and ease of concealment. Aircraft carriers are very destructive but hard to hide in a suitcase, while the proliferation of small arms around the world will almost certainly cost more lives in the next few decades than all other categories of weaponry put together, unless there is a significant nuclear war.

As with the first hunter-gatherers, the overall result of the world's defense spending is to make us all less secure and to divert energy, resources, and inventiveness that could have been put to more peaceful and productive ends; there is good evidence that a country's economic performance suffers when defense spending is escalated.[19] But as with the first hunter-gatherers, this does not mean the countries that do so are being foolish. Again, the evidence suggests that they spend on weapons when they face a threat, and that spending on weapons makes better sense for each country than simply hoping the threat will recede on its own.[20] That is why simple appeals to the prudence of individual countries will never be enough to bring the world's military expenditures down to a less dangerous level, for most individual countries are behaving reasonably, even if in the process they are making each other less secure.

Of course, not all defense expenditure need make your neighbors insecure. Some weapons have greater defensive than offensive potential, and some are designed expressly never to be used. But arms exporters are, above all, businessmen (and women). And businessmen know that, as a rule, there is more money to be made from selling equipment to people who intend to use it than to people who don't.

THE BUSINESS OF GOVERNMENT

Of course, the business of government in the twenty-first century involves much, much more than defense. Although the figures are sensitive to the exact definitions used, to fluctuations from year to year, and to conjectures about the size of the black economy, the share of national income taken in taxes by the government in the rich countries of the world varies from around a third in Japan and the United States to more than two-fifths in Western Europe and around a half in France and Scandinavia. A significant part of this involves transfers, from taxpayers to others, principally recipients of public pensions, unemployment, and social security benefits, but also beneficiaries of a range of subsidies from arts grants to export credits for — yes — arms producers. And if we look just at that part of economic activity that involves consumption of goods and services (excluding both transfers and investment), government in rich countries takes around 20 percent, while in poor countries it takes around 16 percent. Both shares are a lot higher than they were in previous centuries (even poor countries have benefited from modern technology for tax collection and social control). Nevertheless, the power of political command is underwritten in all countries by military power, and the power of political command is in turn at the heart of the power to tax, to spend, and to regulate.

This does not mean governments always get what they want. Indeed, as was described in chapter 1, even governments with massive military potential are often strangely powerless to control the detail of events around them, and the greater the commercial vigor of a nation the more it is likely to be diverse, decentralized, and resistant to control. Nevertheless, governments have sought to regulate activity in a multitude of ways, for good reasons and bad. Chapter 7 showed how the pollution and disease of cities has provoked a range of responses to ensure a cleaner environment at the local level. This has not come about principally through altruism, but rather through the recognition that externalities between the powerful and the powerless bind their fates together. Unless cities are made more healthy for the poor, they will become uninhabitable even by the rich. Similarly, the moves to democratize political systems in the nineteenth and twentieth centuries often sprang not from the generosity or goodwill of the politically powerful but from their fear of revolution if demands for democracy were not met ("Reform, that you may preserve," as Macaulay put it during the passage of the Great Reform Act of 1832).[21]

Yet, like the very societies they seek to regulate, the regulatory policies of all governments have come into being less as the product of a coherent vision than as a series of responses to immediate problems. The business of government is just as much subject to a division of labor as is the business of everything else. Central governments operate with only a cloudy vision of what is happening in local governments (that's one of the reasons why local governments can do some things so much better than central governments can). Even within central governments, officials in agriculture ministries know next to nothing about transport regulation; central banks are increasingly given constitutional independence from oversight by government; competition authorities get on with their job without liaising with ministries of labor or ministries of defense. Sometimes this is the inevitable result of the scale of the task and the consequent need for specialists: a government of amateurs regulating an economy full of specialists would be left hopelessly behind. Sometimes it is the result of a belief that some tasks need consistency and independence from the day-to-day lobbying that accompanies all government activity. Central banking and competition regulation, like the judicial system, depend not just on making wise decisions but on sending credible and consistent signals to the rest of society, signals whose very credibility might be undermined by an obviously political process of implementation. The people charged with these tasks tend, therefore, to be appointed in ways that insulate them from the pressures of daily politics that operate elsewhere in the system. Those pressures of daily politics are themselves the product of multiple conflicting initiatives, by voters, lobbyists, party activists, elected representatives, journalists, all people with axes to grind, careers to make, families to worry about, grudges to nurse. Government in a complex modern society is unimaginable in any other way.

These are all good, indeed unanswerable, arguments. But when we worry about where the division of labor in society may be leading us, we should be wary of supposing that the intervention of government overcomes the problem rather than posing it anew, albeit sometimes in a more tractable form. Collective action—politics, in a word—reproduces through its own operation the very division of labor whose failings it seeks to redress. It comes with its own version of the virtues and vices—creativity, flexibility, tunnel vision—which have made such a spectacular contribution to human development but which simultaneously pose threats to the future of that development. Over the haphazard web of loosely coordinated exchanges between private individuals it lays another haphazard web of loosely coordinated exchanges between coalitions of politically minded individuals. Have we any assurance that the proposed solution is any more reassuring than the original problem?

Faced with poverty, war, and damage to the fabric of our planet, many of the world's citizens at the beginning of the twenty-first century are convinced that conventional solutions have failed. Broadcasting and telecommunications have made us aware of problems more serious than any to which conventional political processes can promise an answer. In response, many citizens are seeking to bypass these political processes, preferring to demonstrate on the streets outside international political meetings rather than influence those meetings through the ordinary mechanisms of voting, lobbying, and arguing with political leaders face to face. The very globalization that enables citizens to be aware of the plight of others on the far side of the world, as well as to organize pressure groups with worldwide reach, seems to many of those citizens to have run out of control.

Are they right? Has the great experiment launched by *Homo sapiens sapiens* ten thousand years ago reached its tolerable limits? And is it even conceivable to call a halt?

CHAPTER 14

Globalization and Political Action

SOLIDARITY AND DIFFERENCE

Imagine a world in which entire communities make a living by digging strawberry ice cream of the finest quality out of the northern tundra and processing it to extract the strawberries. Further south, hitherto unknown societies find outstanding vintage wine flowing in streams and process it to remove the alcohol and recover the natural grape juice. If we were to discover such people, we would no doubt welcome this expansion of the world's ethnographic riches and think them worthy at least of a full-color spread in the *National Geographic*. But, if we could think beyond the exoticism, we would be aware also that they represented a marvelous business opportunity.

At least, let's hope we would. Such a response to the discovery of people with tastes so different from ours might seem sordidly commercial, but it would be a major improvement upon the reaction of many of our forebears. The discovery of people controlling a resource that we value more than they do has led, only too often, to their murder or enslavement. Even in the absence of slavery or genocide, what Adam Smith famously described as the human propensity to "truck, barter and exchange" has always coexisted uneasily with a rival temptation to take, bully, and extort. Smith was an extraordinarily wise and decent man who nevertheless shocked many of his contemporaries by what they saw as his cynical praise for the virtues of solid economic self-interest. In one respect, though, Smith was far from cynical enough, for he drew too little attention to the fragility of the commercial motive in the face of more brutal temptations. Yet he lived in times that were bloody enough, and whose bloodiness sometimes had global consequences. Thus Macaulay unforgettably described Frederick the Great, provoker of (among many others) the War of the Austrian Succession in 1740, when Adam Smith was a young man arriving to begin his studies at Oxford: "In order that he might rob a neighbour whom he had promised to defend, black men fought on the coast of Coromandel and red men scalped each other by the great lakes of North America."[1] Smith himself made many references in his writings to war and its consequences, though these do not seem to have dented his confidence in the strength of human beings' willingness to cut deals.

Romantic conservatives throughout the ages, from Plato through Edmund Burke and Thomas Carlyle down to some of the more high-minded critics of globalization in our own time, such as John Gray,[2] have disdained the commercial spirit as vulgar and philistine. Some have evidently nursed an admiration for the manlier virtues (Burke famously described the young Queen Marie-Antoinette of France in the language of a hazy, semierotic daydream, bemoaning the fact that "ten thousand swords" had not "leaped from their scabbards to avenge even a look that threatened her with insult," and concluding mournfully that "the age of chivalry is gone; that of sophisters, economists and calculators has succeeded, and the glory of Europe is vanished for ever").[3] Yet the manlier virtues have been yoked countless times to the service of murder and extortion, while exchange with someone who is different from us, though it may lack panache, is, in the end, the only civilized thing to do. We can exchange poetry and works of art if we wish (and if they don't prefer Coca-Cola), but exchange we must. The problem of civilized society, though, is how to turn the propensity to truck, barter, and exchange into something stronger than a propensity — into a habit, into second nature. Second nature is the best we can hope for since, as modern evolutionary biology has now shown us (and as Adam Smith was never in a position to know), it is a long way from being our first.

The fantasy of a people who mine ice cream is of course an invention, but less bizarre than it might seem. For all over the world there are people trying to transform, escape, or get rid of things that other people somewhere else are no less keenly trying to acquire: Bangladeshis who have too much water while Bedouins have far too little, European farmers accumulating wheat surpluses while Ethiopian children go hungry, tourists on beaches soaking up the sun that the locals are skulking inside trying to avoid. It is differences that make for a common interest between strangers, differences that give us reasons to exchange. Sometimes, those differences just come about through the accidents of natural bounty; they provide each side with a "comparative advantage" in trade, as David Ricardo expressed it nearly two centuries ago.[4] Sometimes they are just the result of specialization among people who are otherwise pretty much alike. But often they reflect differences of taste, outlook, or vision of the world, differences that give us more reason, rather than less, to exchange. The expression "de gustibus non est disputandum" is best seen as an injunction to think of differences in tastes as an opportunity rather than a threat.

If violence in the human species were an isolated and individual affair, we could perhaps be optimistic that the more different people were, the more the gains from exchange would provide a reason to trade rather than fight. But human violence, like that among chimpanzees, is not only or even mainly the result of quarrels between individuals. It is also, systematically and spectacularly, about violence between groups, whose individuals cooperate among themselves to inflict violence more lethally and cruelly than they could ever do on their own. Groups need to excite and exploit in the service of violence the very same capacity for cooperation that, in other contexts, is the foundation for peace. They do so by emphasizing the similarities among members of the group and their differences from outsiders. They identify convictions (ideas and beliefs shared and reinforced by the group) as different from purely individual tastes and claim that differences of conviction provide an excellent reason to fight. But why should this work? There's an obvious reason for the emphasis on similarity: it allows groups of unrelated individuals to trigger emotions that evolution has favored for the greater cohesion of kin groups (we talk of brothers, sisters, a fatherland). The reason for the emphasis on difference with outsiders is also obvious: evolution has favored ways of targeting our violence toward those who are likely to be unrelated to us and therefore our genetic rivals rather than our allies. These emotions may have served genetic survival during our evolutionary history, but today they threaten the physical survival of everyone.

GLOBALIZATION AND ITS LEGACY

At the beginning of the twenty-first century, "globalization" has become a convenient catch-all term to sum up the multitude of different, often contradictory reasons people have to feel uneasy about the way in which world events are developing. It is widely discussed as though it were a phenomenon of the last few years, even though it has been going on, in one way or another, for much of the last ten thousand years, with waves of intensification beginning five thousand, two and a half thousand, and five hundred years ago, again around a century and a half ago, and yet again after the Second World War. In the country where I live, France, politicians who all bear the indelible marks of globalization in the clothes they wear, the food they eat, the books they read, the technology they use, all nevertheless agree that globalization is a bad thing, even when they agree about very little else.

Although, as we have seen, globalization poses some serious risks to the future of the planet, it's as well to be reminded of the spectacular benefits it has brought to humankind.[5] Studying the societies of the past with the same degree of statistical rigor as we can apply to modern states is not easy. But one important recent study by the economists François Bourguignon and Christian Morrison has tried to estimate the evolution of world income—both its average level and its distribution between rich and poor—over the nearly two centuries since the end of the Napoleonic Wars.[6] Comparing real incomes in the past with those of today is not straightforward, since many things that are available even in poor countries today (electricity, for instance) simply did not exist in past eras. But we can make comparisons in terms of marketable goods and services (food, clothes, housing) that form the bulk of the expenditure of the poor now as they have always done. And the picture Bourguignon and Morrison paint is very striking. A little under a quarter of the world's population lives today in conditions of extreme poverty, which they define as living on less than a dollar per person per day. This is an awful fact about the modern world, but there is nothing specifically modern about such poverty. On the contrary, Bourguignon and Morrison estimate that around 84 percent of the world's population lived in such conditions in 1820. We do not hear much about them, since the novels, diaries, and journalism that influence our perception of that historical period were written by the rich. When the poor appear in the novels of the nineteenth century (by writers such as Balzac, Dickens, and Victor Hugo), they are usually the urban poor, whose factory-blackened clothes and bodies suggest an indictment of the industrial system that was also a product of globalization. The rural poor, who suffered in their hundreds of millions from malnutrition, disease, and early death without going anywhere near a factory, have largely been written out of the script. We need to remember: at all previous stages in the great globalizing experiment launched ten thousand years ago by *Homo sapiens sapiens*, the overwhelming majority of people were desperately poor, and their lives were grim.

More striking even than the picture painted by statistics about real incomes is the evidence that being poor implied in the past a much greater risk of disease and early death. Remember the evidence cited in chapter 7 about Italy's level of infant mortality on the eve of the Second World War, as high as Uganda's is today. This is not an isolated case. In 1860 the rich countries of today had incomes between around $1,300 and $3,200 per person in today's prices. That's between Ghana and Romania on a modern scale. Yet Romania's infant mortality today is around 2 percent and Ghana's around 7 percent; while in the developed countries in 1860 infant mortality lay between 14 percent (for Sweden) and 26 percent (for Austria). Reducing infant mortality for the poor has been one of humanity's remarkable achievements—due not to a magic bullet like the invention of antibiotics but to steady, sustained progress in hygiene, nutrition, and waste disposal as well as the diffusion of medical knowledge across the world as a whole.[7]

It is true that the progress of globalization may threaten some of the world's more poetic idiosyncrasies. On the streets of the cities and towns of South India, women can buy lengths of fine cord threaded with tiny jasmine flowers to put in their hair. The scent of jasmine from the crowds around me, caught on an evening breeze otherwise laden with the noxious smells of the city, is one of the most exhilarating memories I have of India, yet it is possible principally because of the labor of children whose fingers are nimble enough to thread the flowers at a speed that makes the operation profitable. When India's poor have become more prosperous, there will be many fewer children willing to do such work, but the disappearance of their handiwork is something it would be hard honestly to regret. It will not be the only casualty of prosperity, but we should be clear that if globalization causes its disappearance, that will be counted among globalization's successes, not among its failures.

Politicians in ancient Athens were more open about accepting the challenges and benefits of globalization than are many of their successors today. Pericles told Athenians in his funeral oration: "We throw open our city to the world, and never by alien acts exclude foreigners from any opportunity of learning or observing, although the eyes of an enemy may occasionally profit by our liberality; trusting less in system and policy than to the native spirit of our citizens; while in education, where our rivals from their very cradles by a painful discipline seek after manliness, at Athens we live exactly as we please, and yet are just as ready to encounter every legitimate danger."[8] It is a noble and attractive vision, but there is pathos in his final clause. Athens lost the Peloponnesian War, and the fragility of a political and economic system founded on exchange between independent states has haunted the world ever since.

POLITICS AND GROUP LOYALTY

So what does politics have to offer in the face of this fragility? Modern democratic politics is an opportunistic compromise between the talents of man the reasoner and user of symbolic knowledge and man the emotional loyalist of the hunter-gatherer band. Many of the day-to-day tasks of government, at least in reasonably functional industrial states, are undertaken according to a set of rules, framed in terms of abstract categories that are independent of the particular individual applying them. A civil service is the epitome of symbolic reasoning, even if its actual functioning often falls short of the austere objectivity prescribed by the ideal. But the political process itself rarely even aims at such objectivity. Politicians explicitly aim to trigger the emotional responses of the family group, and the resources of television have now strengthened their ability to do so even beyond what used to be possible in the meeting hall or the stadium. A politician speaking on television is cultivating the illusion of speaking to each individual viewer as a kinsman or a friend. The viewer's brain may not be fooled, but the brain may not be the target. Her subliminal responses will be influenced, just as during human evolution our ancestors were influenced to respond warmly to smiles and to laughter, as we saw in chapter 3. "Trust me," says the smiling politician, and we relax a little. "Brothers and sisters," says the concerned-looking politician, and we become concerned in turn, serious, ready for sacrifice. A reference to the fatherland tugs at our reserves of loyalty — how could we be so churlish as to withhold our cooperation now?

Politicians are not alone in this; modern business uses similar techniques to sell its products. Why should the fact that a celebrity endorses a car or a telephone make any difference to whether we shall decide to buy it? Because celebrities give us the illusion of being people we know. They also tap into our wish to belong to powerful and high-status groups and imply to us that by buying the badge that distinguishes members from the rest, we can somehow make it more likely that we really do belong. Our desire for group membership can be very strong: the attraction of high-status groups is self-evident, but in many circumstances even weak, low-status-groups can seem more attractive than the solitary life. It must have served us well during our evolution, since it discouraged us from leaving the bands of our relatives even when personal relations were proving difficult. But it's a wish that makes us vulnerable to manipulative advertising in the very different circumstances of today. None of this means, as Vance Packard's book *The Hidden Persuaders* argued several decades ago, that advertisers and the firms that pay them are all-powerful.[9] After all, they compete against each other for our custom, and we are not passive stooges. Natural selection has also endowed us with brains that can reflect upon our own emotional vulnerabilities.

Nor is this to say that the daily trickery of politics is always to be deplored. Some of it may serve the interests of prosperity and peace. But the fact that similar emotions can be harnessed to both peaceful and aggressive ends means that we cannot tell from the quality of the emotional interaction alone what its overall social consequences will be. When we send our fittest young men to perform in international athletic contests or football tournaments, with politicians declaring their support for the brave youngsters and coordinating displays of patriotic solidarity, are we honing the instincts of warriors or enacting a parody of warfare to divert those instincts from a yearning for the real thing? When politicians declare war on an abstract noun like poverty, drugs, or unemployment, how close are they to mobilizing support for real wars, with real victims?

When the triggers of loyalty within a group work at the expense of cooperation between groups, everyone may lose out. The economist and political scientist Leonard Wantchekon recently performed a brilliant political experiment in his native Benin, when he persuaded rival political parties in the 2001 presidential election campaign to allow him to select a number of different villages to try out the effects of political programs that appealed to the general interests of the nation, as opposed to those that spoke about the same issues (health, unemployment, and so on) in explicitly partisan terms, promising voters in one place jobs and benefits even though these would be at the expense of jobs and benefits for voters elsewhere. The results were clear, and disturbing. When parties offered programs appealing to general interests, they received fewer votes than when they offered partisan programs. Perhaps the voters thought such partisan programs were more credible (because easier to fulfil). At all events, the experiment confirmed what many political scientists have long feared: that campaigning in partisan terms, to exploit the loyalty of a group by fanning its rivalry with other groups, may be a strategy that pays off for the individual politician even if it is damaging for the political system as a whole.[10]

So where does this leave general ideas and noble principles? Does a vision of politics based on evolutionary nostalgia, on the emotions of the hunter-gatherer, have any room for them?

LIBERALISM AND ITS HISTORY

One of the most powerful political ideas to surface in the modern world was liberalism. Most accounts of liberalism would date its origins to between roughly five hundred and roughly three hundred years ago, according to whether they date the birth of an idea to its first major visible influence or to its being explicitly written down. Five hundred years ago saw the discovery of the New World and the birth of Protestantism (Martin Luther's stand before the Diet of Worms took place in 1521). And just over three hundred years ago, between 1689 and 1692, John Locke published his *Two Treatises of Government*, and his three *Letters on Toleration*. In between, much had happened:

the early forms of capitalism had appeared; the English Civil War and its horrible European counterpart, the Thirty Years War, had been fought. Historians have argued at length about the precise nature of the furnace in which liberalism was forged, but most agree that it is a product of the modern, capitalist, Christian West.

Like most political philosophies, liberalism comprises both a vision of the human condition and a set of ideas to live by. In spite of differences about the details, there are strong common themes in the values advanced by various liberal writers. These comprise:

- Core values — liberty most obviously, but also, and to varying degrees, equality and pluralism.
- A procedure for moral reasoning — such as the social contract of Locke and Rousseau, or the "veil of ignorance" proposed by Rawls[11] — whose purpose is to undermine the perceived arbitrariness of appeals to tradition or authority.
- A set of constitutional recommendations to safeguard the core values, such as universal suffrage or a bill of rights.
- A program for political reform, whose content depends on current political circumstances but which always aims to remove existing threats to the exercise of liberty.

The vision of the human condition embodied in liberalism is the fruit partly of a natural psychology, an account of how human beings think and feel. It is also partly the fruit of a view of their social predicament, a story about why human beings who think and feel this way find themselves often in conflict, and what may be done to resolve conflicts in a way that is compatible with the constraints of natural psychology. The standard history of liberalism takes its natural psychology to be the "tabula rasa" (empty slate) theory of the human mind and its account of the social predicament to be modern Western capitalism. Since the former has now been scientifically discredited, and the latter seems wedded to a very particular historical time and place, the ability of liberalism to speak to the concerns of today's world seems — on this view — extremely limited. How can it even understand, let alone meet the challenge of, other philosophies, from socialism to nationalism to Islamic fundamentalism? Is the only alternative what Samuel Huntington has famously and depressingly called a "clash of civilizations"?[12]

Let's look first at how this conventional historical interpretation has been framed. Most historical accounts would see the origins of liberalism in capitalism (and its dependence on what the historian C. B. Macpherson called "possessive individualism"),[13] in the Reformation and its upholding of the sacredness of the individual conscience, and also in shared and horrified reaction to the brutality of the religious wars that wracked Europe in the sixteenth and, especially, the seventeenth centuries.[14] According to this view, capitalism and the Reformation acted as solvents, easing the move from status to contract, from gift to market, from magic to science, from a world of familiars to a world of strangers. They could do this because of a great malleability in human psychology, one noted and celebrated by philosophers from Locke to Russell. At the same time, modernity posed new problems for mankind that required radically new solutions, and it was the job of the prophets of liberalism not only to chart the arrival of modernity but actively to propose solutions to its discontents. So writers such as Locke, Rousseau, Voltaire, and John Stuart Mill were social reformers, drawing on the resources of liberal ideas to put forward both specific solutions to perceived social evils and also a framework of thought within which such solutions made sense. Their writings, and the ferment of ideas to which they contributed, had some momentous consequences:

- the European revolutions of 1789 and 1848;
- the anticolonial movements of the early nineteenth century in Latin America and, albeit with a very long lag, in Africa and Asia in the twentieth century;
- the moves toward free trade by the major European powers, Great Britain and Germany, in the nineteenth century;
- much more recently, the growing tension between rationalism and pluralism, between the wish to tolerate alternative lifestyles and the hope that everything, including lifestyle, is accessible to rational evaluation and criticism. This is a tension that bedevils modern multiculturalism, and that some critics of liberalism have seen as its Achilles heel.[15]

It is critical to this standard history of liberalism that the predicaments and concerns it raises are quite different from those of the ancient world. Benjamin Constant's famous essay on *The Liberty of the Ancients and the Liberty of the Moderns* is perhaps the purest expression of this view,[16] but in one way or another it is central to our view of liberalism as a Western capitalist ideology — a view whose fit with the preoccupations of non-Western, noncapitalist societies and such ideologies as Islam remains very uncertain. Some writers have queried the strength of the division between ancient and modern sensibilities (the philosopher Bernard Williams is an important recent example).[17] But this has not really disturbed the consensus that sees liberalism as rooted in just one of several rival economic, political, and cultural systems, nor the resulting anxiety about the fragility of liberalism's claim to offer inspiration across the globe.

And yet this historical account makes no sense of the fact that human beings have faced the challenge of living with strangers for the last ten thousand years. Pericles' defense of the openness of Athenian society is a perfect expression of a liberal point of view. This point of view may not have received its full philosophical stamp of approval until the writings of Locke, Rousseau, Voltaire, and Hume. But we should not see these writers as the original inventors of solutions to the problem of cohabiting a planet with people who are different from us, who are our rivals, and who nevertheless also share common interests. We should understand those writers instead as codifying and expressing publicly solutions that were already implicit in the human capacities that had enabled people for thousands of years to deal — literally — with strangers.

Seeing liberalism as a set of ideas that are (at least implicitly) ten thousand rather than merely five hundred years old has two great advantages. First, we can see its proper relation to other political ideologies. Socialism is not an *alternative* to liberalism's conception of humankind's social predicament, but rather one proposed means of resolving that predicament — it is a rival to some of the prescriptions of liberal writers rather than to their diagnosis. Both socialism and classical liberalism are compatible with a vision of humanity as needing to find a way to live with strangers; they simply disagree about how much individual enterprise and how much collective action are required for the task. Classical liberalism has frequently been naïve about what could be expected from individual enterprise without collective action. Socialism has been naïve both about the ease of achieving collective action and about the dangers of its being abused for militaristic or politically repressive ends.

Similarly, Islam as a political ideology consists of a set of ideas and values that proved extremely successful at building cohesion in societies under stress at a crucial period in their history. For several centuries Islamic societies led the world in culture, cosmopolitanism, and military strength: as Bernard Lewis has put it, Islam "created a world civilization, polyethnic, multiracial, international, one might even say intercontinental."[18] Some Islamic centers, as in southern Spain before the Christian reconquest, were models of tolerance and — yes — liberalism that have rarely been equaled in any culture since. Islam had evolved a response to the challenge of a world populated with strangers, though one that has proved fragile under the stresses of more recent centuries. That fragility is not accidental, though.[19] The fact that Islam rapidly acquired impressive military and political strength within a few years of its foundation meant that — unlike Christianity — it never needed to develop a philosophy of compromise with secular authorities and could indulge the ambition of a comprehensive regulation of social life. Its periods of tolerance were, therefore, the product of vast self-confidence and the absence of any real internal challenge rather than an ideology that had adapted to the permanent presence of strangers. How Islam will evolve in future decades remains very unclear, but whatever the rhetoric of its more warlike adherents, whatever the attractions of all-out aggression against unbelievers, Islam needs to evolve a new accommodation with strangers and unbelievers if it is to survive in the modern world.

In the same spirit, the antiglobalization movement cannot be interpreted in the literal sense of its title: globalization is a fact of the post-agricultural age, and it cannot be wished away. Antiglobalization has proved a very successful slogan for intragroup solidarity, and like all forms of solidarity based on opposition to a real or imagined external threat, it has to evolve into a basis for cooperation between groups as well as within them. Now that the movement has succeeded in capturing press and media attention, its more thoughtful leaders will need more than ever to begin that task.

The second great advantage of appreciating the true origins of liberalism is that we can appreciate what is valuable in the ideas of the great liberal philosophers without being wedded to their entirely implausible natural psychology. Locke's *tabula rasa* theory of the human mind is not taken seriously in psychology any more, and the nature of plasticity in human mental capacities is now seen as the product of ecological requirements during our prehistory: we are good at learning the kinds of things it was adaptive for us to learn rather than to inherit as hard-wired competencies. And Rousseau's account of the mind of the noble savage makes no sense from an evolutionary perspective. In one almost comically patronizing passage in his essay *On the Origins of Inequality*, he wrote that the soul of "the savage man . . . which nothing disturbs, dwells only in the sensation of its present existence, without any idea of the future, however close that might be, and his projects, as limited as his horizons, hardly extend to the end of the day. Such is, even today, the extent of the foresight of a Caribbean Indian: he sells his cotton bed in the morning, and in the evening comes weeping to buy it back, having failed to foresee that he would need it for the next night."[20] It is hard to see how Caribbean Indians as Rousseau describes them could have survived for a single generation, let alone populated an entire region of the world.

Human beings ten thousand years ago had inherited a psychology that made them intensely suspicious of strangers and capable of savage violence toward them under some circumstances, but able to benefit spectacularly from institutional arrangements that made it reasonable to treat strangers as honorary friends. The ability to abstract, therefore, from purely tribal loyalties and grant strangers the same freedoms as were granted to friends, the capacity to be open to new opportunities and choose freely among them, the willingness to communicate with those who do not share our ways of dressing, eating, and living, and to share a space with those who do not worship our gods — none of these constitute a purely Western capitalist mindset, even if historically it has been Western capitalism that has wrung the most economic mileage out of them. Indeed, these ideas are not sufficient in themselves to constitute a whole mental outlook of any kind, but without them none of the major historical civilizations could have developed.

This also answers our question about how much ideas matter in politics. Ideas as abstractions make almost no difference at all, for politics remains a very tribal activity, based on competition among would-be leaders to find ways of triggering our instincts for loyalty and cooperation. But ideas can be embodied in habits of thought that affect whom we treat as honorary friends and in institutions in which those habits of thought are put to work. As earlier chapters of this book have described in detail, almost all of the institutions of modern society can be understood as dedicated to an utterly unnatural division of labor between strangers. The idea of such cooperation on its own would be powerless without the institutions that make individuals believe in the cooperation of others, but the institutions, in turn, could not work unless they built on a natural disposition in human beings to cooperate within them. The political ideas that humanity will need for its survival in the next century are, therefore, all ideas about how to make these institutions work.

Reflection on this history can help us to make sense of some of the dilemmas of present-day liberalism. How much can modern citizens of industrial society concede to alternative cultural outlooks? As much as is needed to trust them, comes the reply. Reason is not in tension with pluralism, because what is needed to trust strangers is much less than what is needed to enter fully into their cultural outlook. We may or may not like someone else's cultural outlook, but we do not need to make up our minds about it in order to share the same social space with them. Toleration does not imply bland praise for every set of ideas that differs from our own; it simply means refusing to allow differences over ideas to prevent us from dealing with others in a civilized way. Likewise, dislike of someone's culture does not imply we can afford to avoid dealing with them, nor should dealing with them be construed as a threat to our own core values.

Such liberal sentiments may sound admirable, and the fact that they have been in some sense a part of our species' heritage for ten millennia may increase our respect for their pertinence to humanity as a whole rather than just to its prosperous and privileged minorities. But today's world is subjecting these sentiments to new and disturbing stresses. How likely is it that the Great Experiment can survive the unpredictable human energies it has unleashed?

How Fragile is the Great Experiment?

As you are reading these words, somebody you have never met is working hard on your behalf. Almost certainly many people are working for you — an Indian farmer driving bullocks across his land so he can plant the cotton that will be made into the shirt you will buy sometime next year; a Brazilian farmer harvesting the coffee beans for your breakfast next month; a civil servant planning the road improvements close to that dangerous junction you pass on your way to work; a chemist synthesizing molecules to treat the illness that you still do not realize you have. These people do not know you, but they do not need to, even though your life, your health, and your prosperity depend upon them. You have every reason to be grateful for the intimate links that tie them to you.

Possibly too, at this same moment, someone you have never met is working actively on a plan to kill you. Unless you are a well-known public figure, you may not be the specific target of his murderous intention, which may simply be directed at causing random casualties. But in some ways that makes the possibility more worrying, since it is harder for you to know how to make precautions, whom to be wary of, what to avoid. You are likely to develop instead a systematic suspicion of strangers, which may be precisely the intention of your would-be assassin. Since 11 September 2001, American society in particular has seen suspicion of strangers — especially strangers of Middle Eastern appearance and Islamic faith — intensify to a remarkable degree.

Perhaps surprisingly, these risks are much *less* likely to affect you directly than are the many unintentional interactions between you and millions of other strangers across the world who are not working consciously to do you either good or harm. The most important risk is infectious disease. Throughout history, infectious disease has been a far greater threat than violence, and in spite of antibiotics and modern medicine, this remains overwhelmingly true today. According to the World Health Organization, roughly 56 million deaths were recorded worldwide in 2001 — a reasonably typical year. Of these, nearly 11 million were due to infectious or parasitic disease. That's just under 20 per cent. War and violence killed around three-quarters of a million people — a little over 1 per cent.[1] Even in periods of major conflict, war has rarely rivaled disease as a killer: the influenza pandemic of 1918 killed over 20 million people, more than had died in the four previous horrifying years of war. And for all that television brings us face to face with violence across the world, the average risk of violence faced by the world's citizens is almost certainly as low now as it has ever been in our history.[2]

Besides cultivating and transmitting infectious diseases, strangers across the world are also consuming scarce resources, polluting rivers and the atmosphere, deforesting hillsides, congesting cities and scarce agricultural land, running down or poisoning aquifers, strewing the countryside with plastics and depleting energy reserves. They are not paying the full cost of this wanton damage today, leaving you and others to pay some of the cost tomorrow, or next year, or even decades from now. It makes no sense to resent them for behaving like this, for you are almost certainly doing many of these things yourself, or paying other people to do so. But when faced with this alarming catalogue of damage being done to you by strangers, you might be tempted to think that the risks of violence are comparatively small. *Homo sapiens sapiens*, the shy, murderous ape, may be spreading pestilence and pollution on a global scale, but his violent instincts at least seem to have been triumphantly tamed.

And so they have, if we measure them by the statistical risk of violent death at the hands of someone else. In Europe and in the United States, for instance, such deaths make up only a little over half of 1 percent of all deaths. That's much less than those due to traffic accidents and only half of those due to suicide. Even in Africa, the world's most materially and institutionally impoverished region, violent deaths at the hands of others make up only a little over 2 percent of all deaths.[3] And yet such statistics cannot even begin to capture the real impact of violence. First of all, violence and war bring disease, destitution, and environmental damage in their wake even when they do not carve their names in the mortality statistics. And then the *fear* of violence exerts a poisonous and disruptive effect on human relations. Travelers have taken scores, perhaps hundreds of millions fewer airplane journeys as a result of the hijackings of 11 September 2001;[4] the political and military map of the Middle East is being redrawn as a consequence of those events; citizens of the prosperous Western world worry about whether it is safe to take trains and buses or to visit city centers. In Israel and Palestine the fear of death at a stranger's hands has had a chilling effect on everyday life. In Africa, millions of people are condemned to poverty and disease by the inability of the ordinary institutions of society to function without the periodic eruption of violence. In short, for every death at a stranger's hands there are many thousands of living victims. Their newly awakened fear of strangers disrupts the whole web of relations that bind people together in a healthy modern society and undermines all the institutions on which such a society depends, from schools to hospitals, shops, government departments, and the legal system. The more pervasive are the threads in this web of relations, the more corrosive is the effect of any single incident of violence on our capacity for trust.

Worse, many of the stresses caused by disease and by environmental degradation may themselves come to provoke conflict. There are two main ways this is likely to happen. First, through the general disruption caused to people's livelihoods by degraded environments and dwindling natural resources, the resulting frustration of such people, and their disillusionment with peaceful routes to prosperity. Secondly, through ethnic tensions set up when groups migrate to escape the pressure of environmental scarcity.[5] In turn these conflicts may disrupt the institutions that might otherwise be able to manage environmental resources in a reasonably efficient and sustainable way—no one can expect wise or farsighted policies for water conservation to emerge from a society in civil war. For instance, conflicts over access to water have seriously worsened relations between Israelis and Palestinians in the West Bank and Gaza. About 40 percent of Israel's groundwater use depends on aquifers that lie principally under the West Bank,[6] and it is mournfully clear that the current state of tension leaves little chance of reaching a fair and efficient agreement on the conservation and sharing of water in the future.

At the same time, technology is affecting the likelihood of future violence in two main ways. First of all, the worldwide reach of technologies of communication—television and the internet, those two great weapons of mass distraction—has given those who use violence in the struggle for scarce resources a vast audience for their campaigns, as well as much better information about the most vulnerable targets. Such technologies do not just change the stakes for those whose use of violence is strictly prudent and instrumental; they also provide a temptingly dramatic stage, and a seductively compelling narrative, for those prepared to risk death for violent ends. Modern society has, in part, turned humanity's violent tendencies inward, so that, astonishingly, more people today are killed by their own hand than by the hand of others: nearly a million people in the world commit suicide every year. The overwhelming majority are people who do so in a state of depression, friendless and alone. Fortunately, perhaps, the crippling effects of depression on the capacity for foresight and planning mean that few such people will ever be able to put their decision to kill themselves to a precise military or political end. But not all who commit suicide are depressed; some are clinically schizophrenic, while others without the benefit of a formal diagnosis appear to believe that the reward for their actions will be glory, whether in a real heaven or in the virtual heaven of the websites and the cable networks. As modern communications penetrate around the world, we should not be surprised if growing numbers of the deluded, allied perhaps to a minority of the desperate, succumb to the allure of a spectacular exit before the world's television cameras.

Secondly, the progress of military technology — if "progress" is the appropriate word at this point — means that those inclined toward violence have increasingly destructive ways of inflicting it upon their victims. Some of the people who once used fists can now use knives; some of those who once used knives can now use guns; some of those who once used guns can now use bombs. Admittedly, some of the threats of high-tech terrorism seem overrated. It's unlikely, for instance, that biological terrorism will cause even a tiny fraction of the deaths that occur routinely from infectious diseases invented by nature, without any malign intent, through random experimentation in her own millions of laboratories — though the fear generated by biological terrorism is likely to be out of proportion to any casualties it will cause. Less clear is whether nuclear weapons are likely to find their way into the hands of terrorists able and willing to deliver them to the cities of the industrialized world. They represent a tempting source of hard currency and influence for those states that own them, and it would be foolish to bet against their being long held in secure custody. But high technology may be a lesser threat than the steady, unspectacular spread around the world of familiar, standard-issue weaponry that will allow much greater compass to any single act of rage, aggression, or revenge. A world in which any person's act of rage could destroy or terrorize an entire apartment block, street, or neighborhood would be unable to sustain the close proximity to strangers that is at the heart of modern life. And even if in practice such acts of rage were rare, and a balance of terror prevailed in each street, a world in which every citizen could resist the demands of the police, the law courts, and the tax authorities with weaponry that was a match for the state's own would be a world in which civic institutions as we know them could no longer function.

Perhaps, then, the character that has principally defined states for the last few centuries — namely, their monopoly of coercion within a stable territory — may now be coming under serious challenge. This might seem no more than the logical evolution of modern society — monopolies are coming under challenge from smaller and nimbler competitors everywhere, from telecommunications to steel markets to the domains of information and ideas — but it would have more disturbing consequences. An easier, more competitive supply of weapons imposes more dangerous externalities on others than an easier, more competitive supply of telecoms or steel. It would also limit the ability of the state to function as the counterweight to market exchange through its powers to raise taxes and regulate the operation of markets. Not everyone would regret this limitation. But the infrastructure of modern society, which we think we can afford to disdain because it is so familiar that we are scarcely aware of its existence, would crumble without the coercive potential of the modern state.

Whether the Great Experiment survives much past its first ten thousand years will depend, therefore, on the answers to three main questions:

First, can states survive as monopolies of coercion within their own territorial frontiers?

Second, can they combine the openness and flexibility needed by modern industrial societies with the trust in strangers that has been so laboriously established over previous centuries?

Third, can they find ways to create between themselves an analogous version of the trust in strangers that they seek to create among their citizens?

The first question amounts to asking whether the state can protect people from external threats better than any other institution. The second amounts to asking whether states can protect their own citizens from each other. The third amounts to asking whether states can protect themselves from each other confidently enough to cooperate rather than live in fear.

THE SURVIVAL OF THE STATE

All monopolies depend for their survival as monopolies either on some technological advantage over their competitors or on the inherited privileges derived from a special relationship with the state. The state itself cannot rely on such inherited privileges, of course. So its survival will depend on whether it continues to enjoy intrinsic organizational advantages over other institutions that can exercise coercion, such as terrorist organizations, religious orders, or even just isolationist citizens with heavy weaponry in their back yards. Surprisingly, perhaps (in an age when new technologies are transforming organizations in so many domains of life), the continued organizational superiority of the nation-state looks rather likely for the foreseeable future.

Why? Developing effective military technology still requires control over territory. A terrorist group operating in a network of cells can make simple bombs or develop chemical or biological weapons, but these are undiscriminating devices that cannot be used in self-defense or as a way to pursue systematic bargaining for political ends. Such a group cannot deliver massive destructive power to a precise target some distance away — the necessary condition for credible military bargaining with a powerfully armed nation-state — unless it controls territory of its own. Even owning pirated stocks of weapons-grade uranium is useless to an organization unless it can develop this into a weapon undisturbed, hide the weapon from preemptive attack, and then deliver it to its target. All this requires the organization to have undisputed control over a significant area of land. But to control territory it is not enough to be rich or to have superior technological skills. The organization also needs people, to patrol its borders, to manage its internal structure and activities, to protect it from subversion. These people need somewhere to live, and they need the infrastructure of life — schools, hospitals, leisure activities — which the organization must either rely on the state to provide or must provide for itself. Any organization that can provide these things for itself is already operating on a scale of ambition and internal coercion to make it, in all essentials, a state, and states will never be viable in a hostile environment unless they have significant populations (statelets such as Monaco or Liechtenstein survive because they are not in hostile environments). In short, defense needs a good deal of territory; managing territory needs a good many people; so in defense there remains a real advantage to being large. Just how large a viable state has to be is an open question, and the thresholds of viable size may be falling in the modern world (just as they have risen and fallen at various stages in history).[7] These thresholds are also open to bloody and protracted negotiation, with periods of stalemate in which zones can be occupied by guerrilla organizations able to resist the demands of central government but unable to create a properly functioning state of their own, as in the areas of Sri Lanka occupied by the Liberation Tigers of Tamil Eelam or those of Colombia occupied by the Revolutionary Armed Forces of Colombia.[8] But it is unlikely that the thresholds of viability have fallen so far as to create any credible alternative to something very like the state as we know it today.

The Survival of Trust within Nation-States

Even so, can nation-states continue to assure our trust in strangers? As Raymond Chandler pointed out, it can be easier to rule a country than a city. A future is imaginable in which nation-states can patrol their borders against invasions but are powerless to stop infiltrations; in which people are safe from foreign armies but live in terror of their neighbors; in which a trip to the grocery store becomes a hazardous and adrenaline-fueled venture, as the hunt must once have been for our Paleolithic ancestors.

One of the strengths of our trust-building institutions, as they were described in the early chapters of this book, is how decentralized they are. We ourselves are the real police; those who wear uniforms are just the special forces, playing a crucial but minority role in overseeing the billions of daily interactions between strangers in our modern world. The barriers to violent or opportunistic behavior consist mostly in habits learned early in life and performed almost unthinkingly before an audience of other people rather like ourselves. While this makes them prone to frequent, small disruptions—the stuff of countless human-interest stories in local newspapers and television reports—large disruptions are rare. The system has no real command center and therefore no single point of vulnerability. To disrupt the trust-building institutions of modern society requires subjecting many of them to frontal assault, as in wartime. Some terrorist organizations aim to do almost this, to reproduce through precision assaults on visible and symbolically charged targets the sense of vulnerability characteristic of a society at war. To the extent that they can succeed, this will be because even a decentralized system has certain symbolic centers, damage to which harms our willingness to trust our fellow citizens.[9] It will not be because any individual target (even, say, a capital city) is in itself critical to the functioning of our institutions of trust.

Researchers have devoted much effort in recent years to studying the properties that make networks (like computer, power, or transportation networks) robust against disruption.[10] They have stressed the importance of an architecture that allows some links within a network to do the job of others that may be damaged through accident or design. Some networks function efficiently under normal conditions through an architecture built around hubs that connect many different links. Major airports, for instance, allow even complex journeys through an air transportation network to be made with only one or two interconnections: by flying through Chicago, you can get to many destinations with just one stop. If there are too few such hubs, the network can break down dramatically when one of them fails. The more hubs there are, the more robust is the network against disruption (you can reroute through another hub). But the cost is redundancy—building more links than you normally need.

Occasional malevolent assaults on the hubs of our society are likely to happen for the foreseeable future. Technology and the global spread of weapons may make some of these assaults spectacularly deadly. And to the extent that we are connected to others as never before in our history, we all face such threats from a greater variety of directions. But such assaults have always been a hazard of human life, and in many ways modern society has fewer irreplaceable hubs than in the past. Medieval European societies had monarchs who embodied authority and legitimacy in their own person and whose assassination could provoke massive bloodletting. Most modern societies invest authority and legitimacy in presidents or equivalent officeholders who can be replaced by vice presidents at a moment's notice without major social breakdown. These transitions are not always smooth: charismatic individual leaders may seem irreplaceable, and others may choose to try and make themselves so by deliberate practice of personalized politics. (When Indian prime minister Indira Gandhi was assassinated in 1984 by a Sikh member of her own bodyguard, thousands of people were killed in ethnic violence between Hindus and Sikhs.) But modern society is nevertheless founded on the shared presumption that individuals count for less in their contribution to social trust than do the roles they play. If this were not so, we would need to learn far too much about too many individuals to be able to trust any of them.

This is true of political officeholders, and it is also true at the humble level of individual interaction. In a smoothly functioning modern society, you can trust me to transact reasonably with you not because of my character and personality (about which you know little and care less), nor because you share my religion or my politics (which may repel you), nor because you know my family, but simply because of the social space we share. If it is to survive future challenges, such a social space needs construction through institutions (including systems of education) that are blind to all the particularities of individuals except those that are strictly necessary for their interaction. In a word, it requires a degree of impartiality. Members of any one tribe, religion, family, nationality, or ethnic group need to be sure that when they encounter strangers, it is safe to deal with them. It is in this sense that education needs to be secular, multiethnic, liberal, a challenge that education systems in many countries have yet properly to face. Indeed, the secular character of education has been coming under increasing assault in some countries that wish to see schools reclaimed as the preserve of communitarian and religious values. Whatever the merits of transmitting particular sets of communitarian and religious values to one's children, schools in the twenty-first century need above all to teach children the one vital skill for the survival of humanity, namely, how to live peacefully and profitably with people whose community and religion are not one's own. Awareness of religion and ethnicity need not be banished from the schoolroom, but the schoolroom must be a place where ethnic groups learn how to meet and mingle rather than to fight. Concretely, to take an example that has been much discussed in France, where I live, a properly secular education seems less threatened by the headscarf, a mark of religious affiliation in which some Islamic girls take pride, than by the veil, which is a barrier to the facial recognition that underlies human interaction and that we use to signal our willingness to treat strangers as honorary friends. There is much controversy about such issues, about how much of our ethnic identity we can legitimately take with us into public spaces, and about how likely it is that secular systems of education can be made to work. But that we need them to work somehow is an almost inescapable implication of the irreversible intermingling of strangers in the modern world: it is too late now to unmix the eggs from the omelette and put them back into their shells.

It would be naïve to think that a system of trust-building institutions that is decentralized enough to be robust against disruption will always be impartial enough to inspire the confidence of strangers. Indeed, it is a mark of decentralized institutions that those who wish to use them for partial and communitarian ends can always try to do so. We can be sure that some countries will live through periods of ethnic violence and suspicion, which will discredit their institutions, doing damage that may take years or decades to repair. What is virtually certain, though, is that no country can hope to live peacefully and prosperously unless it finds ways to reconcile its citizens to mutual trust. And even that is only part of the task. Countries that have resolved their internal challenges still have to learn how to trust each other.

TRUST BETWEEN NATION-STATES

The last decade of the twentieth century saw the political and economic collapse of one of the two superpowers that had sustained the Cold War, the spread of democratic institutions to many countries that had not previously enjoyed them (particularly in central and eastern Europe), the creation of many new institutions of cooperation between nation-states (from the International Criminal Court to the World Trade Organization), the signing of international treaties on such matters as the control of global warming, and a highly visible and activist role for the United Nations. If trust between nations could be measured by the proliferation of agreements, the future would surely be bright.

Yet in one crucial respect international trust is becoming harder, not easier to build. The United States is now militarily predominant over the whole world to a degree unprecedented in history and paralleled in any part of the world only by the hegemony of the Roman empire two millennia ago. Trust grows more naturally between two wolves than between a wolf and a sheep, and no amount of sincere protestation addressed from wolf to sheep can alter this melancholy fact. Of course, if the United States were able to function reasonably wisely in the world without the trust of other countries, this might not matter very much. Some press comment by influential Americans both before and after the U.S.-led invasion of Iraq in 2003 suggested that this was a widely held American view.[11] Not only did many Americans believe that the cooperation of other countries mattered little; they also seemed to believe that the United States would police the world with prudence and wisdom for the foreseeable future.

This is a dangerous mistake, for two reasons. One is that the United States will need the full and enthusiastic cooperation of other countries if its prosperity and liberties are to be preserved. This is not just a matter of American dependence on foreign energy reserves and other imported goods and on the mobility of American goods and ideas around the world. It is also a matter of the need for other countries, in particular the emerging superpowers China and India, to cooperate in solving problems where externalities matter on a world scale, notably in the protection of the environment. American military predominance will not on its own persuade China and India to cooperate in controlling global warming; it may even make cooperation more difficult. Most of all, if individual Americans are to be physically present in the rest of the world, they will need physical protection there, whether they come as guests or as policemen. Even policemen need to move comfortably among strangers, and even policemen rely on a largely voluntary cooperation, most of the time, from the societies in which they move. And yet, in the old paradox described by Hegel, the more powerful the policeman, the harder it is for him to command the free assent on which the creative exercise of his power depends.

The second reason it is a mistake to believe the United States need not be concerned about its military predominance is that domestic political checks may not prevent that predominance from being exercised in reckless and self-defeating ways. The knowledge that military aggression carries a high risk of casualties is the best restraint against the exercise of that aggression. This is true (as we have seen) for groups of marauding chimpanzees, and it is no less true for us, their biological relatives. Without such risks, aggressive wars, fought for plausible but ultimately foolish reasons, are eventually inevitable. Relying on moral restraint is not enough, for as we have also seen warfare draws upon and inspires genuinely impressive feats of altruism — even when the warfare is aggressive and imprudent. Even aggressive wars are fought with a moral fervor. Nor are purely political checks enough. Decisions about acts of war typically rely on intelligence information that is impossible for citizens to verify, as was demonstrated by the debate in the United States and the United Kingdom over whether Iraq possessed weapons of mass destruction. This means that political leaders rely on appeals to the trust of citizens, who are in a weak position to determine whether that trust has been justified in any particular case. It is of little assurance to note the United States' "fervent devotion to liberty,"[12] precisely because the more convinced are the citizens that their leaders are devoted to liberty, the harder it will be for them to question any decision in favor of war.

In one respect, though, the asymmetry between the United States and its rivals provides a reason for optimism. Nearly four decades ago, the economist Mancur Olson analyzed, in *The Logic of Collective Action*, the incentives for members of a group to contribute to public goods. These are goods that benefit the entire group and from which no members can be excluded if they fail to contribute. The incentive of members to free-ride on the contributions of others is well known — we saw it at work in chapter 13. But Olson also drew attention to what might happen if there was significant inequality between group members. Members who were economically powerful, gaining a significant share of the benefits from public goods, would tend to make large contributions, thereby further diminishing the already low willingness of weaker members to make any contribution at all. As Olson put it, somewhat provocatively, "there is a systematic tendency for 'exploitation' of the great by the small."[13] Powerful members might wish they could persuade others to contribute more, but their own need for the public good makes them contribute enough to satisfy the weaker members' inclination to pay.

The political leaders of the United States would no doubt recognize Olson's description of their plight, and the phrase "the exploitation of the great by the small" would perhaps strike a responsive chord. They might consider his analysis to apply mainly to areas where the United States already intervenes in the world and seeks to share the cost (as in the military intervention in Iraq). But it has lessons equally for areas where the United States is reluctant to pursue cooperative action, perhaps thinking itself insulated from the consequences of inaction. Recent events may have begun to persuade American leaders and citizens that they are less insulated than they once believed. Olson's logic may persuade them that they need to contribute to the building of international stability even without the contributions of other nations. They have yet to be persuaded, though, that international stability requires the trust of others to be won, that it cannot simply be delivered, a fait accompli, by an overwhelmingly powerful nation as its gift to the world.

The implication of these arguments is that, paradoxically, the United States itself has a strong interest in international institutions that constrain its power and discretion. This is a version, projected onto an international scale, of a fundamental argument that has appeared repeatedly in this book. When modern man goes out into a city to mingle with strangers, he is bound by a multitude of constraints that prevent him from asserting his Paleolithic personality. When a stranger offers him food, he cannot simply seize it as his prize but must meekly sign a credit-card slip. When the credit card company asks for settlement of his account, he cannot proudly tell them to go hang but must pay up, or face endless petty nuisances that — most of the time — are a credible incentive to comply. When another stranger picks his pocket, he must report the theft patiently to the police rather than seeking out the perpetrator and killing him along with all his tribe. In short, bourgeois prudence has driven out panache, and modern society is unimaginable in any other way. The stronger and more unchallenged is any one individual, the more he needs these petty and unexciting constraints. Without them, he will find the marketplace empty, and the few strangers he ever meets will be cowed and fearful, plotting revenge behind his back for the humiliations he imposes on them to their face.

If the Great Experiment is to survive an era of globalization, environmental degradation, and arms proliferation, international relations will need petty and unexciting constraints of just this kind, and the United States will need them most of all. For all that international diplomacy resounds to high-minded declarations, it is all about compromises and cutting deals; the activities of the marketplace of nations. But the United States and its leaders have still to be convinced that the marketplace of nations needs trust-building institutions as profoundly as do the ordinary market-places of the modern world. It is a mark of the wound suffered by the United States on the 11 September 2001 that a country that has mastered better than any other the transformation of the frontier spirit into the bourgeois virtues should have become so impatient with the demands of bourgeois prudence in its dealings with the rest of the world.

It's time to sum up. Contrary to what one might conclude from the excitable tone of much recent press comment, globalization and its challenges are not new but a continuation of social developments of at least the last ten thousand years. The conceptual habits we need to deal with these challenges are not new either, and the fact that they have been more explicitly articulated in the last three centuries perhaps indicates that they are so instinctive and familiar that it has often been easy to overlook them. But their being instinctive and familiar does not prevent them being fragile. On the contrary, the practical intelligence that has evolved among human beings is one that is skilled at manipulating the natural environment, and also at managing the interactions of small groups of individuals who see each other frequently and know each other well. It is only in the last ten thousand years that human beings have had to come to terms on a significant scale with the impact of strangers, and it is only in the last two hundred or so that this impact has become a dominant fact of everyday life. To manage the hazards imposed on us by the actions of strangers has required us to deploy a different skill bequeathed to us by evolution for quite different purposes, the capacity for abstract symbolic thought. Modern political institutions temper their appeals to the deep emotions, to family and clan loyalty, with just enough abstract reasoning to help *Homo sapiens sapiens*, the shy, murderous ape, emerge from his family bands in the savanna woodland in order to live and work in a world largely populated by strangers. This experiment is still young, and needs all the help it can get.

Notes

INTRODUCTION

1. The main phases in human evolution are discussed accessibly in Klein & Edgar 2002, more technically in Klein 1999. The latter uses the subspecies name *Homo sapiens sapiens* to refer to fully modern humans (those of when we have evidence only in the last fifty thousand years), leaving open whether earlier humans should also be considered members of *Homo sapiens*; I follow this usage here.

2. See Ridley 1996, especially chapter 2.

3. Ants are sisters, but share three-quarters of their genes, as explained in Hölldobler & Wilson 1994, pp. 95–106.

4. This theory was due originally to Hamilton 1964, and the classic popular exposition is given in Dawkins 1976.

5. When biologists speak of individuals "sharing" genes, they are referring to those genes that vary across members of the same species. The great majority of human genes are common to the whole species; indeed, most are shared with other primates. For the theory of kin selection, what matters is the probability that two individuals share a mutation that first appeared in the genome of their most recent common ancestor. This probability is given by the proportion of genes that have been inherited from their most recent common ancestor, instead of from other ancestors—even if the ones inherited from other ancestors are, at most loci, the same gene.

6. See Dawkins 1976 for sticklebacks, Wilkinson 1990 for vampire bats, and Pusey & Packer 1983 for lions. The theory explaining such behavior, known as "reciprocal altruism," is due to Trivers (1971).

7. See Bishop 1992, pp. 125, 192.

8. Of course, if one counted same- *and* opposite-sex ancestors, potentially doubling the numbers at each generation, the total would be vastly greater.

9. See Cavalli-Sforza 2000, pp. 45–46.

10. The evolution of human consciousness is brilliantly discussed in Mithen 1996, though discoveries are being made so fast that it must be hoped a second edition will not be long in appearing (similar remarks apply a fortiori to the pioneering work of Humphrey 1984). Klein & Edgar 2002 gives a clear account of the main questions and uncertainties surrounding the evolution of symbolic capacity in man. Deacon 1997 is a comprehensive account of the challenges facing an evolutionary account of symbolic ability. Tomasello 1999 links human cultural capacities to an evolved ability to put ourselves in the position of the psychological responses of others. This ability was adaptive because it improved our powers to predict and it had dramatic consequences for the cumulative nature of our culture because it enormously increased our ability to imitate the

behavior of those others. These arguments are discussed in more detail in chapter 11.

11. On the dating of the last common ancestors of living human beings, see Cavalli-Sforza 2000, pp. 77–82 (incidentally, the last common maternal ancestor and the last common paternal ancestor almost certainly never met, let alone had children together).

12. Klein 1999, pp. 517–24, after discussing possible objections to the claim, concludes that the behavioral capacities of Cro-Magnon man very likely marked a fundamental departure from those of Neanderthal man, although some archaeological puzzles remain.

13. The puzzle of multiple discoveries of agriculture is discussed in Richerson, Boyd, & Bettinger 2001. See also the prologue to part 4.

14. Blackmore 1999 emphasizes that we cannot conclude that the evolution of human institutions (which are one form of the behavior patterns she calls, following Dawkins 1976, "memes") is beneficial for human beings, or even for their genes. She argues that "what makes us different [from other animals] is our ability to imitate" and stresses that once behavior patterns are imitated, "something is passed on. This 'something' can then be passed on again, and again, and so take on a life of its own." Memes evolve, in other words, for the good of the memes and not for the good of anyone or anything else. Nevertheless, we can investigate whether human psychology, as shaped by natural selection, makes it easier for certain memes to spread than for others; the extent to which meme evolution is thus constrained by psychology is an empirical question.

CHAPTER 1. WHO'S IN CHARGE?

1. The startling character of cooperative exchange involved in the production of even simple objects is not a new observation; see, for example, the discussion of pencils in Friedman & Friedman 1990, pp. 11–13.

2. Terkel 1974.

3. Hamermesh 2003 has studied routine as a characteristic of different kinds of work and documents its links to income and education levels. He describes these links as "yet another avenue by which standard measures of income inequality understate total economic inequality."

4. Hacking 1990 is a fascinating account of the rise of statistics as a discipline and the wonder provoked in its practitioners by the apparent regularity of human behavior in large numbers.

5. However, the proportion of jobs in rich countries lost through international competition is by most estimates smaller than the proportion lost through technical change. See Bourguignon et al. 2002 for a summary of these issues.

6. See the discussion in Sivéry 2000, especially pp. 44–47; also De Vries 1976, especially chapter 2 and pp. 159–64. I am grateful to Sheilagh Ogilvie for these references.

7. Packard 1957.

8. Klein 2001—Naomi, not Richard.

9. Cited in Jones 1988, p. 151.

PROLOGUE TO PART 2

1. See Wrangham & Peterson 1996, and the more detailed discussion of this evidence in chapter 3.

2. Though not quite indistinguishable: human brain size has fallen since around fifty thousand years ago, and some of this fall may have taken place in the last twelve thousand years. A recent and controversial theory (see Wrangham 2003) suggests this may have been due to a process like the domestication of animals, in which particularly violent or antisocial individuals had their breeding possibilities reduced through ostracism. Domesticated animals typically have brains smaller than their wild relatives. It is too early yet to say whether this theory will prove persuasive, but we can be confident that it will not remove the need to explain how human institutions have managed to tame the violence of which our species is still capable.

CHAPTER 2. MAN AND THE RISKS OF NATURE

1. Suppose that of a population of 200 million, 20 million have a certain condition. Then a test with 99 percent reliability, applied to the whole population, will generate 19.8 million true positives and 1.8 million false positives. This means that if you test positive, you have a probability of just over 90 percent of having the condition. If the condition is much rarer, affecting only 20,000 in the population, then the test will generate 19,800 true positives and 1.98 million false positives. This means that even if you test positive, the probability you have the condition is still only a little over 1 percent, namely, 19,800 as a proportion of 1.98 million plus 19,800.

2. See Hacking 1990.

3. Dunbar 1992.

4. Ricardo 1817.

5. See Perrin 1979 for an account of how Japan gave up guns in the mid-sixteenth century and reverted to the sword.

6. Klein & Edgar 2002.

7. Ridley 1996, pp. 197ff.

8. Originally by Peltzman (1975). See also Evans & Graham 1991. Peterson et al. (1994) make a similar investigation of airbags. However, Sen & Mizzen (2001) have provided some reasons to be skeptical about the size of the effects measured in other studies. They point out that sometimes seatbelt use or the purchase of cars with airbags may be prompted by drivers' recognition of preexisting dangers, so the measured association may mean that high risk causes the adoption of safety measures, rather than vice versa.

9. Adams (1995), who writes accessibly about the theory of risk compensation in general.

10. For the evolution of European economies away from peasant self-sufficiency, see De Vries 1974 for the Netherlands; De Vries 1976, especially chapter 2, for Europe more generally; Britnell 1997 for England; and Ogilvie 2000 for an overview, especially pp. 94–108. I am grateful to Sheilagh Ogilvie and Leigh Shaw-Taylor for these references. Leigh Shaw-Taylor has also shown me un-

published evidence from English poll tax records suggesting that as early as 1381, peasants numbered a quarter or less of the population in many villages and were typically outnumbered by craftsmen and traders. For more anecdotal information about North America, used to support a theory of historical changes in self-sufficiency, see Locay 1990.

11. Dutta & Seabright 2002.

12. Anderson 2000, pp. 326–28.

CHAPTER 3. MURDER, RECIPROCITY, AND TRUST

1. Dostoyevsky 1865.

2. On the evidence that men are, on average, more violent than women, see Daly & Wilson 1988, Wrangham & Peterson 1996, Barash & Lipton 2002, and Ghiglieri 1999; Barash 2002 provides a summary. Needless to say, all such comparisons are based on averages of behavior patterns in the populations in question and do not imply biological determinism in any individual case.

3. So, of course, does killing a related member of the same sex and species, but the rivalry is less intense because of the shared genes.

4. Act 4, scene 3.

5. Evidence from a preindustrial society (specifically, the Yanomamo of Venezuela) that men who kill others have more children is found in Chagnon 1988, though it is also a plausible inference from other ethnographic studies, such as Meggitt 1977. Robarchek and Robarchek (1998, p. 133) cite data that appear to support this inference, though they themselves have doubts about its validity.

6. Andersson 1994 discusses the theory of sexual selection at length. It is discussed specifically in relation to violence in Ghiglieri 1999.

7. Evidence about infanticide in primates is set out in De Waal 2001, especially at pages 27, 30, 60–61, and 88–89. It is also discussed, in relation to primate and human violence more generally, in Ghiglieri 1999, especially pp. 129–33, though Ghiglieri overlooks the evidence that bonobos are strikingly less violent than chimpanzees. Diamond 1993, pp. 290–94, discusses the relevance for humans of intraspecies violence in nonhuman species and gives a graphic description of the violence witnessed by Jane Goodall and her team. This violence is also described by Ghiglieri (pp. 172–77), who points out that in the chimpanzee groups he observed, recorded violence was lower than in the Goodall groups, apparently because the former had reached a more stable accommodation between groups: each group had enough males to make defense possible without making attack attractive. The best (and best-written) overview of human and great-ape violence is certainly Wrangham & Peterson 1996, which is more balanced and less sensationalist than its title ("Demonic Males") might lead one to expect.

8. Lorenz 1963.

9. The evidence about human violence in general is controversial, and questions about causality (such as whether there is an "instinct" for violence) are even more controversial than questions about the incidence of violence at particular times and places. For the argument I advance in this chapter it is enough to

show that human societies have usually been violent in the absence of institutions for deterring violent behavior. Ember 1978 is an early survey of warfare (inter alia) among hunter-gatherers, and Gat 2000a,b among preindustrial societies more generally. Ferguson & Gat (2000) debate the reliability of this evidence. Gat 1999 also contains evidence about the nature and purposes of such violence. A sobering overview of the human species' capacity for murderous violence is Diamond 1993, chapter 16. Robarchek & Robarchek (1997) compare two societies that, at the time of observation, had very different violence levels, though the more peaceful community (the Semai Senoi of Malaysia) had in previous years been successfully recruited into the anticommunist armies used by the British colonial administration, where they became ruthless and efficient killers (Ghiglieri 1999, p. 185).

10. Ember 1978.
11. Leblanc 1999.
12. Meggitt 1977.
13. See Seabright 1993 for a survey.
14. Summarized in Fehr & Gächter 2000a.
15. Fehr et al. 1993.
16. Fehr & Gächter 2000b.
17. Ibid.
18. Basu 1984.
19. Durant 1926, p. 307. I am grateful to Stanley Engerman for pointing this out to me.
20. However, the strength of the reciprocity motivation may have important implications for the ways in which cooperative behavior can be encouraged in practice. For instance, there is evidence that increasing penalties for tax evasion may sometimes result in reduced tax compliance, because it is interpreted by previously honest taxpayers as a signal that many others are dishonest, thereby prompting them to reduce their own compliance; see Kahan 2003.
21. Cosmides & Tooby 1992.
22. This argument is due originally to Frank (1988).
23. Owren & Bachorowski 2001.
24. There are other theories of the evolution of laughter, not necessarily incompatible with the one outlined here. For instance, Ramachandran & Blakeslee (1999) propose that laughter evolved to signal to other members of a social group that a feared threat (from a predator, for instance) is in fact not serious; this could explain why we laugh in relief. This could in turn account for the use of laughter to signal to a listener that the person laughing is not himself a threat.
25. Gray & McNaughton 2000, chapter 4.
26. It's true that drinks tend to be served after agreements are signed, but trust is as important after the agreement as before: each party still needs to decide whether it can trust the other to stick to the agreement.
27. Mark Greenberg points out that what biologists call the handicap principle may also be at work; by drinking alcohol in your company, I am signaling that I am so confident in my skill at discerning your trustworthiness that I am willing to disable it with a powerful depressant drug. This can work both to reassure you that I intend to trust you (by behaving in a trustworthy manner

myself) *and* to warn you how quickly you will be discovered if you betray that trust.

28. A fascinating early contribution to this literature is Axelrod 1984.

29. Somewhat confusingly, the literature has started to refer to this as "strong reciprocity," to indicate that it persists even when the parties will not knowingly encounter each other again. However, if they knew they would see each other again, it would not count as reciprocity at all, merely as calculation. I therefore prefer, for consistency, to continue to use the term "reciprocity," it being understood that this is of the kind that does persist even when the parties will not knowingly meet again.

30. Opportunists might or might not be calculators. Alternatively, they could be those in whom reciprocity was triggered by evidence that they would encounter the person concerned in the future and inhibited by evidence that they would not, without the process being under conscious control.

31. See Fehr & Henrich 2003.

32. Wilson & Sober 1994; Gintis 2000.

33. Fehr & Gächter 2000a.

34. Wrangham 2003.

35. Gambetta 1993. The theory of the mafia as an organized response to problems of establishing trust has been applied to Russian conditions by Varese (1994, 2001).

36. Bowles 1991.

37. Granovetter 1972. Barabási 2002 is a very good introduction to this and other work on the properties of networks: how they form and grow, and what makes them effective, stable, and resistant to external threats.

38. See Wirth 1938, for example. Biggar 2002 is a recent collection of essays in which the elegiac strain is clearly heard.

39. This view is most famously associated with Douglass North and Robert Paul Thomas (see North & Thomas 1973 and North 1990).

40. See epilogue to parts 1 and 2, note 14, below.

41. The passages from Jacobs [1961] 1992 are on pp. 31–32 and p. 40. Jacobs's ideas about cities are explored in more detail in chapter 7.

CHAPTER 4. MONEY AND HUMAN RELATIONSHIPS

1. This discussion, including many of the examples cited, draws from the introduction to Seabright 2000 and from Ledeneva & Seabright 2000.

2. Buchan 1997, p. 24.

3. Monnerie 1996, pp. 47–69.

4. Ibid., p. 63.

5. This theory is due to Marin et al. (2000).

6. See the LETSYSTEMS web page at http://www.gmlets.u-net.com.

7. Buchan 1997, p. 281.

8. Wiener 1982. For Athens, see Hall 1998, p. 58, and chapter 7 below.

9. See Polanyi 1944 for a very influential expression of this point of view.

10. Tourneur 1607, act I, scene 1.

11. Buchan 1997, p. 20.
12. Balzac 1847.
13. Amis 1984.

CHAPTER 5. HONOR AMONG THIEVES

1. The suggestion that banks may have come into existence before money is entirely a conjecture on my part, and it is extremely unlikely that evidence will be found to corroborate or disprove it, since both banks and money may well have preceded writing. Davies (2003) shows that the first *documented* banks were in Mesopotamia and did indeed serve as storehouses for grain. The first documented *private* banks appear in Athens, in the late fifth century B.C. (Cohen 1992, p. 42).
2. Sheilagh Ogilvie tells me this certainly occurred in sixteenth-century Bohemia.
3. Similar behavior tends to be observed when there are rumors of a gasoline shortage.
4. Cornett & Saunders 1998, pp. 329–33. Joseph Mollicone, the bank president who sparked the crisis, was convicted in 1993 of embezzlement and sentenced to thirty years in prison; he was released in July 2002 (*Financial Times*, 24 July 2002).

CHAPTER 6. PROFESSIONALISM AND FULFILMENT IN WORK AND WAR

1. Calvino 1991, pp. 20–23.
2. Quotations from the proceedings are from Marrus 1997, especially pp. 182, 206, 217. The English version is given as in Marrus, even where the translation is evidently slightly faulty (as in "pity with" instead of "pity for"). Overy 2001 is a fascinating account of the interrogation of Nazi leaders prior to the trial, reproducing many original transcripts.
3. Brendon 2000, p. 404.
4. The evolution of human mental capacities, especially for broad, abstract reasoning, is the subject of Mithen 1996, whose main focus is the development of consciousness; on Mithen's view many of these mental capacities are by-products of skills that evolved for ecological adaptation and social interaction. Miller (2000) proposes sexual selection as an explanation: far from being a by-product, human mental abilities were actively selected by females. In fact, the two theories are less starkly opposed than they may appear: the particular forms of mental capacity that were sexually selected were not necessarily the ones we see today, and sexual interaction was surely one of the most important forms of social interaction driving the evolutionary process.
5. Hall 1998, pp. 48, 58.
6. An intriguing account of this process in the U.S. Navy is given in Hutchins 1995, especially pp. 6–26.

7. Dumont 1981.

8. Donne 1997, pp. 126–27.

9. Durkheim's theory of suicide is set out in Durkheim 1897. He proposed four types of suicide, distinguishing notably between egoistic suicide, which was driven by lack of social integration in modern society, and anomic suicide, which was driven by lack of social regulation. A sense of some of the empirical and conceptual controversy still surrounding these ideas can be gained from the readings in Lester 1994, though the discussions of the empirical material are neither very clear nor (to my mind) very convincing.

10. Furedi 2002.

11. Terkel 1974, pp. 203–4.

12. This is documented in Hamermesh 2003, which shows from surveys of labor market behavior that variety in one's work and life is valuable to people and is one of the fruits of education.

13. Perec 1978, pp. 94–95 (my translation).

14. Amnesty International 2001.

15. Gusterson 1996. This was drawn to my attention by Luhrmann 2000, itself a brilliant account of the subtle but far-reaching consequences of a certain professional training, namely, in psychiatry.

16. Terkel 1986.

17. Richerson & Boyd 1998.

18. The most recent at time of writing is the U.S.-led invasion of Iraq in March–April 2003. The photographer Laurent van der Stockt, interviewed by Michel Guerrin in *Le Monde* (13/14 April), describes the killing by U.S. Marines of civilians, including women and children, who evidently posed no threat to the troops but were in some sense simply in the way.

EPILOGUE TO PARTS 1 AND 2

1. See Perloff 2001, chapter 10, for a textbook discussion, and Mas-Colell et al. 1995, chapter 10, for a rigorous but difficult technical treatment. For an enjoyable nontechnical introduction to economic thinking see Coyle 2002.

2. A very readable tour of the many different kinds of market in real economies is McMillan 2002.

3. These points are given an excellent and reasonably simple textbook treatment in Milgrom & Roberts 1992, especially chapter 4. Aoki 2001 is a fuller and more detailed textbook covering these themes.

4. See Rodrik 1997 for a skeptical view of globalization and Bourgignon et al. 2002 for a more general overview.

5. See McCulloch et al. 2001 and Bourguignon et al. 2002, especially chapter 4, for summaries of the evidence on trade, globalization, and world poverty and inequality.

6. Smith 1759 and Smith 1776.

7. Dougherty 2002. See also Rothschild 2001.

8. See Riley 2001 for a survey and Perloff 2001, chapter 19, for a textbook treatment.

9. Akerlof 1970.

10. See the summary in Seabright 1993.

11. Kreps & Wilson 1982.

12. See Hörner 2002 for a recent model of self-regulation via competition for reputation-building. An up-to-date textbook treatment of the economics of regulation is given in Viscusi, Vernon and Harrington 2000.

13. See Tirole 1996 and Seabright 1997.

14. The classic work in this literature is Putnam 1993; Putnam 2000 applies the ideas to contemporary American society. Dasgupta & Serageldin 1999 provides a comprehensive overview of the issues.

15. This work is reviewed in Fehr & Gächter 2000a.

16. Case, Lin & McLanahan 2000 and Cox 2001, for example. Bergstrom 1996 discusses the significance of kin selection for the economics of the family, and Robson 2001 surveys what evolutionary biology has to say about economic preferences and the nature of economic rationality. Cronk, Chagnon, & Irons 2000 consists of essays exploring adaptive explanations for phenomena documented by anthropologists; Dunbar, Knight, & Power 1999 also contains much interesting material. Hirshleifer 1977 is an early and still very readable discussion of the links between biology and economics, and Ghiselin 2001 provides a large bibliography.

17. See Henrich et al. 2001 for a fascinating cross-cultural experiment.

18. That the character of societies can be far removed from the intentions of individuals is something of a truism in sociology; see Barnes 1995 for a survey of the main sociological approaches to understanding social interaction. This concept was central to the work of Durkheim, especially his book *On the Division of Labour in Society* (1893). Kaufmann 1995 describes the general insights of complex systems theory into the nature of self-organizing structures.

PROLOGUE TO PART 3

1. Beckerts, Holland, & Deneubourg 1994, p. 181, cited by Stan Franklin in a web essay at www.msci.memphis.edu/~franklin/coord.html. See also Hölldobler & Wilson 1994, pp. 107–22, for similar observations about ants. Explicit analogies between ants and markets are explored in Kirman 1993.

2. Smith 1776, p. 473. Hirschman 1977 is an account of how various writers saw the importance of harnessing, rather than repressing, human self-interest.

3. Rothschild 2001, p. 119.

CHAPTER 7. THE CITY, FROM ANCIENT ATHENS TO MODERN MANHATTAN

1. An interesting account (and critique) of the thinking behind planned cities is in Scott 1998, chapter 4.

2. Hall 1998, p. 68.

3. Ibid., p. 234.

4. Ibid., p. 235.

5. Ibid., p. 238.

6. Hughes 1992, p. 155. This book should be read by everyone interested in cities, even those who have never been to Barcelona.

7. Jacobs 1961, pp. 50–51.

8. Ibid., p. 56.

9. Hall 1998, chapter 3.

10. Dr. Snow's cholera map is reproduced in Tufte 1983, p. 24 and Tufte 1997, pp. 30–31. The latter has an excellent discussion on pp. 27–37 of Snow's inferences from the map and whether these were in fact responsible for the end of the epidemic. Such issues are also brought out on the John Snow website maintained by Ralph R. Frerichs at the UCLA Department of Epidemiology at http://www.ph.ucla.edu/epi/snow.html#SNOWHEADS

11. Dutta & Seabright 2002.

12. Borges 1951, p. 423. I have not been able to find the original in Gibbon, and knowing Borges' taste for whimsy am skeptical that I ever shall.

13. Corbin 1982.

14. Susskind 1988, pp. 3–4.

15. In any one place the children of the rich, being better fed, were somewhat less vulnerable to disease than those of the poor (though not much less so). But the rich were more likely to live in cities, where mortality rates were higher than in the country. See Dutta & Seabright 2002.

16. McGranahan 1993, p. 105.

17. Dutta & Seabright 2002.

18. Mayhew 1861, 2:136.

19. Ibid., 2:142–44.

20. Diamond 1997, especially chapter 11.

21. Libecap & Hansen 2001.

22. Chandler [1950] 2002.

CHAPTER 8. WATER

1. European Commission 1992.

2. See Ward 2002. Homer-Dixon 1999 presents a more systematic analysis of the various kinds of violent conflict to which environmental crises can give rise.

3. Robbins 1936.

4. Falkenmark et al. 1989.

5. Gleick 2002, p. 100, figure 4.2.

6. Schama 1987, pp. 22–25.

7. Hanson 1988.

8. Gleick 1993, tables C18, C19, C21, C23, C24.

9. Gleick 2002, tables 6, 7.

10. Begg et al. 1993, p. 146 and Malle 1996.

11. The focal role of inland seas was a central theme of Braudel 1972 and more recently Ascherson 1995 and Horden & Purcell 2000.

12. Dumont 1981.

13. Baumann 1969.

14. Auden 1979, pp. 184–87.

15. Opinion poll evidence comparing perceptions of general environmental

issues across countries is given in Worcester 1995, especially pp. 20–24. Evidence for the high ranking of water within general environmental issues in Britain appears in Corrado & Ross 1990, table 6. The Lima opinion poll is cited in Worcester & Corrado 1991, p. 11. I am most grateful to Robert Worcester and Michele Corrado, both of MORI, for making these sources available to me.

16. See Ward 2002. Gleick 2002, pp. 194–208, has a valuable chronology of water conflicts in modern history, also available on the website http://www.worldwater.org.

17. The water rights systems in the United States are discussed in Rogers 1993 and Clyde 1989.

18. Wittfogel 1957.

19. Wade 1987.

20. Landes 1983, pp. 22–23. An obvious difficulty with this argument is that the mechanical clock and the culture he describes may both have been effects of some other cause.

21. Coase 1974.

22. Coase 1960.

23. See, for instance, Shleifer & Vishny 1993.

24. Hermann et al. 1988.

CHAPTER 9. PRICES FOR EVERYTHING?

1. This is not just the simple median of all the different traders' estimates but the median weighted by the number of contracts each trader holds.

2. Gibbon 1776, chapter 5, entitled "The Sale of the Empire by the Praetorians."

3. Ibid.

4. Klemperer 1999, note 21.

5. Hendricks & Porter 1988.

6. Mauss 1950.

7. Davis 2001.

8. McCloskey 1976.

9. De Soto 2000.

10. Gann 2001.

11. The comparative study of British and American blood transfusion systems—one relying on donations, the other to a much greater extent on sales— was the subject of a classic study by Titmuss (1970), who claimed that paying people to give blood was inefficient as well as unethical, because it resulted in higher levels of infected blood and less willingness to provide blood among people who would otherwise have been willing to do so for free. See also the review essays by Solow (1971) and Arrow (1972).

CHAPTER 10. FAMILIES AND FIRMS

1. The classic source for this question about the boundaries of firms is Coase 1937. One of the collections in which it is republished, Putterman & Kroszner

1996, contains many useful essays dealing with this and related questions. Hart 1995, especially part 1, is a good undergraduate-level overview; Williamson 1985 a less formal one, and a classic reference for what has come to be known as "transactions cost economics." Aoki 2001 is a comprehensive recent monograph reviewing contributions to the economics of institutions in the transactions cost tradition. Mokyr 2002, particularly chapter 4, provides an excellent historical perspective on the impact of technical change on the size and character of firms since the industrial revolution.

2. On output, see Bourguignon & Morrison 2002, table 1; on energy and freshwater, see McNeill 2000, tables 1.5 and 5.1.

3. The exceptions include, not just plantation agriculture in the Americas, but also the great European feudal estates; it is also true that even family farms have often been active in labor markets, hiring in or hiring out labor according to the rhythms of the agricultural year.

4. The material on Henry Ford in this chapter is drawn from Hall 1998, chapter 13.

5. A remarkable exception is reported by Jones (1988): "before the birth of Christ an ironmaster in Szechuan was employing 1,000 men" (p. 74).

6. On the economic and social foundations of European military efficiency, see Hanson 1989, which studies Athenian infantry prowess, and Hanson 2001, which undertakes a longer historical comparison.

7. Hutchins 1995, pp. 6–7.

8. Ibid., p. 6.

9. See Buder 1970.

10. Jones 1988: "the silk industry in Italy was carried out in four- and six-storey mills as early as the sixteenth century" (p. 23).

11. Hall 1998, pp. 330–31.

12. Ibid., p. 414.

13. Ibid., p. 409.

14. Ibid., p. 411.

15. Aoki 2001, p. 108.

16. Hall 1998, p. 409.

17. Ibid., p. 405.

18. Landes 1998, p. 306. See also Hall 1998, pp. 404–5. Jones 1988 has used the converse argument to point to the absence of mass demand as a reason why a number of episodes of striking economic growth in the premodern world were not sustained: "concentration on products for which there could be no mass demand and from which there were few spin-offs slowed an economic advance that was *technically* within the reach of some organized society" (p. 72).

19. Lamoreaux, Raff, & Temin 2002 gives an interesting account of the evolution of the textile and other light industries in early nineteenth-century New England, from a structure based on families and family control to a more centralized factory system. For example, owners of the new large mills built in the second and third decades of the century "needed many more workers than could be obtained from local farm households[;] they had to convince young, unmarried women from all over New England to come work temporarily in the mills. In order to make factory employment more attractive to this group, they invested in boarding houses and educational institutions."

20. Statistics about the size of U.S. businesses from the U.S. Census Bureau at http://www.census.gov/epcd/www/smallbus.html#EmpSize.

21. Chandler 1990. See also the review essay by Teece (1993).

22. Fukuyama 1995, particularly in application to China at pp. 69–82.

23. There exist categories of nonvoting shares, though the law prevents the firm's directors from treating these differently as far as dividend payments are concerned.

24. For an analysis of this episode and its aftermath, see Berglof & Burckardt 2003.

25. Even McDonald's relies on franchising to combine standardization with some of the flexibility that is one of the virtues of the small.

26. Teece 1993, especially footnote 52, emphasizes that firms facing identical technological conditions could have quite different capacities for coordinating their production, differences that could persist over many decades.

27. Chandler 1977.

28. Lamoreaux, Raff, & Temin 2002 provides an overview of these developments and an outline of an alternative synthesis.

29. Hutchins 1995 describes in detail how the different cognitive tasks involved in the navigation of a large naval vessel are not concentrated in the mind of a single individual but are distributed throughout the members of the ship's crew, and analyzes the coordinating mechanisms that turn this distributed process into a recognizably coherent response to a cognitive problem.

30. See Cooper 1998.

31. Mowery & Ziedonis 2001.

32. John Sutton's theories about firm size are set out in Sutton (1998); an application to questions of globalization was given in his Royal Economic Society public lecture, the text of which is not available but is loosely based on a British Academy lecture (Sutton 2001).

CHAPTER 11. KNOWLEDGE AND SYMBOLISM

1. The story of the Chauvet cave, along with pictures of the artworks and a discussion of the archaeological and geological context, can be found online at http://www.culture.fr/culture/arcnat/chauvet/fr/.

2. Mithen 1996 cites Glyn Isaac as describing how "for almost a million years, toolkits tended to involve the same essential ingredients seemingly being shuffled in restless, minor, directionless changes" (p. 19).

3. The evolution of human culture is a central theme of Klein & Edgar 2001; the authors support the hypothesis of African origins but favor the hypothesis of a relatively sudden transformation. McBrearty & Brooks (2000) argue strongly in favor of a more gradual African evolution. Mithen 1996 has an excellent account of the challenge of explaining the development of human cultural and cognitive capacities, as well as an intriguing hypothesis about how it might have happened.

4. This remains a speculation, though, and it is hard to see what evidence could, realistically, confirm or refute it.

5. Not all specialists would accept this characterization: Sue Blackmore, for instance, tells me, in a personal communication, that she doesn't see why symbolic representation is necessary for imitation. My own view is that imitation as such had been a feature of human behavior long before the developments we can describe as culture (all those unchanging stone tools), but it was the fluidity of symbolic recombination that gave imitation the explosive potential so grippingly described in Blackmore 1999.

6. And the brain itself uses symbols which are not necessarily images to represent external objects (see Ramachandran & Blakeslee 1999, chapter 4, for a particularly clear and intuitive account of this point of view). So a more general reliance on symbols rather than more specifically on images for communication is a natural extension of our biological capacities from the perceptual sphere to the sphere of communication.

7. Klein 1999, pp. 348–49; Mithen 1996, pp. 160–61. One of the key pieces of evidence is the structure and position of the larynx, which in humans carries a much greater risk of choking than in apes. This risk implies that there must already have been adaptive benefits from the greater capacity of the human larynx to produce sounds suitable for language; otherwise there would have been strong selective pressures against its evolution.

8. Whiten et al. 1999; Whiten & Boesch 2001.

9. Diamond 1992, pp. 133–35. It is likely that the increased life span co-evolved with increased brain size, since larger brains do not instantly increase fitness but, rather, raise the returns to learning, which is a type of investment. This would therefore have increased the overall adaptive value of longer life expectancy, since it gave a longer period in which learning investments would be productive. See Kaplan, Hill, Lancaster, and Hurtado 2000 and Robson & Kaplan 2003.

10. The citations about the impact of printing are from Eisenstein 1982, which was reissued in abridged form as Eisenstein 1993. A fine social history of printing is Febvre & Martin 1997, while Martin 1994 connects the history of printing with that of writing and literacy more generally.

11. This is compatible with a large increase in absolute rewards for those whose talents appeal to a geographically dispersed audience who can be brought together by the cheap reproduction and diffusion of information goods. I recall reading somewhere that Joseph Losey's movie version of *Don Giovanni* has been seen by more people than have seen the live opera in the more than two centuries since Mozart wrote it.

12. Frank 1999, p. 38. A previous book by the same author (Frank 1996) was devoted entirely to such markets and their effects on society. The underlying idea was first developed by Rosen (1981).

13. See Boldrin & Levine 2003, chapter 1.

14. Bessen & Maskin 2000.

15. See Carlton & Waldman 1998 and Bernheim & Whinston 1998.

16. Boldrin & Levine 2003.

17. I'm not, of course, the first to have this idea. Most days my email inbox contains advertisements for products purporting to do at least some of these things—yet somehow I'm still a frog.

18. Chapter 8, note 22, above.

19. Kremer & Snyder 2003 have argued that a similar problem explains why private-sector pharmaceutical companies invest less in vaccines than in curative drugs.

20. Stokes 1965, p. 30. The analogy is interesting even if one does not accept his psychoanalytic, and specifically Kleinian, framework (Melanie Klein this time, not Richard, nor even Naomi).

21. Gray, Feldon, Rawlins, Hemsley, & Smith 1991. The ability to screen out irrelevant information is known as "latent inhibition."

22. Cognitive psychologist Colin Martindale has advanced the theory that the changing characteristics of all artistic movements can be explained by pressure for novelty generated by the habituation of artistic audiences to familiar stimuli (Martindale 1990); such a theory seems naturally suited to explaining an increasing shrillness of artistic movements as they struggle to compete in a symbolically overpopulated space of public attention. An interesting comparison is with David Galenson's recent book about two different styles of artistic creativity, the experimental and the conceptually innovative (Galenson 2001).

23. Jones 1988, especially pp. 176ff., and Landes 1998. For a skeptical view, see Pomeranz 2000.

24. Landes 1998, pp. 94, 96.

CHAPTER 12. EXCLUSION

1. Brendon 2000, pp. 79–81.

2. A discussion of Walker Evans's relation to the Farm Security Administration is at http://xroads.virginia.edu/~UG97/fsa/farm.html.

3. Shiller 2000, p. 153; his research on word-of-mouth communication in stock markets is reported at pp. 154–57.

4. On Alan Greenspan's contribution to the stock market bubble of the late 1990s, read Paul Krugman's op-ed piece from the *New York Times*, 4 September 2002, at http://www.startribune.com/stories/1519/3208079.html, and the *Economist* of 7 September 2002, pp. 14 and 80, as well as Greenspan's defense of his record at http://www.federalreserve.gov/boarddocs/speeches/2002/20020830/default.htm. Galbraith 1990 is an account of a number of episodes of financial euphoria and a warning of the ease with which people can believe in the possibility of becoming effortlessly rich.

5. "Manipuram" and "Kovilur" are fictitious names for real villages where I lived for nearly a year in 1985 and which I revisited in 1990 and 1992. Research findings from these villages have resulted in several publications, one of which is Seabright 1997. Bliss & Stern 1983 is a detailed and fascinating case study of the North Indian village of Palanpur, revisited in Lanjouw & Stern 1998. The best general-purpose textbook on economic development is Ray 1998, though Basu 1998 has some excellent chapters, particularly the early ones. Bardhan & Udry 1999 is a good advanced undergraduate textbook on institutional aspects of economic development.

6. Assortative matching is discussed nontechnically in chapter 5 of Cohen

1998 and technically in Shimer & Smith 2000. It has been applied to under-standing a wide range of phenomena, including growing inequality in household income (Deaton 1995; Lerman 1996), poverty traps in developing economies (Kremer 1993), peer-group lending in poor countries (Ghatak 1999), rising divorce rates (Weiss 1993), transmission rates of HIV infection (Dow and Philipson 1996), racial and class segregation in the schooling system (Benabou 1994) and the changing employment structure of U.S. firms (Kremer & Maskin 1996; Acemoglu 1998; Mailath, Samuelson, and Shaked 2000).

7. One piece of evidence suggesting this may be an important phenomenon is presented in Hamermesh 1999, who argues that measures of job satisfaction — which are likely to be very sensitive to the quality of a person's coworkers — have become more unequal in both the United States and Germany in recent years.

8. Kremer 1993.

9. An introduction to the economics of networks is given in Economides 1996, downloadable from his website http://www.stern.nyu.edu/networks/site.html, which also contains a mass of relevant material. Shy 2001 is a good advanced undergraduate textbook on network externalities and the economics of network industries.

10. Depression statistics are available at http://www.prairiepublic.org/features/healthworks/depression/stats.htm. Suicide statistics for the United States are at http://www.suicidology.org/stats2001/1999datapage2.pdf; suicide statistics for the world as a whole at http://www5.who.int/mental_health/main.cfm?p=0000000149.

11. An introduction to the theory of principal-agent relationships is in James Mirrlees' Nobel lecture (Mirrlees, 1997); an excellent but advanced text is Laffont & Martimort 2002. Holmstrom & Milgrom 1991 applies the theory to multiple tasks, where some tasks are more easily monitored than others. Applications to multitasking are discussed in Seabright 1999.

12. Bursztajn, Feinbloom, Hamm, and Brodsky 1990, p. 414. This is an interesting discussion of medical decision-making, with many case studies. Chapter 10 is entitled "Trust" and describes many of the difficulties facing doctors in reconciling their wish to establish trust with patients and the need to make hard-headed resource-allocation decisions.

13. Holmstrom & Milgrom 1991.

14. Luhrmann 2000, p. 243.

15. Ibid., p. 260.

16. Ibid., p. 17.

17. For discussion of evidence that life for the poor is less miserable now than in earlier ages, see Dutta & Seabright 2002. For evidence that adjusting GDP to take account of nonmarket aspects of welfare has an overall positive impact on estimates of income growth, see Crafts 2003.

18. For an example of the romanticization of mental illness, see Laing 1960; for a more subtle and historically wide-ranging version, see Foucault 1965. Kakar 1982 is a more nuanced account of the different ways in which American and Indian societies both conceptualize mental illness and respond to individuals with certain presenting conditions.

EPILOGUE TO PART 3

1. Schelling 1978 is a superb introduction to the issues.

2. Krugman 1991 remains the best introduction to this literature. For more recent work, see the book by Fujita, Krugman and Venables (1999) and the review essay by Neary (2001).

3. Seabright 1993 and Portney 2000 are two introductory essays; Pearce & Turner 1990, a textbook treatment, Dasgupta 1993 and 2001, two comprehensive monographs; and Dasgupta & Mäler 1997, a set of essays about problems of environment and development.

4. See McMillan 2002 for a very readable introduction.

5. Farrell 1987 provides a very clear account of the reasons why asymmetries of information prevent efficient bargaining of the kind necessary for the Coase theorem to hold.

PROLOGUE TO PART 4

1. I have developed the argument about defense and the adoption of agriculture more fully in Seabright 2003. Evidence about the existence of multiple independent adoptions is summarized in Richerson, Boyd, & Bettinger 2001, and the rapid spread of agriculture around the world is documented in Bellwood 1996 and Cavalli-Sforza, Menozzi, & Piazza 1994. Yet, as Mithen (1996) points out, earlier humans had sophisticated biological knowledge, so that it does not seem likely that the problem lay in lack of skill. Existing theories are dominated by two hypotheses: that of a late Pleistocene food crisis caused by population pressure (Cohen 1977) and that of rapid climate change including global warming (Richardson, Boyd, & Bettinger 2001). The first is problematic because of evidence that hunter-gatherers were able to control population growth through various measures, including infanticide. According to Cohen & Armelagos (1984), the second may only be a necessary and not a sufficient condition for adoption of agriculture, given the evidence about the health of early farmers. Given that evidence, climate change might not have increased agricultural productivity enough to make its adoption inevitable. As Mithen points out, many previous episodes of comparable climate change had not led to agriculture. Two additional theories help explain why adoption of agriculture could have led to a "point of no return," though neither explains the initial adoption. Bar-Yosef and Belfer-Cohen (1989) suggest that sedentism removed constraints to population growth and made a return to hunting and gathering impossible. Winterhalder & Lu (1995) suggest that more intense hunting by already sedentary communities would have depleted big game, with the same consequence of rendering a return to hunting and gathering impossible. And Mithen himself offers his account of an evolving human consciousness as a way of explaining why modern humans might have been more aware of the possibilities of agriculture than their biologically sophisticated, but less symbolically creative, forebears: they knew about wild animals and plants but were not used to thinking of them as potentially domesticable.

So my suggestion that defense needs imposed important externalities is best seen as a way to reconcile the evidence about the health of early farmers with the possibility that climate change might nevertheless have made agriculture sufficiently productive to become strongly attractive to individual communities.

2. Ferguson 1773, p. 218. I owe both this and my acquaintance with Ibn Khaldun (1377) to the excellent book by Gellner (1994), on pp. 62–63 of which I originally came across the reference to Ferguson.

CHAPTER 13. STATES AND EMPIRES

1. Cavalli-Sforza 2000, pp. 104–13. Renfrew 1989 is a treatment of the puzzle of the origins of Indo-European languages that also depends on the hypothesis of a gradual spread of a technology (in this case, a linguistic technology) carried by the spread of agriculture.

2. The claim that almost no societies refrained from enslaving others at some time in their history, and that slavery became more likely the wealthier the society concerned, was due at first to Nieboer (1900, especially pp. 255–61, 286–88, 294, 303, 306, and 417–27). I am grateful to Stanley Engerman for this reference. The classic source for the economics of slavery is Fogel & Engerman 1974.

3. Gat 2003.

4. Hanson 1989, pp. xxiv–xxv.

5. Pericles' description of the Peloponnesians comes from Thucydides, book 1, chapter 141; in the edition by Strassler (1998), p. 81.

6. Hanson 2001, pp. 274–75.

7. Kennedy 1989.

8. White 1966.

9. Scott 1998, pp. 64–73.

10. This view is reviewed and rejected in Keeley 1996, especially pp. 121–26.

11. For the annihilation of the aboriginal Australians and Tasmanians and the Hereros, see Diamond 1992, pp. 278–88.

12. Hochschild 1999, passim, but especially chapter 15.

13. The argument that asymmetries in size and strength explain violence between adults in some species is discussed in Wrangham & Peterson 1996, pp. 156–72. The evidence on gorilla infanticide is at pp. 146–51.

14. Hanson 2001, pp. 273–75.

15. Cohen 1992, pp. 43–44.

16. Cave & Coulson 1936, pp. 104–5

17. Landes 1998, p. 339. It is not entirely clear what Landes means by this last remark—perhaps that no European state was without powerful enemies who were always trying to achieve a military advantage.

18. The website of the Stockholm International Peace Research Institute is at http://www.sipri.se.

19. Barro & Sala-i-Martin 1995.

20. Aizenman & Glick 2003. This evidence suggests that military spending is good for economic growth once the nature of the military threats faced by a

country is taken into account. Of course, this may be true on average even if for certain countries military spending is useless or counterproductive or serves the interests only of a narrow elite.

21. Aidt, Dutta & Loukoianova 2002.

CHAPTER 14. GLOBALIZATION AND POLITICAL ACTION

1. Macaulay 1857.
2. Gray 1998.
3. Burke 1790.
4. Ricardo 1817.
5. Rodrik 1997 places more emphasis on the risks of globalization; though see also Bourguignon et al. 2002.
6. Bourguignon & Morrison 2002.
7. Dutta & Seabright 2002.
8. Quoted in Thucydides' history of the Peloponnesian War, book 2, chapter 39; in the edition by Strassler (1998), p. 113.
9. Packard 1957.
10. Wantchekon 2002.
11. Rawls 1975.
12. Huntington 1993.
13. Macpherson 1962.
14. The importance of the religious wars is particularly emphasized by Tully (1980, 1993).
15. Sandel 1982 and Gray 2000, for example.
16. Constant 1819.
17. Williams 1993.
18. Lewis 2002, p. 6.
19. Lewis 2003 is one of several writers to develop this argument.
20. Rousseau 1755, p. 90.

CONCLUSION. HOW FRAGILE IS THE GREAT EXPERIMENT?

1. World Health Organization 2002, Annex 2. In addition, infectious agents are suspected of involvement in a number of cancers that are recorded as non-communicable diseases (see Price-Smith 2002, p. 37).
2. For the influenza pandemic, see Price-Smith 2002, p. 6. Keeley 1996, especially pp. 89–94 reviews evidence suggesting that prehistoric and preindustrial societies had casualty rates from warfare that were much higher even than the wartime casualty rates of industrial societies.
3. For European and African rates for 2001, see World Health Organization 2002, annex 2; for U.S. rates for 1999, see the WHO mortality database at http://www3.who.int/whosis/mort/table1_process.cfm. U.S. traffic-accident mortality is around a third higher than the suicide rate, while in Europe it is around 25 percent lower.

4. For statistics on journeys taken by air, see the website of the U.S. Bureau of Transportation Statistics at http://www.bts.gov/oai/indicators/SysMovAgv.html; such figures can measure the fall in traffic after 11 September 2001 but cannot, of course, tell us how much of that fall was due to the events of that day.

5. See Homer-Dixon 1999.

6. Ibid, p. 75.

7. Radical technological innovations could conceivably change this in the future — targeted viruses that can kill massive numbers of people but do not need sophisticated delivery mechanisms might be one way — but this remains entirely speculative.

8. Geoffrey Hawthorn tells me the story of a popular Venezuelan rock band that was asked by the FARC to play for them. The band said it required twenty thousand dollars, a decent stadium to play in, and safe passage to and from Caracas. No problem, said the FARC. The band had its fee, a private jet to and from the venue, and at the venue itself a large stadium with state-of-the-art sound and lighting. In itself trivial, but indicative of how much nonstates can confidently control.

9. Gladwell 2000 provides an excellent account of the way in which ideas (including panics) can spread, emphasizing the role of certain key individuals with large numbers of links to others and a strong persuasive power. This means that societies can have hubs in the realm of ideas even if their physical and formal organizational hubs are few.

10. See Barabási 2002 for an introduction.

11. To cite only one of many instances, see "America's destiny is to police the world," by Max Boot, *Financial Times*, 17 February 2003.

12. Ibid.

13. Olson 1965, p. 29.

Bibliography

Acemoglu, Daron. 1998. "Changes in Unemployment and Wage Inequality: An Alternative Theory and Some Evidence." National Bureau of Economic Research (Cambridge, Mass.) working paper no. 6658.

Adams, John. 1995. *Risk*. London: UCL Press.

Aidt, Toke, Jayasri Dutta, and Elena Loukoianova. 2002. "Democracy Comes to Europe: Franchise Extension and Fiscal Outcomes 1830–1939." University of Cambridge, mimeo.

Aizenman, Joshua, and Reuven Glick. 2003. "Military Expenditure, Threats and Growth." National Bureau of Economic Research (Cambridge, Mass.) working paper no. 9618.

Akerlof, George. 1970. "The Market for Lemons: Qualitative Uncertainty and the Market Mechanism." *Quarterly Journal of Economics* 84: 488–500.

Amis, Martin. 1984. *Money*. Harmondsworth, U.K.: Penguin.

Amnesty International. 2001. *Stopping the Torture Trade*. London: Amnesty International.

Anderson, David. 2000. "Surrogate Currencies and the 'Wild' Market in Central Siberia." In Seabright 2000.

Andersson, Malte. 1994. *Sexual Selection*. Princeton: Princeton University Press.

Aoki, Masahiko. 2001. *Toward a Comparative Institutional Analysis*. Cambridge: MIT Press.

Arrow, Kenneth J. 1972. "Gifts and Exchanges." *Philosophy and Public Affairs* 1 (2): 343–62.

Ascherson, Neal. 1995. *Black Sea*. London: Jonathan Cape.

Auden, W. H. 1979. *Selected Poems*. Edited by Edward Mendelson. London: Book Club Associates.

Axelrod, Robert. 1984. *The Evolution of Co-operation*. New York: Basic Books.

Balzac, Honoré de. [1847] 1988. *Splendeurs et Misères des Courtisanes*. Paris: Livres de Poche.

Barabási, Albert-László. 2002. *Linked: The New Science of Networks*. Cambridge, Mass.: Perseus Publishing.

Barash, David. 2002. "Evolution, Males and Violence." *Chronicle Review*. Downloadable from http://chronicle.com/free/v48/i37/37b00701.htm.

Barash, David, and Judith Lipton. 2002. *Gender Gap: The Biology of Male-Female Differences*. Piscataway, N.J.: Transaction Publishers.

Bardhan, Pranab, and Christopher Udry. 1999. *Development Microeconomics*. Oxford: Oxford University Press.

Barnes, Barry. 1995. *The Elements of Social Theory*. Princeton: Princeton University Press.

Barro, Robert, and Xavier Sala-i-Martin. 1995. *Economic Growth*. Cambridge: MIT Press.

Bar-Yosef, O., and A. Belfer-Cohen. 1989. "The Origins of Sedentism and Farming Communities in the Levant." *Journal of World Prehistory* 3: 447–97.

Basu, Kaushik. 1984. *The Less-Developed Economy: A Critique of Contemporary Theory.* Oxford: Blackwell and Oxford University Press.

———. 1998. *Analytical Development Economics.* Cambridge: MIT Press.

Baumann, D. 1969. "Perception and Public Policy in the Recreational Use of Domestic Water Supply Reservoirs." *Water Resources Research* 5 (1969): 543.

Beckerts, R., O. Holland, and J.-L. Deneubourg. 1994. "From Local Actions to Global Tasks: Stigmergy in Collective Robotics." In Rodney Brooks and Pattie Maes, eds., *Artificial Life IV: Proceedings of the Fourth International Workshop on the Synthesis and Simulation of Living Systems.* Cambridge: MIT Press.

Begg, David, et al. 1993. *Making Sense of Subsidiarity.* London: Centre for Economic Policy Research.

Bellwood, P. 1996. "The Origins and Spread of Agriculture in the Indo-Pacific Region." In David Harris, ed., *The Origins and Spread of Agriculture and Pastoralism in Eurasia.* Washington, D.C.: Smithsonian Institution.

Bénabou, R. 1994. "Human Capital, Inequality, and Growth: A Local Perspective." *European Economic Review* 38 (3–4): 817–26.

Berglof, Erik, and Michael Burckardt. 2003. "Break-Through in European Take-Over Regulation?" *Economic Policy*, no. 36.

Bergstrom, Ted. 1996. "Economics in a Family Way." *Journal of Economic Literature* 34: 1903–34.

Bernheim, Douglas, and Michael Whinston. 1998. "Exclusive Dealing." *Journal of Political Economy* 106 (1): 64–104.

Bessen, J., and E. Maskin. 2000. "Sequential Innovation, Patents & Imitation." MIT working paper number 00/01.

Biggart, Nicole Woolsey, ed. 2002. *Readings in Economic Sociology.* Oxford: Blackwell.

Bishop, C., ed. 1992. *The Way Nature Works.* New York: Macmillan.

Blackmore, Susan. 1999. *The Meme Machine.* Oxford: Oxford University Press.

Bliss, Christopher, and Nicholas Stern. 1983. *Palanpur.* Oxford: Clarendon Press.

Boldrin, Michele, and David Levine. 2003. "The Case against Intellectual Monopoly." University of California of Los Angeles, draft book manuscript. First two chapters downloadable from http://www.dklevine.com/.

Borges, Jorge Luis. [1951] 2000. "The Argentine Writer and Tradition." In *Selected Non-Fictions*, translated by Esther Allen, Suzanne Levine and Eliot Weinberger; London, Harmondsworth: Penguin. Originally, El Escritor Argentino y la Tradición, lecture given at Colegio Libre de Estudios Superiores, Buenos Aires.

Bourguignon, François, and Christian Morrison. 2002. "Inequality in World Incomes 1820–1992." *American Economic Review* 92(4): 727–44.

Bourguignon, François, et al. 2002. *Making Sense of Globalization: A Guide to the Economic Issues.* Centre for Economic Policy Research Policy Paper no. 8. London: CEPR.

Bowles, Samuel. 1991. "What Markets Can—and Cannot—Do." *Challenge*, July/August, pp. 11–14.

Braudel, F. 1972. *The Mediterranean and the Mediterranean World in the Age of Philip II*. London and New York: Harper Colophon.

Brendon, Piers. 2000. *The Dark Valley: A Panorama of the 1930s*. London: Pimlico Press.

Britnell, Richard. 1997. *The Commercialisation of English Society, 1000–1500*. 2nd ed. Manchester: Manchester University Press.

Buchan, James. 1997. *Frozen Desire: An Enquiry into the Meaning of Money*. London: Picador.

Buder, Stanley. 1970. *Pullman: An Experiment in Industrial Order and Community Planning*. Oxford: Oxford University Press.

Burke, Edmund. [1790] 1999. *Reflections on the Revolution in France*. Oxford: Oxford University Press.

Bursztajn, Harold, Richard Feinbloom, Robert Hamm, and Archie Brodsky. 1990. *Medical Choices, Medical Chances: How Patients, Families and Physicians Can Cope with Uncertainty*. London: Routledge.

Calvino, Italo. [1991] 2000. *Why Read the Classics?* translated by Martin McLaughlin. London: Vintage. Originally published as *Perché Leggere i Classici*. Milan: Arnoldo Mondadori.

Carlton, D., and M. Waldman. 1998. "The Strategic Use of Tying to Preserve and Create Market Power in Evolving Industries." National Bureau of Economic Research (Cambridge, Mass.) Discussion paper no. 6831.

Case, Anne, I-Fen Lin, and Sara McLanahan. 2000. "How Hungry Is the Selfish Gene?" *Economic Journal* 110 (466): 781–804.

Cavalli-Sforza, Luigi Luca. 2000. *Genes, People and Languages*. Translated by Mark Seielstad. Berkeley: University of California Press.

Cavalli-Sforza, Luigi Luca, Paolo Menozzi, and Alberto Piazza. 1994. *The History and Geography of Human Genes*. Princeton: Princeton University Press.

Cave, Roy, and Herbert Coulson. [1936] 1965. *A Source Book for Medieval Economic History*. New York: Biblo & Tannen.

Chagnon, Napoleon. 1988. "Life Histories, Blood Revenge and Warfare in a Tribal Population." *Science*, 239: 985–92.

Chandler, Alfred. 1977. *The Visible Hand: The Managerial Revolution in American Business*. Cambridge: Harvard University Press, Belknap Press.

———. 1990. *Scale and Scope: The Dynamics of Industrial Capitalism*. Cambridge: Harvard University Press, Belknap Press.

Chandler, Raymond. [1950] 2002. "The Simple Art of Murder." New York: Vintage.

Clyde, S. 1989. "Adapting to the Changing Demand for Water Use through Continued Refinement of the Prior Appropriation Doctrine: An Alternative Approach to Wholesale Reallocation." *Natural Resources Journal* 29: 435–56.

Coase, Ronald. [1937] 1996. "The Nature of the Firm." *Economica* 4: 386–405. Reprinted in Coase 1988 and in Putterman & Kroszner 1996.

———. 1960. "The Problem of Social Cost." *Journal of Law and Economics* 3: 1–44. Reprinted in Coase 1988.

———. 1974. "The Lighthouse in Economics." *Journal of Law and Economics* 2: 357–76. Reprinted in Coase 1988.

———. 1988. *The Firm, the Market and the Law*. Chicago: University of Chicago Press.

Cohen, Daniel. 1998. *The Wealth of the World and the Poverty of Nations*. Cambridge: MIT Press.

Cohen, Edward E. 1992. *Athenian Economy and Society: A Banking Perspective*. Princeton: Princeton University Press.

Cohen, M. N. 1977. *The Food Crisis in Prehistory*. New Haven: Yale University Press.

Cohen, M. N., and G. J. Armelagos. 1984. *Paleopathology at the Origins of Agriculture*. New York: Academic Press.

Constant, Benjamin. [1819] 1980. "De la Liberté des Anciens Comparée a Celle des Modernes." In *De La Liberté chez les Modernes*. edited by Marcel Gauchet. Paris: Livres de Poche.

Cooper, Gail. 1998. *Air-Conditioning America: Engineers and the Controlled Environment, 1900–1960*. Baltimore: Johns Hopkins University Press.

Corbin, Alain. [1982] 1994. *The Foul and the Fragrant: Odour and the Social Imagination*. London: Picador. Originally published as *Le Miasme et la Jonquille*. Paris: Editions Aubier Montaigne.

Cornett, Marcia Millon, and Anthony Saunders. 1998. *Fundamentals of Financial Institutions Management*. New York: McGraw-Hill.

Corrado, Michele, and Miranda Ross. 1990. "Green Issues in Britain and the Value of Green Research Data." London: MORI.

Cosmides, Leda, and John Tooby. 1992. "Cognitive Adaptations for Social Exchange." In J. Barkow, L. Cosmides, and J. Tooby, eds., *The Adapted Mind*. New York: Oxford University Press.

Cox, Donald. 2001. "How Do People Decide to Allocate Transfers among Family Members?", Boston College, working paper.

Coyle, Diane. 2002. *Sex, Drugs and Economics: An Unconventional Introduction to Economics*. New York: Texere.

Crafts, Nicholas. 2002. "UK Real National Income 1950–1998: Some Grounds for Optimism." *National Institute Economic Review*, July.

Cronk, Lee, Napoleon Chagnon, and William Irons. 2000. *Adaptation and Human Behavior: an Anthropological Perspective*. New York: Aldine de Gruyter.

Daly, Martin, and Margo Wilson. 1988. *Homicide*. New York: Aldine de Gruyter.

Dasgupta, Partha. 1993. *An Inquiry into Well-Being and Destitution*. Oxford: Clarendon Press.

———. 2001. *Human Well-Being and the Natural Environment*. Oxford: Clarendon Press.

Dasgupta, Partha, and Karl-Göran Mäler, eds. 1997. *The Environment and Emerging Development Issues*. Oxford: Clarendon Press.

Dasgupta, Partha, and Ismail Serageldin. 1999. *Social Capital: A Multi-Faceted Perspective*. Washington D.C.: World Bank.

Davies, Glyn. 2003. *A History of Money: From Ancient Times to the Present Day*. 2nd ed. Cardiff: University of Wales Press.

Davis, Natalie Zemon. 2000. *The Gift in Sixteenth Century France*. Madison: University of Wisconsin Press.

Dawkins, Richard. 1976. *The Selfish Gene*. Oxford: Oxford University Press.

Deacon, Terrence. 1997. *The Symbolic Species: The co-evolution of Language and the Human Brain*. London: Allen Lane.

Deaton, A. 1995. "Inequality within and between Households in Growing and Aging Economies." In M.-G. Quibria, ed., *Critical Issues in Asian Development: Theories, Experiences and policies*. Hong Kong, Oxford, and New York: Oxford University Press for the Asian Development Bank, 1995.

De Soto, Hernando. 2000. *The Mystery of Capital: Why Capitalism Triumphs in the West and Fails Everywhere Else*. New York: Basic Books.

De Vries, Jan. 1974. *The Dutch Rural Economy in the Golden Age, 1500–1700*. New Haven: Yale University Press.

———. 1976. *The Economy of Europe in an Age of Crisis, 1600–1750*. Cambridge: Cambridge University Press.

De Waal, Frans. 2001. *Tree of Origin: What Primate Behavior Can Tell Us about Human Social Evolution*. Cambridge: Harvard University Press.

Diamond, Jared. 1992. *The Third Chimpanzee*. New York: Harper Collins.

———. 1997. *Guns, Germs and Steel: The Fates of Human Societies*. New York: Norton.

Donne, John. 1997. *No Man Is an Island: a Selection from the Prose of John Donne*. Edited by Rivers Scott. London: Folio Society.

Dostoyevsky, Fyodor. [1865] 1996. *Crime and Punishment*. Translated by David McDuff. Harmondsworth, U.K.: Penguin.

Dougherty, Peter. 2002. *Who's Afraid of Adam Smith? How the Market Got its Soul!* New York: John Wiley.

Dow, W., and T. Philipson. 1996. "An Empirical Examination of the Implications of Assortative Matching on the Incidence of HIV." *Journal of Health Economics* 15 (6): 735–49.

Dumont, Louis. 1981. *Homo Hierarchicus*. 2nd ed. Translated by Basia Gulati. Chicago: University of Chicago Press.

Dunbar, Robin. 1992. "Neocortex Size as a Constraint on Group Size in Primates." *Journal of Human Evolution* 20: 469–93.

Dunbar, Robin, Chris Knight, and Camilla Power. 1999. *The Evolution of Culture*. New Brunswick: Rutgers University Press.

Durant, Will. [1926] 1983. *The Story of Philosophy: The Lives and Opinions of the World's Greatest Philosophers*. New York: Simon & Schuster.

Durkheim, Emile. [1897] 1998. *De la Division du Travail Social*. 5th ed. Paris: Quadrige, Presses Universitaires de France.

———. [1897] 1999. *Le Suicide*. 10th ed. Paris: Quadrige, Presses Universitaires de France.

Dutta, Jayasri, and Paul Seabright. 2002. "Competition and the Spread of Knowledge in Economic Growth." University of Toulouse, mimeo.

Economides, Nicholas. 1996. "The Economics of Networks: A Survey." *International Journal of Industrial Organization* 14: 673–99.

Ehret, Christopher. 1998. *An African Classical Age: Eastern & Southern Africa in World History, 1000 B.C. to A.D. 400*. Oxford: James Currey.

Eisenstein, Elizabeth. 1982. *The Printing Press as an Agent of Change: Communications and Cultural Transformation in Early Modern Europe.* 2 vols. Cambridge: Cambridge University Press.

———. 1993. *The Printing Revolution in Early Modern Europe.* Canto ed. Cambridge: Cambridge University Press.

Ember, Carol. 1978. "Myths about Hunter-Gatherers." *Ethnology* 17: 439–48.

European Commission. 1992. *Commission Decision of 22 July 1992 Relating to a Proceeding under Council Regulation (EEC) No. 4064/89 (Case No. IV/M. 190 — Nestlé/Perrier) (92/553/EEC).* Downloadable from http://europa.eu.int/comm/competition/mergers/cases.

Evans, W., and J. Graham. 1991. "Risk Reduction or Risk Compensation? The Case of Mandatory Safety Belt Use Laws." *Journal of Risk and Uncertainty* 4: 61–73.

Falkenmark, M., J. Lundqvist, and C. Widstrand. 1989. "Macro-Scale Water Scarcity Requires Micro-Scale Approaches: Aspects of Vulnerability in Semi-Arid Development." *Natural Resources Forum* 13: 258–67.

Farrell, J. 1987. "Information and the Coase Theorem." *Journal of Economic Perspectives* 1 (2): 113–29.

Febvre, Lucien, and Henri-Jean Martin. 1997. *The Coming of the Book: The Impact of Printing 1450–1800.* Translated by David Gerard. London: Verso Books.

Fehr, Ernst, Georg Kirchsteiger, and Arno Riedl. 1993. "Does Fairness Prevent Market Clearing? An Empirical Investigation?" *Quarterly Journal of Economics* 108: 437–60.

Fehr, Ernst, and Simon Gächter. 2000a. "Fairness and Retaliation: the Economics of Reciprocity." *Journal of Economic Perspectives* 14: 159–81.

———. 2000b. "Cooperation and Punishment in Public Goods Experiments." *American Economic Review* 90: 980–94.

Fehr, Ernst, and Joseph Henrich. 2003. "Is Strong Reciprocity a Maladaptation? On the Evolutionary Foundations of Human Altruism." Centre for Economic Policy Research (London) discussion paper no. 3860.

Ferguson, Adam. [1773] 1996. *An Essay on the Origin of Civil Society.* Cambridge: Cambridge University Press.

Ferguson, Brian, and Azar Gat. 2000. "Debate: The Causes and Origins of 'Primitive Warfare.'" *Anthropological Quarterly* 73 (3): 159–68.

Fogel, Robert, and Stanley Engerman. 1974. *Time on the Cross: the Economics of American Negro Slavery.* New York: Little, Brown.

Foucault, Michel. 1965. *Madness and Civilization: A History of Insanity in the Age of Reason.* New York: Vintage.

Frank, Robert. 1988. *Passions within Reason: The Strategic Role of the Emotions.* New York: Norton.

———. 1996. *The Winner-Take-All Society: Why the Few at the Top Get So Much More than the Rest of Us.* Penguin USA.

———. 1999. *Luxury Fever.* Princeton: Princeton University Press.

Friedman, Milton, and Rose Friedman. 1990. *Free to Choose: A Personal Statement.* San Diego: Harvest Books.

Fujita, Masahisa, Paul Krugman, and Anthony Venables. 1999. *The Spatial Economy: Cities, Regions and International Trade*. Cambridge: MIT Press.

Fukuyama, Francis. 1995. *Trust: The Social Virtues and the Making of Prosperity*. London: Hamish Hamilton.

Furedi, Frank. 2002. *Paranoid Parenting*. Chicago: Chicago Review Press.

Galbraith, John Kenneth. 1990. *A Short History of Financial Euphoria*. New York: Whittle Books.

Galenson, David. 2001. *Painting Outside the Lines: Patterns of Creativity in Modern Art*. Cambridge: Harvard University Press.

Gambetta, Diego. 1993. *The Sicilian Mafia: The Business of Private Protection*. Cambridge: Harvard University Press.

Gann, Jennifer. 2001. "Hey Brother Can You Spare a Kidney: Adverse Selection and Forbidden Markets." University of Toulouse, mimeo.

Gat, Azar. 1999. "The Pattern of Fighting in Simple, Small-Scale Prestate Societies." *Journal of Anthropological Research* 55: 563–83.

———. 2000a. "The Human Motivational Complex: Evolutionary Theory and the Causes of Hunter-Gatherer Fighting. I. Primary Somatic and Reproductive Causes." *Anthropological Quarterly* 73 (1): 20–34.

———. 2000b. "The Human Motivational Complex: Evolutionary Theory and the Causes of Hunter-Gatherer Fighting. II. Proximate, Subordinate, and Derivative Causes." *Anthropological Quarterly* 73 (2): 74–88.

———. 2003. "Why City States Existed? Riddles and Clues of Urbanization and Fortifications." University of Tel Aviv, mimeo.

Gellner, Ernest. 1994. *Conditions of Liberty: Civil Society and Its Rivals*. London: Hamish Hamilton.

Ghatak, M. 1999. "Group Lending, Local Information and Peer Selection." *Journal of Development Economics* 60 (1): 27–50.

Ghiglieri, Michael. 1999. *The Dark Side of Man: Tracing the Origins of Male Violence*. Cambridge, Mass.: Perseus Publishing.

Ghiselin, Michael. 2001. "A Bibliography for Bioeconomics." *Journal of Bioeconomics* 2: 233–70.

Gibbon, Edward. [1776] 1993. *The Decline and Fall of the Roman Empire*. New York: Knopf.

Gintis, Herbert. 2000. "Strong Reciprocity and Human Sociality." *Journal of Theoretical Biology* 213: 103–19.

Gladwell, Malcolm. 2000. *The Tipping Point: How Little Things Can Make a Big Difference*. New York: Little, Brown.

Gleick, P. 1993. *Water in Crisis: A Guide to the World's Freshwater Resources*. New York: Oxford University Press.

———. 2002. *The World's Water: The Biennial Report on Freshwater Resources 2002–3*. Washington, D.C.: Island Press.

Granovetter, Mark. 1972. "The Strength of Weak Ties." *American Journal of Sociology* 78: 1360–80.

Gray J. A., J. Feldon, J.N.P. Rawlins, D. R. Hemsley, and A. D. Smith. 1991. "The Neuro-Psychology of Schizophrenia." *Behavioral and Brain Sciences* 14: 1–84.

Gray, J. A., and Neil McNaughton. 2000. *The Neuropsychology of Anxiety: An Enquiry into the Functions of the Septo-Hippocampal System.* 2nd ed. Oxford Psychology Series, no. 33. Oxford: Oxford University Press.

Gray, John. 1998. *False Dawn: The Delusions of Global Capitalism.* New York: New Press.

———. 2000. *Two Faces of Liberalism.* New York: New Press.

Gusterson, Hugh. 1996. *Nuclear Rites.* Berkeley: University of California Press.

Hacking, Ian. 1990. *The Taming of Chance.* Cambridge: Cambridge University Press.

Hall, Peter. 1998. *Cities in Civilisation.* London: Weidenfeld & Nicolson.

Hamermesh, Daniel. 1999. "The Changing Distribution of Job Satisfaction." IZA (Bonn) discussion paper no. 42.

———. 2003. "Routine." National Bureau of Economic Research (Cambridge, Mass.) working paper no. 9440.

Hamilton, William. 1964. "The Genetical Evolution of Social Behaviour." *Journal of Theoretical Biology* 7: 1–52.

Hanson, Royce. 1988. "Water Supply and Distribution: The Next 50 Years." In J. Ausubel and R. Herman, eds., *Cities: Infrastructure and the Vital Systems.* Washington, D.C.: National Academy Press.

Hanson, Victor Davis. 1989. *The Western Way of War: Infantry Battle in Classical Greece.* Berkeley: University of California Press.

———. 2001. *Carnage and Culture: Landmark Battles in the Rise of Western Power.* New York: Doubleday.

Hart, Oliver. 1995. *Firms, Contracts and Financial Structure.* Oxford: Clarendon Press.

Hendricks, Kenneth, and Robert Porter. 1988. "An Empirical Study of an Auction with Asymmetric Information." *American Economic Review* 78: 865–83.

Henrich, Joseph, Robert Boyd, Samuel Bowles, Colin Camerer, Ernst Fehr, Herbert Gintis, and Richard McElreath. 2001. "In Search of Homo Economicus: Behavioral Experiments in Fifteen Small-Scale Societies." *American Economic Review* 91: 73–78.

Herman, R., et al. 1988. "The Dynamic Characterization of Cities." In J. Ausubel and R. Herman, eds., *Cities: Infrastructure and the Vital Systems.* Washington, D.C.: National Academy Press.

Hirshleifer, Jack. 1977. "Economics from a Biological Viewpoint." *Journal of Law and Economics* 20: 1–52.

Hirschman, Albert O. [1977] 1997. *The Passions and the Interests.* Princeton: Princeton University Press.

Hochschild, Adam. 1999. *King Leopold's Ghost.* London: Macmillan.

Hölldobler, Bert, and Edward Wilson. 1994. *Journey to the Ants: A Story of Scientific Exploration.* Cambridge: Harvard University Press, Belknap Press.

Holmstrom, Bengt, and Paul Milgrom. 1991. "Multi-Task Principal-Agent Analysis: Incentive Contracts, Asset Ownership and Job Design." *Journal of Law, Economics & Organization* 7: 24–52.

Homer-Dixon, Thomas. 1999. *Environment, Scarcity and Violence.* Princeton: Princeton University Press.

Horden, Peregrine, and Nicholas Purcell. 2000. *The Corrupting Sea: A Study of Mediterranean History*. Oxford: Blackwell.

Hörner, Johannes. 2002. "Reputation and Competition." *American Economic Review* 92 (3): 644–63.

Hughes, Robert. 1992. *Barcelona*. London: Harvill Press.

Humphrey, Nicholas. 1984. *Consciousness Regained*. Oxford: Oxford University Press.

Huntington, Samuel. 1993. "The Clash of Civilizations?" *Foreign Affairs*, Summer.

Hutchins, Edwin. 1995. *Cognition in the Wild*. Cambridge: MIT Press.

Ibn Khaldun, Abu Zaid. [1377] 1969. *The Muqadimmah*. Translated by Franz Rosenthal. Princeton: Princeton University Press.

Jacobs, Jane. [1961] 1992. *The Death and Life of Great American Cities*. New York: Vintage Books. Originally New York: Random House.

Jones, E. L. 1988. *Growth Recurring: Economic Change in World History*. Oxford: Oxford University Press.

Kahan, Dan. 2003. "The Logic of Reciprocity: Trust, Collective Action and Law." University of Yale, mimeo.

Kakar, Sudhir. 1982. *Shamans, Mystics and Doctors: A Psychological Inquiry into India and Its Healing Traditions*. New York: Knopf.

Kaplan, Hillard, Kim Hill, Jane Lancaster, and Magdalena Hurtado. 2000. "A Theory of Human Life History Evolution: Diet, Intelligence and Longevity." *Evolutionary Anthropology* 9 (2): 156–85.

Kaufmann, Stuart. 1995. *At Home in the Universe*. New York: Oxford University Press.

Keeley, Lawrence. 1996. *War before Civilization: The Myth of the Peaceful Savage*. Oxford: Oxford University Press.

Kennedy, Paul. 1989. *The Rise and Fall of the Great Powers*. London: Fontana.

Kirman, Alan. 1993. "Ants, Rationality and Recruitment." *Quarterly Journal of Economics* 108: 137–56.

Klein, Naomi. 2001. *No Logo*. London: Flamingo.

Klein, Richard. 1999. *The Human Career: Human Biological and Cultural Origins*. 2d ed. Chicago: University of Chicago Press.

Klein, Richard, with Blake Edgar. 2002. *The Dawn of Human Culture: A Bold New Theory on What Sparked the "Big Bang" of Human Consciousness*. New York: John Wiley.

Klemperer, Paul. 1999. "Auction Theory: A Guide to the Literature." *Journal of Economic Surveys* 13 (3): 227–86.

Kremer, Michael. 1993. "The O-Ring Theory of Economic Development." *Quarterly Journal of Economics* 108 (3): 551–75.

Kremer, Michael, and Eric Maskin. 1996. "Wage Inequality and Segregation by Skill." National Bureau of Economic Research (Cambridge, Mass.) working paper no. 5718.

Kremer, Michael, and Christopher Snyder. 2003. "The Revenue Consequences of Vaccines versus Drug Treatments." Harvard University, mimeo.

Kreps, David, and Robert Wilson. 1982. "Reputation and Imperfect Information." *Journal of Economic Theory* 27: 863–94.

Krugman, Paul. 1991. *Geography and Trade*. Cambridge: MIT Press.

Laffont, Jean-Jacques, and David Martimort. 2002. *The Theory of Incentives*. Princeton: Princeton University Press.

Laing, R. D. 1960. *The Divided Self*. London: Tavistock.

Lamoreaux, Naomi, Daniel Raff, and Peter Temin. 2002. "Beyond Markets and Hierarchies: Towards a New Synthesis of American Business History." National Bureau of Economic Research (Cambridge, Mass.) working paper no. 9029.

Landes, David. 1983. *Revolution in Time: Clocks and the Making of the Modern World*. Cambridge: Harvard University Press.

———. 1998. *The Wealth and Poverty of Nations*. London: Little, Brown.

Lanjouw, Peter, and Nicholas Stern, eds. 1998. *Economic Development in Palanpur over Five Decades*. Oxford: Clarendon Press.

Leblanc, Steven. 1999. *Prehistoric Warfare in the American Southwest*. Salt Lake City: University of Utah Press.

Ledeneva, Alena, and Paul Seabright. 2000. "Barter in Post-Soviet Societies: What Does It Look Like and Why Does It Matter?" In Seabright 2000.

Lerman, R. 1996. "The Impact of the Changing U.S. Family Structure on Child Poverty and Income Inequality" *Economica* 63 (250), suppl.: S119–39.

Lester, David. 1994. *Emile Durkheim: Le Suicide 100 Years Later*. Philadelphia: Charles Press.

Lewis, Bernard. 2002. *What Went Wrong? Western Impact and Middle Eastern Response*. Oxford: Oxford University Press.

———. 2003. *The Crisis of Islam: Holy War and Unholy Terror*. London: Weidenfeld & Nicolson.

Libecap, Gary, and Zeynep Hansen. 2001. "U.S. Land Policy, Property Rights and the Dust Bowl of the 1930s." National Bureau of Economic Research (Cambridge, Mass.) conference paper. Downloadable from http://www.nber.org/~confer/2001/si2001/libecap.pdf.

Locay, Luis. 1990. "Economic Development and the Division of Production between Households and Markets." *Journal of Political Economy* 98: 965–82.

Lorenz, Konrad. [1963] 1974. *On Aggression*. New York: Harvest Books.

Luhrmann, Tanya. 2000. *Of Two Minds: The Growing Disorder in American Psychiatry*. New York: Knopf.

Macaulay, Thomas Babington. 1857. "Frederick the Great." In *Biographical Essays*. Leipzig: Bernhard Tauchnitz.

Macpherson, C. B. 1962. *The Political Theory of Possessive Individualism*. Oxford: Clarendon Press.

Mailath, Robert, Lawrence Samuelson, and Avnar Shaked. 2000. "Endogenous Inequality in Integrated Labor Markets with Two-Sided Search." *American Economic Review* 90: 46–72.

Malle, K.-G. 1996. "Cleaning Up the River Rhine." *Scientific American* 274: 54–59.

Marin, Dalia, Daniel Kaufmann, and Bogdan Gorochowskij. 2000. "Barter in Transition Economies: Competing Explanations Confront Ukrainian Data." In Seabright 2000.

Marrus, Michael. 1997. *The Nuremberg War Crimes Tribunal: A Documentary History*. Boston anf New York: Bedford/St. Martin's.

Martin, Henri-Jean. 1994. *The History and Power of Writing*. Translated by Lydia Cochrane. Chicago: University of Chicago Press.

Martindale, Colin. 1990. *The Clockwork Muse: The Predictability of Artistic Change*. New York: Basic Books.

Mas-Colell, Andreu, Michael Whinston, and Jerry Green. 1995. *Microeconomic Theory*. New York: Oxford University Press.

Mauss, Marcel. [1950] 1990. *The Gift: The Form and Reason for Exchange in Archaic Societies*. Translated by W. D. Halls. New York: Norton, originally published as *Essai sur le Don*. Paris: Presses Universitaires de France.

Mayhew, Henry. [1861–62] 1968. *London Labour and the London Poor*. New York: Dover Publications. Facsimile of original edition published by Griffin Bohn & Company.

McBrearty, Sally, and Alison S. Brooks. 2000. "The Revolution That Wasn't: A New Interpretation of the Origin of Modern Human Behavior." *Journal of Human Evolution* 39: 453–563.

McCloskey, D. 1976. "English Open Fields as Behavior Towards Risk." *Research in Economic History* 1 (Fall): 124–70.

McCulloch, Neil, L. Alan Winters, and Xavier Cirera. 2001. *Trade Liberalization and Poverty: a Handbook*. London: Centre for Economic Policy Research.

McGranahan, G. 1993. "Household Environmental Problems in Low-Income Cities." *Habitat International* 17: 105–21.

McMillan, John. 2002. *Reinventing the Bazaar: A Natural History of Markets*. New York: Norton.

McNeill, J. R. 2000. *Something New under the Sun: An Environmental History of the Twentieth Century*. New York: Norton.

Meggitt, Mervyn. 1977. *Blood Is Their Argument: Warfare among the Mae Enga Tribesmen of the New Guinea Highlands*. Mountain View: Mayfield.

Milgrom, Paul, and John Roberts. 1992. *Economics, Organization and Management*. New York: Prentice-Hall.

Miller, Geoffrey. 2000. *The Mating Mind: How Sexual Choices Shaped the Evolution of Human Nature*. New York: Anchor Books.

Mirrlees, James. 1997. "The Economics of Carrots and Sticks." *Economic Journal* 107 (444): 1311–29.

Mithen, Steven. 1996. *The Prehistory of the Mind*. London: Thames & Hudson.

Mokyr, Joel. 2002. *The Gifts of Athena: Historical Origins of the Knowledge Economy*. Princeton: Princeton University Press.

Monnerie, Denis. 1996. *Nitu: Les Vivants, les Morts et le Cosmos selon la Société de Mono-Alu (Iles Salomon)*. Leiden: CNWS Research School.

Mowery, D., and A. Ziedonis. 2001. "The Geographic Reach of Market and Non-Market Channels of Technology Transfer: Comparing Citations and Licenses of University Patents." National Bureau of Economic Research (Cambridge, Mass.) working paper no. W8568.

Neary, Peter. 2001. "Of Hype and Hyperbolas: Introducing the New Economic Geography." *Journal of Economic Literature* 39: 536–61.

Nieboer, H. J. [1900] 1971. *Slavery as an Industrial System*. Burt Franklin.

North, Douglass. 1990. *Institutions, Institutional Change and Economic Performance*. Cambridge: Cambridge University Press.

North, Douglass, and Robert Paul Thomas. 1973. *The Rise of the Western World: A New Economic History*. Cambridge: Cambridge University Press.

Ogilvie, Sheilagh. 2000. "The European Economy in the Eighteenth Century." In T.W.C. Blanning. ed., *The Short Oxford History of Europe*, vol. 12, *The Eighteenth Century: Europe 1688–1815*. Oxford: Oxford University Press.

Olson, Mancur. [1965] 1971. *The Logic Of Collective Action: Public Goods and the Theory of Groups*. Rev. ed. Cambridge: Harvard University Press.

Overy, Richard. 2001. *Interrogations: The Nazi Elite in Allied Hands, 1945*. Harmondsworth, U.K.: Penguin Books.

Owren, Michael, and Jo-Anne Bachorowski. 2001. "The Evolution of Emotional Expression: A 'Selfish-Gene' Account of Smiling and Laughter in Early Hominids and Humans." Chapter 5 of Tracy Mayne, and George Bonnano, eds., *Emotions*. New York: Guilford Press.

Packard, Vance. [1957] 1985. *The Hidden Persuaders*. New York: Pocket Books.

Pearce, David, and R. Kerry Turner. 1990. *Economics of Natural Resources and the Environment*. Baltimore: Johns Hopkins University Press.

Peltzman, S. 1975. "The Effects of Automobile Safety Regulation." *Journal of Political Economy* 83 (4): 677–725.

Perec, Georges. 1979. *La Vie Mode d'Emploi*. Paris: Hachette.

Perloff, Jeffrey M. 2001. *Microeconomics*. 2d ed. Boston: Addison Wesley Longman.

Perrin, N. 1979. *Giving Up the Gun: Japan's Reversion to the Sword 1543–1879*. Boston: Godine.

Peterson, S., G. Hoffer, and E. Millner. 1994. "Are Drivers of Airbag-Equipped Cars More Aggressive? A Test of the Offsetting Behaviour Hypothesis." *Journal of Law and Economics* 38: 251–65.

Polanyi, Karl. [1944] 2001. *The Great Transformation: The Political and Economic Origins of Our Time*. Boston: Beacon Press.

Pomeranz, Kenneth. 2000. *The Great Divergence: China, Europe and the Making of the Modern World Economy*. Princeton: Princeton University Press.

Portney, Paul. 2000. "Environmental Problems and Policy 2000–2050." *Journal of Economic Perspectives* 14: 199–206.

Price-Smith, Andrew. 2002. *The Health of Nations: Infectious Disease, Environmental Change, and Their Effects on National Security and Development*. Cambridge: MIT Press.

Pusey, A. E., and C. Packer. 1983. "The Once and Future Kings." *Natural History* 92: 54–63.

Putnam, Robert. 1993. *Making Democracy Work: Civic Traditions in Modern Italy*. Princeton: Princeton University Press.

———. 2000. *Bowling Alone: The Collapse and Revival of American Community*. New York: Simon & Schuster.

Putterman, Louis, and Randall Kroszner. 1996. *The Economic Nature of the Firm: A Reader*. Cambridge: Cambridge University Press.

Ramachandran, V. S., and Sandra Blakeslee. 1999. *Phantoms in the Brain*. New York: Harper Collins.

Ray, Debraj. 1998. *Development Economics*. Princeton: Princeton University Press.

Rawls, John. 1975. *A Theory of Justice*. Oxford: Clarendon Press.

Renfrew, Colin. 1989. *Archaeology and Language: The Puzzle of Indo-European Origins*. Harmondsworth, U.K.: Penguin.

Ricardo, David. [1817] 1996. *On the Principles of Political Economy and Taxation*. New York: Prometheus Books.

Richerson, Peter, and Robert Boyd. 1998. "Complex Societies: The Evolutionary Origins of a Crude Superorganism." University of California Davis, mimeo.

Richerson, Peter, Robert Boyd, and Robert Bettinger. 2001. "Was Agriculture Impossible during the Pleistocene but Mandatory during the Holocene? A Climate Change Hypothesis." *American Antiquity* 66 (3): 387–411.

Ridley, Matt. 1996. *The Origins of Virtue*. Harmondsworth, U.K.: Viking Penguin.

Riley, John. 2001. "Silver Signals: Twenty-Five Years of Screening and Signaling." *Journal of Economic Literature* 39: 432–78.

Robarchek, Clayton, and Carole Robarchek. 1997. *Waorani: The Contexts of Violence and War*. Fort Worth, Tex.: Harcourt Brace College Publishing.

Robbins, Lionel. [1936] 1984. "On the Nature and Significance of Economic Science." London: Palgrave Macmillan.

Robson, Arthur. 2001. "The Biological Basis of Economic Behavior." *Journal of Economic Literature* 39: 11–33.

Robson, Arthur, and Hillard Kaplan. 2003. "The Evolution of Human Life Expectancy and Intelligence in Hunter-Gatherer Economies." *American Economic Review* 93: 150–69.

Rodrik, Dani. 1997. *Has Globalization Gone Too Far?* Washington, D.C.: Institute for International Economics.

Rogers, P. 1993. *America's Water: Federal Roles and Responsibilities*. Cambridge: MIT Press, 1993.

Rosen, Sherwin. 1981. "The Economics of Superstars." *American Economic Review* 71: 845–58.

Rothschild, Emma. 2001. *Economic Sentiments*. Cambridge: Harvard University Press.

Rousseau, Jean-Jacques. [1755] 1984. *Discourse on the Origins of Inequality*. Translated by Maurice Cranston. Harmondsworth, U.K.: Penguin.

Sandel, Michael. 1982. *Liberalism and the Limits of Justice*. Cambridge: Cambridge University Press.

Schama, Simon. 1987. *The Embarrassment of Riches: An interpretation of Dutch Culture in the Golden Age*. London: Collins.

Schelling, Thomas. 1978. *Micromotives and Macrobehavior*. New York: Norton.

Scott, James. 1998. *Seeing Like a State: How Certain Schemes to Improve the Human Condition Have Failed*. New Haven: Yale University Press.

Seabright, Paul. 1993. "Managing Local Commons: Theoretical Issues in Incentive Design." *Journal of Economic Perspectives* 7: 113–34.

———. 1997. "Is Co-operation Habit-Forming?" In Partha Dasgupta, and Karl-Göran Mäler, eds., *The Environment and Emerging Development Issues*. Oxford: Clarendon Press.

———. 1999. "Skill versus Judgment and the Architecture of Organizations." *European Economic Review* 44: 856–68.

———. 2003. "Agriculture, Warfare and the Division of Labour." University of Toulouse, mimeo.

———. 2000. *The Vanishing Rouble*. Cambridge: Cambridge University Press.

Sen, A., and B. Mizzen. 2001. "To Encourage or Not to Encourage Seat-Belt Use." University of Waterloo, mimeo. Downloadable from http://economics.uwaterloo.ca/sen/traffic%20paper-RESTAT.pdf.

Shiller, Robert. 2000. *Irrational Exuberance*. Princeton: Princeton University Press.

Shimer, R., and L. Smith. 2000. "Assortative Matching and Search." *Econometrica* 68 (2): 343–69.

Shleifer, Andrei, and Robert Vishny. 1993. "Corruption." *Quarterly Journal of Economics* 108: 599–617.

Shy, Oz. 2001. *The Economics of Network Industries*. Cambridge: Cambridge University Press.

Sivéry, Gérard. 2000. "Rural Society." In David Abulafia, ed., *The New Cambridge Medieval History*, vol. 5, *c. 1198–c. 1300*. Cambridge: Cambridge University Press.

Smith, Adam. [1759] 2000. *The Theory of Moral Sentiments*. Amherst, N.Y.: Prometheus Books.

———. [1776] 1991. *An Inquiry into the Nature and Causes of the Wealth of Nations*. New York: Prometheus Books.

Solow, R. 1971. "Blood and Thunder." *Yale Law Journal* 80 (2): 170–83.

Stokes, Adrian. 1965. *The Invitation in Art*. London: Tavistock Press.

Strassler, Robert, ed. 1998. *The Landmark Thucydides: A Comprehensive Guide to the Peloponnesian War*. New York: Touchstone Books.

Susskind, Patrick. 1988. *Perfume*. Translated by John Woods. New York: Knopf.

Sutton, John. 1998. *Technology and Market Structure*. Cambridge: MIT Press.

———. 2001. "Rich Trades, Scarce Capabilities: Industrial Development Revisited." Downloadable from http://www.res.org.uk/pdf/SuttonLEC.pdf.

Teece, David. 1993. "The Dynamics of Industrial Capitalism: Perspectives on Alfred Chandler's Scale and Scope." *Journal of Economic Literature* 31: 199–225.

Terkel, Studs. 1974. *Working*. Harmondsworth, U.K.: Penguin.

———. 1986. *The Good War: An Oral History of World War II*. Harmondsworth, U.K.: Penguin.

Tirole, Jean. 1996. "A Theory of Collective Reputation, with Applications to the Persistence of Corruption and to Firm Quality." *Review of Economic Studies* 63: 1–22.

Titmuss, R. 1970. *The Gift Relationship*. London: Allen & Unwin.

Tomasello, Michael. 1999. *The Cultural Origins of Human Cognition*. Cambridge: Harvard University Press.

Tourneur, Cyril. [1607] 1996. *The Revenger's Tragedy*. Manchester: Manchester University Press.

Trivers, Richard. 1971. "The Evolution of Reciprocal Altruism." *Quarterly Review of Biology* 46: 35–57.

Tufte, Edward R. 1997. *The Visual Display of Quantitative Information*. Cheshire, Conn.: Graphics Press.

———. 1997. *Visual Explanations*. Cheshire, Conn.: Graphics Press.

Tully, James. 1980. *A Discourse on Property: John Locke and His Adversaries*. Cambridge: Cambridge University Press.

———. 1993. *An Approach to Political Philosophy: Locke in Contexts*. Cambridge: Cambridge University Press.

Varese, Federico. 1994. "Is Sicily the Future of Russia? Private protection and the Rise of the Russia Mafia." *Archives Européennes de Sociologie* 35: 224–58.

———. 2001. *The Russian Mafia: Private Protection in a New Market Economy*. Oxford: Oxford University Press.

Viscusi, W. Kip, John Vernon, and Joseph Harrington. 2000. *Economics of Regulation and Antitrust*. 3d ed. Cambridge: MIT Press.

Wade, R. 1987. *Village Republics*. Cambridge: Cambridge University Press.

Wantchekon, Leonard. 2004. "Clientelism and Voting Behavior: Evidence from a Field Experiment in Benin." *World Politics*, forthcoming.

Ward, Diane Raines. 2002. *Water Wars: Drought, Flood, Folly and the Politics of Thirst*. New York: Riverhead Books.

Weiss, Y. 1993. "The Formation and Dissolution of Families: Why Marry? Who Marries Whom? And What Happens upon Divorce?" Foerder Institute for Economic Research (Tel Aviv) working paper 15/93.

White, Lynn. 1966. *Medieval Technology and Social Change*. Oxford: Clarendon Press.

Whiten, A., J. Goodall, W. C. McGrew, T. Nishida, V. Reynolds, Y. Sugiyama, C. Tutin, R. Wrangham, and C. Boesch. 1999. "Cultures in Chimpanzees." *Nature* 399: 682–85.

Whiten, A., and C. Boesch. 2001. "The Cultures of Chimpanzees." *Scientific American* 284: 48–55.

Wiener, Martin. 1982. *English Culture and the Decline of the Industrial Spirit 1850–1980*. Cambridge: Cambridge University Press.

Wilkinson, G. S. 1990. "Food Sharing in Vampire Bats." *Scientific American* 262: 276–82.

Williams, Bernard. 1993. *Shame and Necessity*. Berkeley: University of California Press.

Williamson, Oliver. 1985. *The Economic Institutions of Capitalism: Firms, Markets and Relational Contracting*. New York: Free Press.

Wilson, David, and Elliott Sober. 1994. "Re-Introducing Group Selection to the Human Behavioral Sciences." *Behavioral and Brain Sciences* 17: 585–654.

Winterhalder, B., and F. Lu. 1995. "A Forager-Resource Population Ecology Model and Implications for Indigenous Conservation." *Conservation Biology* 11: 1354–64.

Wirth, Louis. 1938. "Urbanism as a Way of Life." *American Journal of Sociology* 44: 1–24.

Wittfogel, K. [1957] 1981. *Oriental Despotism*. New York: Vintage Random House.

Worcester, Robert. 1995. "A Comparative Examination of Green Activism in 22 Countries." London: MORI.

Worcester, Robert, and Michele Corrado. 1991. "Attitudes to the Environment: a North-South Analysis." London: MORI.

World Health Organization. 2002. *The World Health Report 2002*. Geneva: World Health Organization. Downloadable from http://www.who.int/whr/2002/en/.

Wrangham, Richard. 2003. "The Evolution of Cooking: A Talk with Richard Wrangham." Downloadable from www.edge.org.

Wrangham, Richard, and Dale Peterson. 1996. *Demonic Males: Apes and the Origins of Human Violence*. Boston: Mariner Books.

Index

Coulson, H., 276n.16
Couturiers Sans Frontières, 14
Cox, D., 267n.16
Coyle, D., 266n.1
Crafts, N., 274n.17
Cronk, L., 267n.16
culture, evolution of, 175

Daly, M., 262n.2
Dasgupta, P., 267n.14, 271n.3
Davies, G., 265n.1
Davis, N. Z., 148, 269n.7
Dawkins, R., 259 nn. 4 and 6, 260n.14
De Soto, H., 151, 269n.9
De Vries, J., 260n.6, 261n.10
De Waal, F., 262n.7
Deacon, T., 259n.10
Deaton, A., 273n.6
decentralization, 134, 251
Deneubourg, J.-L., 267n.1
Denmark, 203
depression, 202, 203, 247
Diamond, J., 119, 262 nn. 7 and 9,
  268n.20, 272n.9, 276n.11
diamonds, 166
Dickens, C., 115, 236
disease, 6, 22, 42, 44, 115, 185, 204, 230,
  245, 246, 247; in cities, 114; condi-
  tional probability and, 33; poverty and,
  236; resistance to, 119
division of labor. See specialization
Donne, J., 92, 266n.8
Dostoyevsky, F., 49, 262n.1
double coincidence of wants, 74
Dougherty, P., 100, 266n.7
Douglass, C., 39
Dow, W., 273n.6
Dumont, D., 266n.7, 268n.12,
Dunbar, R., 37, 261n.3, 267n.16
Du Pont Corp., 165
Durant, W., 263n.19
Durkheim, E., 92, 266n.9
Dutta, J., 262n.11, 268 nn. 11, 15, and
  17, 274n.17, 277 nn. 2 and 7

East India Company, 157
Edgar, B., 259 nn. 1 and 10, 261n.6,
  271n.3
education, 252
Egypt, 156, 177
Eisenstein, E., 178, 183, 272n.10

Ember, C., 53, 262n.9, 263n.10
Emerson, R. W., 181
empire, 90, 124, 213, 223; Chinese, 224;
  European, 225; Greek, 223; Roman,
  143, 146, 224; Soviet, 25
Engerman, S., 276n.2
environment. See pollution
erosion, 120
ethnic tensions, 247
Evans, W., 191
evolution. See natural selection
experiments, economic, 55
externalities, 44, 99, 105, 112, 230, 245;
  assortative matching, 200; examples,
  19; pollution, 19, 112; soil erosion,
  120; traffic, 112; water, 129

Falkenmark, M., 268n.4
Farrell, J., 271n.5
fashion, 20, 22
Febvre, L., 272n.10
Federal Deposit Insurance Corporation
  (FDIC), 83
Fehr, E., 55, 62, 101, 263 nn. 14–17, 264
  nn. 31 and 33, 267 nn. 15 and 17
Feinbloom, R., 274n.12
Feldon, J., 272n.12
Ferguson, A., 212, 226, 276n.2
Finland, 203
firms, 6, 20, 55, 105, 137, 141, 153–57,
  161–71, 183, 186, 189, 198, 199, 200,
  238; American, nineteenth and twen-
  tieth century, 165; central planning of,
  172; in experiments, 55; history of,
  154, 157; as information channel, 209;
  institutions and financing of, 163; limits
  of technology in, 168; size of, 160, 161,
  169; and standardization, 159, 160,
  166; structure of, 166; technology and,
  169; transfer of knowledge through,
  187; trust and, 161, 162
Fisher, I., 195
Florence, Italy, 109, 114, 118
Fogel, R., 276n.2
Ford, H., 154, 158, 159
Fossey, D., 226
Foucault, M., 274n.18
France, 123, 157, 174, 218, 230
Frank, R., 179, 263n.22, 272n.12
free ride, 131, 218
Friedman, M., 260n.1